IBERIAN AND LATIN AMERICAN STUDIES

Melancholy and Culture

Series Editors
Professor David George (University of Wales, Swansea)
Professor Paul Garner (University of Leeds)

Editorial Board
David Frier (University of Leeds)
Lisa Shaw (University of Liverpool)
Gareth Walters (University of Exeter)
Rob Stone (Swansea University)
David Gies (University of Virginia)
Catherine Davies (University of Nottingham)

IBERIAN AND LATIN AMERICAN STUDIES

Melancholy and Culture

Essays on the Diseases of the Soul in Golden Age Spain

by

ROGER BARTRA

Translated from Spanish by
CHRISTOPHER FOLLETT

UNIVERSITY OF WALES PRESS
CARDIFF
2008

© Roger Bartra, 2008

All rights reserved. No part of this book may be reproduced, stored in a retrieval system, or transmitted, in any form or by any means, electronic, mechanical, photocopying, recording or otherwise, without clearance from the University of Wales Press, 10 Columbus Walk, Brigantine Place, Cardiff, CF10 4UP.

www.uwp.co.uk

British Library Cataloguing-in-Publication Data

A catalogue record for this book is available from the British Library.

ISBN 978-0-7083-2010-5

The right of Roger Bartra to be identified as author of this work has been asserted by him in accordance with sections 77 and 78 of the Copyright, Designs and Patents Act 1988.

This book is a revised edition of *Cultura y melancolia: Las enfermedades del alma en la España del Siglo de Oro* (Bacelona: Anagrama, 2001)

Typeset by Columns Design Ltd, Reading
Printed and bound in Great Britain by CPI Antony Rowe, Wiltshire

Contents

Series Editors' Foreword	vii
Acknowledgements	ix
Introduction	1
Chapter 1 Myths of Melancholy	**9**
1. Translation and its metaphors	11
2. Myth and evolution	17
3. The adust humours: an overview	26
Chapter 2 The Golden Age of Melancholy: **A Sixteenth-Century Physician at the Frontiers of Madness**	**41**
1. A Baroque physician explores the house of the soul	41
2. The Little Book of Melancholy	52
3. The courtly sickness	63
4. The Devil's bath	71
5. The dark night of melancholy	83
6. Love sickness	96
7. The sorrow of the Jews	107
8. Ill-tempered instruments	113
9. Decadence and *Angst*	121
Chapter 3 Melancholy and Christianity: **On Don Quixote's Sadness**	**165**
Bibliography	207
Index	227

Maigre immortalité noire et dorée,
Consolatrice affreusement laurée,
Qui de la mort fais un sein maternel,
Le beau mensonge et la pieuse ruse!
Qui ne connaît, et qui ne les refuse,
Ce crâne vide et ce rire éternel!

Paul Valéry, *Le cimetière marin*, XVIII.

Series Editors' Foreword

Over recent decades, the traditional 'languages and literatures' model in Spanish departments in universities in the United Kingdom has been superceded by a contextual, interdisciplinary and 'area studies' approach to the study of the culture, history, society and politics of the Hispanic and Lusophone worlds – categories which extend far beyond the confines of the Iberian Peninsula, not only to Latin America but also to Spanish-speaking and Lusophone Africa.

In response to these dynamic trends in research priorities and curriculum development, this series is designed to present both disciplinary and interdisciplinary research within the general field of Iberian and Latin American Studies, particularly studies which explore all aspects of **Cultural Production** (inter alia literature, film, music, dance, sport) in Spanish, Portuguese, Basque, Catalan, Galician and the indigenous languages of Latin America. The series also aims to publish research on the **History and Politics** of Hispanic and Lusophone worlds, both at the level of region and that of the nation-state, as well as on **Cultural Studies** which explore the shifting terrains of gender, sexual, racial and postcolonial identities in those same regions.

Acknowledgements

This book is the product of a journey into the past; it was undertaken by an anthropologist with the support of historians. The expedition into the Golden Age of Spain was carried out thanks to a grant awarded by the Rockefeller Foundation and the Department of History of the Universidad Iberoamericana in Mexico City. The collaboration that took place within the Cultural History Program, aimed at exploring the 'grammar of memory', was for me highly stimulating and fruitful. I should like to thank the coordinator of the programme, Ilán Semo, and the directors of the History Department, Valentina Torres Septién and Guillermo Zermeño, for their enthusiastic support and their acute commentaries on my work. I also wish to express my thanks to Perla Chinchilla, the Program's Academic Secretary, and to Alfonso Mendiola, a teacher in the Department, for their collaboration and pertinent observations. My thanks must, naturally, extend to all the colleagues who ensured that my time spent at the Universidad Iberoamericana was a period of calm, appropriate for my study and reflection. The generous cooperation of the historian Manuel Pérez Regordán, a profound connoisseur of the life and historical development of Arcos de la Frontera, has been of the utmost importance; he kindly helped familiarize me with his town, bringing back to life for me times gone by and making available to me valuable and little-known information.

My research assistants, supported by the Mexican National System of Researchers (Sistema Nacional de Investigadores), were an indispensable aid to my work; Germán Franco was in charge of the transcription and edition of several texts by Drs Andrés Velásquez, Pedro de Mercado, Alonso López de Hinojosos, Agustín Farfán and Juan de Barrios; Francisco Barrenechea was responsible for the revision and translation of the numerous classical references, mainly in Latin, which appear in the texts of these physicians. All collaborated, too, with valuable comments and suggestions.

Andrés Velásquez's *Libro de la melancolía* was published for the first time since its original edition of 1585 as part of my book *El Siglo de Oro de la melancolía*; that book, which is a forerunner of the one the reader now has in their hands, also includes fragments of the works of the other physicians cited. In the arduous task of compiling information I was also helped by Dorotea Bieńko, Xochiquetzal Marsilli and Liliana Aguirre. I put the final touches to this book in Barcelona, thanks to my reception as a professor in the Faculty of Humanities of the Universitat Pompeu Fabra, at the invitation of Dr Dolores Folch. I am most grateful also for the hospitality of my friends Josep Alujas, Jordi Borja and Manuel Vázquez Montalbán, who made my stay in Barcelona most enjoyable.

My conversations with Simon Brailowsky, an outstanding neurophysiologist, were a great stimulus to my reflections. Unfortunately, before this book saw the light, Brailowsky met a tragic end which greatly deepened the melancholy of his friends. The friendship of another outstanding doctor, Arnaldo Kraus, has been a constant stimulus on these journeys among the ancient territories of pain and suffering. The observations of Christopher Follett, who has translated this book into English, have helped me to enrich the text. The psychiatrist Héctor Pérez-Rincón, with his stimulating texts and advice, guided me in the study of the history of mental illnesses. The United States poet Sam Abrams, a profound connoisseur of Spanish literature, has been the bedside physician who has guided my steps through a difficult terrain. During this expedition into the past, my friends Christopher Domínguez and José Ramón Enríquez also watched over, so to speak, my literary and spiritual health. I am enormously grateful to all of them for what they have done for me.

Introduction

As the page is turned on the second millennium and the twenty-first century gets under way, melancholy is fast spreading as a subject of reflection and a cause of concern. This is no chance accident of intellectual history. Important political changes drive us rapidly away from the known territories of modernity and create a cultural vertigo as we gaze into the mouth of the abyss which yawns before our eyes. For this reason many find themselves drawn towards the study of melancholy, that fascinating constellation of ancient problems and anxieties which the West, throughout its history, has kept alive in its memory. It is often said that the period of anxiety that followed the Second World War has given way to an Age of Melancholy, set off by the fear of final catastrophes, nuclear wars, ecological collapse, demographic explosions, or other disorders proper to post-industrial society.[1] But we must bear in mind that melancholy has a long history, and that its golden age is to be found in the Renaissance.[2]

During the long and tense post-war period that has been the second half of the twentieth century, many important works on melancholy have been written and disseminated, from the appearance of *Saturn and Melancholy* by Klibansky, Panofsky and Saxl, the *Histoire du traitement de la mélancolie des origines à 1900* by Jean Starobinski and *La mélancolie* by Hubertus Tellenbach, to the more recent books by Jackson, Kristeva, Lepenies and Screech.[3] However, the texts that set out to study the history of this disorder give little or no attention to the subject of melancholy in the Spanish Golden Age, in spite of the enormous importance of Spanish thinking on the subject.[4] The present book seeks to contribute towards filling this void, and to demonstrate that the subject of melancholy in the Spanish Golden Age is an indispensable link in a chain that may help us to understand the appearance of the black humour in Europe at the dawn of modernity.

The first chapter expounds some problems of theory and interpretation. As the reader will discover, from my starting-point in one of the most enigmatic accidents of fortune in the history of science I find my way into the hotly debated field of the influence of culture in the formulation of paradigms. Examination of the cultural roots of scientific concepts has alarmed many researchers, who have reacted against the excesses of those writers who see nothing more than 'mental constructions' and 'inventions' in the history of knowledge.[5] I have also availed myself of the subject of melancholy as an approach to the very thorny problem of artificial intelligence as a possible model for the functioning of the human mind, as well as a basis for offering an evolutionist interpretation of the way myths work in science.

During the late sixteenth and early seventeenth centuries, texts on melancholy began to circulate in Europe that were aimed at the general reading public, not just at specialists in mental illnesses. The most well-known are those by Robert Burton and Jacques Ferrand, published during the first quarter of the seventeenth century, written in English and French respectively, rather than in Latin, as was the normal practice among physicians. It is a little-known fact, however, that the first book on melancholy written in a vernacular language was, as far as we know, that produced by the Spanish doctor Andrés Velásquez: the *Libro de la melancolía*, published in 1585, just a year before the treatise by Timothy Bright, which was known to Shakespeare.[6] The present book takes Velásquez's work as a starting point from which to scrutinize the broad panorama of melancholy in Spain throughout the sixteenth and seventeenth centuries – the Golden Age of Spanish letters. Through the eyes of this Andalusian physician, and the little we know of his life, I have set out to draw a map of that country's black humour. The study of the strange circumvolutions of the Baroque brain as depicted by the physicians and writers of the Golden Age allows me to affirm that melancholy was one of the fundamental axes of Renaissance culture.

The importance of the subject of melancholy in Shakespeare's *Hamlet* or in the *Essays* of Montaigne is well known. Of equal importance is that which pervades the pages of Cervantes's *Don Quixote*, a subject to which I devote the last chapter of this book. There I examine the problem of religious melancholy and its relation with the survival of certain pre-Christian canons; I am guided by the idea that Don Quixote's sadness is a key element in the long history of melancholy, one that has not been sufficiently taken into account by those interested in the problem. I also consider in that essay the moral anxiety caused by the strange and forgotten sin of acedia, and discuss the possible diagnoses of the mysterious illness suffered by the Knight of La Mancha.

Melancholy is a phenomenon linked to a broad and complex cultural constellation, one which extends far beyond the psychiatric and neurological considerations that have attempted to confine it within the terms of what is referred to as 'depression', a mental illness defined technically as an affective disorder and associated with deficits in the neurotransmitter amines in the brain. On the other hand, I do not believe that melancholy is an illness similar to the menacing anarchy depicted by Matthew Arnold, and which was to be dealt with through refinements in culture.[7] I see no opposition between culture and melancholy parallel to that noted by Raymond Williams in the contrast, in English thought, between high culture and bourgeois society.[8] I do not conceive culture as the totality of aesthetic expressions of the elements that society considers most elevated – 'high culture' as Arnold understood it – and which has also been analysed by Edward Said within the context of the cultural manifestations of imperialism, another threat proper to modernity.[9] It is not my wish to restrict this study to the way in which a mental disorder finds expression through the medium of culture. Psychiatrists tend to see culture as the sieve which simultaneously filters and lends its own colours to the manifold manifestations of a pathological phenomenon which assails mankind throughout the world.[10]

I do not believe that culture is the antidote *against* the chaos of melancholy; I do not wish to limit myself to studying a culture *of* melancholy, nor to a mere observation of melancholy *in* culture. I think of melancholy, rather, *as* culture and – to a certain degree – of culture *as* melancholy. Thus, my reflections on melancholy in the Spanish Golden Age are conceived, rather, in the spirit of books such as Klibansky, Panofsky and Saxl's *Saturn and Melancholy*, Screech's *Montaigne and Melancholy* and Lepenies's *Melancholie und Gesellschaft*, for these are studies that link melancholy with the mythology, biography or society they set out to analyse.

As will no doubt have been observed, the texts I have cited all include in their titles the copulative conjunction 'and', which I also use in the title of the present book. I take pleasure in using it to make closer – ironically, admiringly and metaphorically – my links with the said texts and at the same time to suggest literally the union of melancholy with culture, like a conjunction of two heavenly bodies that occupy the same celestial house, and like a *copula* or copulation (in the carnal rather than the logical sense) in the work of cultivating the black humour for the purpose of observing its numerous fruits. My point of view is an anthropological one. For this reason I am fascinated by the arguments raised by a classic study by two western psychiatrists of the social origins of depression: on the basis of case-studies in Sri Lanka Brown and Harris formulate a picture of this mental illness as a response to the loss of an important source of positive values, which brings with it a general sense of hopelessness in one's life; this generalization of despair is, according to them, the central core of the depressive disorder.[11] This account has met with the objections of a Sri Lankan Buddhist, also an excellent anthropologist, who points out that this picture does not correspond to a description of a depressive Buddhist, but rather to that of a good Buddhist, who regards hopelessness as an appropriate reaction to the nature of the world, and for whom salvation consists precisely in understanding and overcoming the lack of hope, not in denying its existence.[12]

Thus, for the Buddhist, melancholy is not an illness but an existential condition deriving from the suffering and sadness that emanate naturally from life itself: the only way of overcoming the melancholy of the world is via nirvana. The Sri Lankan anthropologist I refer to, Gananath Obeyeserkere, states that in the West the effects characterizing depression are relatively free-floating, while in other cultures they form an intrinsic part of broad cultural and philosophical conglomerates. He is mistaken; I believe the latter to be true also of the West, for all the efforts made by modern psychiatry to isolate the depressive syndrome and enclose it within the limits established by the manuals.[13] But in order to comprehend this fact it is necessary to reconnect the idea of depression with that of melancholy, its illustrious predecessor, in order thus to open the doors of the immense and complex cultural conglomerate which agglutinates around the black humour. Only thus can we appreciate the fact that depression as described in the psychiatric manuals is no more than a small facet of a cultural canon of great breadth and extension which underlies the whole of Western history. A great psychiatrist, Ludwig Binswanger, thanks to his phenomenological orientation, became aware of this problem, and made the attempt to distinguish the illness from the existential anxiety. And let us also remember that, before it become entitled *La nausée*, the influential novel by Sartre was called *Melancholia*.[14]

Melancholy is a living problem that permeates contemporary culture.[15] More than once, over the last few years, I have wondered whether that melancholy Spain, whose black humours crystallized during the *Siglo de Oro* and which were celebrated or deplored for centuries as one of the characteristics proper to the Spanish identity, still exists. I am interested in the enigma of Spanish melancholy partly because I have devoted much time to examining the myth of melancholy as an ingredient of Mexican national culture.[16] I have been able to ascertain, besides, that in a number of European cultures the same myth has been cherished as a value intimately linked to national identity. The English of the Elizabethan and Jacobean periods seem to have wished to appropriate for themselves the melancholy that emanated from Spain in order to make of it a national monument, which eventually acquired literary form in Robert Burton's celebrated *The Anatomy of Melancholy*. Undoubtedly, one of the distinctive marks of the German Renaissance is the famous engraving by Dürer representing the Angel of Melancholy. The French constructed *la tristesse* in emulation of the English 'spleen', and the Romantics, of course, carried the worship of the melancholy sentiment to a degree never witnessed before or since. It is possible that the Florentine Neoplatonists were the first to promote the resurgence of Ancient Greek melancholy, supported by the Arab and Jewish philosophical tradition. And the long Golden Age in Spain was one of the cultural processes that contributed most decisively to the consolidation in the West of the black humour as one of the motive forces of society and politics. The immense black sun of Spanish melancholy during that period cast its rays over the whole of Western culture with such strength that its lengthened shadows reach down even to our own days.

But when we direct our gaze towards contemporary Spanish culture, it is not easy to find traces of ancient melancholy; it would appear, then, that the archetype has vanished: what traces remain of the obscure paths of the mystics and the cabbalistic signs of the Jewish physicians? Where are the sad demons hidden that used to lie in wait across each frontier? Where is the memory of melancholic kings and chimerical courtiers? Where are to be found the heirs of monks tortured by acedia and Arab sages who cured lycanthropy with the prescriptions of Avicenna? I cannot help wondering where in modern Spain that melancholy Spain of earlier times lies buried. As an anthropologist by profession, and one devoted to the investigation of the history of myths, I propose here an archaeological expedition into the ruins of Spanish melancholy, with the hope of finding there, buried, some keys to the kind of malaise that we experience today. As we are dealing apparently with an illness, I have chosen some aspects of the medical tradition – which formed an essential part of Renaissance thought – in order to peer into the constitution of the cultural texture of Golden Age Spain. That period is still for many a kind of enlightenment *avant la lettre*, and the black sun of melancholy is like a star that illuminates the way towards an ill-fated modernity. All this, I fear, in order to discover that that sun is in reality the black hole left by the implosion of a foreign body.

This intriguing Spanish mystery brings us to formulate further questions. How can a country live without hating foreigners and those in general whom it regards as alien to it? How can a society exist without being overcome by tedium and apathy? How can political and cultural elites avoid the boredom of living in a courtly space of technocratic power which could well do without them? How can culture grow without mystical dreams and longings, based on nothing more than the expansion of information technology and the media networks? In short, how can Spain be post-modern?

For reasons such as these I take pleasure in retiring into the past and submerging myself in the Golden Age of Spanish melancholy in search of the answers I do not find today. And with the hope, perhaps, of unearthing the roots of the black tree of melancholy.

NOTES

[1] G. L. Klerman, 'Is this the Age of Melancholy?', *Psychology Today*, 12 (1979), 36–42, 88–9; Olle Hagnel *et al.*, 'Are we entering an age of melancholy?', *Psychological Medicine*, 12 (1982), 279–98; Anthony J. Marsella *et al.*, 'Cross-cultural studies of depressive disorders: an overview', in *Culture and Depression* (Berkeley: University of California Press, 1985).

[2] Jean Starobinski, *Histoire du traitement de la mélancolie des origines à 1900* (Basilea: J. R. Geigy, 1960), p. 38.

[3] Raymond Klibansky, Erwin Panofsky and Fritz Saxl, *Saturn and Melancholy*, pub. originally in English in 1964 (my references throughout are to the revised French version of 1989, *Saturne et la Mélancolie*

(Paris: Gallimard); Starobinski, *Histoire du traitement de la mélancolie des origines à 1900*; Hubertus Tellenbach, *La mélancolie* (Paris: Presses Universitaires de France, 1979), pub. in German in 1961; Stanley W. Jackson, *Melancholia and Depression. From Hippocratic Times to Modern Times* (New Haven: Yale University Press, 1986); Wolf Lepenies, *Melancholy and Society* (Cambridge: Harvard Unversity Press, 1992); Julia Kristeva, *Soleil noir. Dépression et mélancolie* (Paris: Gallimard, 1987); M. A. Screech, *Montaigne and Melancholy* (London: Penguin, 1991).

4   Three books which deal with the subject of melancholy in the Spanish *Siglo de Oro* must be mentioned: Teresa Scott Soufas, *Melancholy and the Secular Mind in Spanish Golden Age Literature* (Columbia: University of Missouri Press, 1990); Christine Orobitg, *L'humeur noire. Mélancolie, écriture et pensée en Espagne au XVIe et au XVIIe siècle* (Bethesda, MD: International Scholars Publications, c.1997); and the more general but nonetheless interesting book by Guillermo Díaz-Plaja, *Tratado de las melancolías españolas* (Madrid: Sala, 1975). I should add an important work, published after I published my book in Spanish: Felice Gambin, *Azabache. Il dibattito sulla malinconia nella Spagna dei Secoli d'Oro* (Pisa: Edizioni ETS, 2005).

5   See, for example, the polemics unleashed by the physicist Alan Sokal, which he himself details, together with Jean Bricmont, in their book *Impostures intellectuelles* (Paris: Odile Jacob, 1997).

6   *A Treatise of Melancholy* by Timothy Bright was published in London by the Huguenot editor Thomas Vautrollier in 1586. A modern edition is available, translated into French and edited by Eliane Cuvelier.

7   Matthew Arnold viewed culture in these terms: 'Culture, disinterestedly seeking in its aim at perfection to see things as they really are, shows us how worthy and divine a thing is the religious side in man, though it is not the whole of man' (p. xxxvii); and concluded: 'culture is the most resolute enemy of anarchy, because of the great hopes and designs for the State which culture teaches us to nourish' (p. 197). *Culture and Anarchy. An Essay in Political and Social Criticism* ([1869] New York: Macmillan, 1916).

8   Raymond Williams, *Culture and Society, 1780–1950* (Harmondsworth: Penguin, 1961).

9   Edward W. Said, *Culture and Imperialism* (New York: Knopf, 1993).

10 In this connection see the anthology of texts prepared by Arthur Kleinman and Bryan Good, *Culture and Depression* (Berkeley: University of California Press, 1985).

11 G. S. Brown and T. Harris, *The Social Origins of Depression: A Study of Psychiatric Disorder in Women* (New York: Free Press, 1978), p. 235.

12 Gananath Obeyesekere, 'Depression, Buddhism, and the work of culture in Sri Lanka', in *Culture and Depression* (Berkeley: University of California Press, 1985) p. 134.

13 One of the most influential definitions is that of the *Diagnostic and Statistical Manual of Mental Disorders* (4th edn, 2000), of the American Psychiatric Association. In order to mark a distance with respect to the merely psychiatric definitions and to lay emphasis on my interest in the links between culture and the diseases of the spirit I have employed the

ancient term *soul* in the subtitle of this book; I use this word in allusion to the mind, the consciousness or the ego, without implying thereby any religious or metaphysical intention.

14 Ludwig Binswanger uses the term *Schwermut* to represent a broad concept comprising both the clinical form of melancholic illness and the form known as existential (as a form of *Dasein*). See also his *Mélancolie et manie. Études phénoménologiques* (Paris: Presses Universitaires de France, 1987), pp. 16 and 38. The editors at Gallimard, after twice rejecting the manuscript of *Melancholia*, changed the title and suppressed several passages (Annie Cohen-Solal, *Sartre, 1905–1980* (Barcelona: Edhasa, 1990), pp. 162–7).

15 A tour among the modern literary forms of melancholy can be enjoyed in the beautiful and intense book by Alberto Ruy Sánchez, *Con la literatura en el cuerpo. Historias de literatura y melancolía* (Mexico City: Taurus, 1995). A good overall historical panorama, presented from a modern perspective, may be found in László F. Földényi, *Melancolía* (Barcelona: Circulo de Lectores, 1996). Another general, very compact, view is to be found in Carlos Gurméndez, *La melancolía* (Madrid: Espasa-Calpe, col. Austral, 1990).

16 See Bartra, *The Cage of Melancholy*. I am also interested in the subject because, as a child of Catalan parents exiled in Mexico, I am affected by indefinable longings. Curiously enough, the Valencian historian Gaspar Escolano (1560–1619) spoke of the 'Saturnine melancholy' of the Catalans (*Décadas de la historia de Valencia*, IV, ch. 23, p. 436). See Ángel G. Loureiro's interesting reflections (in 'España maníaca', *Quimera*, 167 (1998), 15–20) regarding the modern repercussions of the subject of melancholy; and also Christine Orobitg, 'La typologie des nations et l'espagnol mélancolique: notes pour l'interpretation d'un cliché'.

Chapter 1

Myths of Melancholy

*To my parents, Agustí and Anna,
who taught me the first myths*

When physicians entered the hidden chambers of the soul in order to scrutinize the functioning of the brain and the secrets of the mentally ill, theologians became wary and kept a severe and close look over the movements of the intruders. Also under suspicion were those who attempted, in their mystical transports, to abandon the dwelling place of the soul, as did St John of the Cross, who used to escape during the darkness of night, as he related, when the house was in total stillness. The physicians, on the other hand, were accustomed to entering into the house of the soul in the midst of the most intense spiritual upheaval. Dr Huarte de San Juan, with his *Examen de ingenios para las ciencias* of 1575, was one of those physicians who trespassed upon the house of the soul in his desire to discover the material causes of the spiritual behaviour of human beings. His extraordinary book did not escape the attentions of the Inquisition, which obliged him to expurgate a considerable amount of his text for the 1594 edition. Theology, nevertheless, did benefit considerably from the pagan contributions explaining the functioning of the body: Hippocratic-Galenic medicine established an explanation – a paradigm, as T. S. Kuhn would say – which remained essentially immutable throughout more than two millennia in the most varied cultural and religious ambiances. This does not imply the lack of important discussions and disagreements among physicians, theologians and those with an interest in natural philosophy. Nevertheless, Hippocratic theory provided a resistant net of meanings and interpretations, with a corpus well established by Galen, enabling communication to take place between Greek, Roman, Persian, German, Italian, French, Spanish and English physicians, despite the enormous temporal, religious and cultural distances that separated them. This scientific corpus, in a certain manner, operated as a sophisticated apparatus for translation which facilitated communication between physicians and other thinkers, such as astronomers and theologians, and even between surgeons and pharmacists and their patients, who recognized in medical practices a logical correspondence with everyday experience.

In order to reflect on the peculiarities of this mediating apparatus, I should like to offer a mental experiment which began as an exercise in science fiction. I constructed this imaginary case as an aid towards explaining cultural and political mediations. This is the story, which is situated in the twenty-sixth century:

> The extraterrestrials, who have recently arrived on our planet from a distant world – which we shall call Odorn – are already on the point of extinction when, after analysing many millions of possible permutations, some scientists by pure chance stumble upon a structural key enabling them to translate the strange olfactory signals with which the extraterrestrials communicate. These beings have a very advanced material culture, but, it seems, little skill in the semiotic arts. The human scientists construct a specialized computer which translates the olfactory signs into the different languages of Earth; the apparatus also translates human messages into the olfactory codes. Thanks to the structuralist genius, a fertile exchange of ideas begins, interplanetary treaties are signed and it is even possible to avoid conflicts which would no doubt have threatened the survival of earthly civilization, since the Odornians have a highly sophisticated destructive power at their command. From time to time, very occasionally, strange inconsistencies appear in the translation, but the cybernetic apparatus is furnished with a self-referring system of corroborations and corrections which resolves such incidents.
>
> After many decades of friendly relations between Odornians and human beings, an expedition of terrestrial anthropologists, on the first visit by men to the planet Odorn, discovers that nearly all the nouns, verbs and adjectives expressed in olfactory terms correspond to objects completely different from those indicated by the cybernetic device, and they realize that its efficacy is grounded on strange metaphorical processes that they do not properly understand. The team of anthropologists decides – we shall never know whether for good or for ill – to carefully conceal their discovery. They believe that the marvellous structural cipher discovered by chance could

well function for several centuries, as was the case with Ptolemy's false model for interpreting the universe, and they renounce the opportunity to become the Copernicans of interplanetary communication. On their return to Earth they publish a curious book of olfatory ethnography, which makes much of the anthropologists' experiences regarding the fragrant and aromatic erotic customs that emanate from Odornian society, perhaps with the purpose of diverting the readers from the semiotic problems. The anthropologists do allow themselves, however, some linguistic experiments, such as the translation of a text by Galen (*De instrumento odoratus*) which, curiously, turns out to be very popular among the inhabitants of Odorn. This is the only insinuation, surreptitiously emitted by the anthropologists, that something odd is occurring with the translating apparatus: they have decided that for a long time to come generations of anthropologists shall jealously guard the secret of Odorn.[1]

My idea is that the model of melancholy, together with the humoural theory that upholds it, is similar – although operating in a different manner – to the cybernetic device used for interplanetary communication: it was a structured ensemble of rules and concepts aimed at explaining the phenomena of sickness which allowed a wide-ranging communication to take place among all those interested in the functioning of the human body; but its correspondence with natural reality was precarious in the best of cases, and non-existent on most occasions. Paracelsus raised his voice to warn that the humoural mediating apparatus was inadequate, and even proceeded, in 1527, to burn the books of Avicenna and Galen before the gates of the University of Basle. But the physicians paid no attention to him, regarding him as mad. As I shall discuss below, these mediating peculiarities indicate that at the centre of scientific paradigms we may find mythical structures with a considerable metaphorical power.

1. Translation and its metaphors

Behind the notion of melancholy we may recognize a highly complex system of signs and symbols capable of articulating very diverse problems. Its functioning is remarkably similar to that of a thermodynamic system able to reduce its entropy at the cost of the environment. This is a system – like the apparatus for translating

Odornian – capable of ordering and then rearranging its surroundings so as to feed its processes of symbolic codification without modifying the self-referential mechanisms. Could we, perhaps, apply to melancholy the general theory of systems, such as it was developed by Bertalanffy, who – as it happens – was also not impermeable to the influence of mysticism?[2] Indeed, a sociologist has applied system theory to melancholy's twin, passionate love. Niklas Luhmann has defined love in systemic terms, as a generalized symbolic medium of communication, and has demonstrated brilliantly and suggestively the way in which the evolution of the semantics of passionate love was able to absorb, for example the revaluation of sexuality produced by the French Enlightenment, in contrast with the Puritan moralizing that was only capable of giving rise to the Victorian malformation of sexuality.[3] The expression *love as passion* derives in fact from the efforts of ancient physicians and theologians to define love as a melancholic illness; but this is a derivation of contrary sign, where the original sense of passion as a negative effect, an illness or perturbation which disorders the normal functions of an organ, is transmuted to denote a positive and irresistible attraction towards the object of amorous desire.[4]

Melancholy was certainly a coherent system capable of giving sense to mental suffering and disorder; it provided a medium for describing and communicating feelings of loneliness and a way of giving expression to the experience of non-communication. Renaissance physicians developed, on the basis of Galenism, a closed code for interpreting the signs of madness and melancholy, while at the same time offering an explanation and a treatment, and providing also a model of communication and behaviour, capable of subsuming both the growing feelings of loneliness and Catholic dogma regarding free will. All in all, the code of melancholy was able to lodge and give impulse to the new expressions of modern individuality that accompanied personal isolation faced with the aleatory conditions so often imposed by social disorder. Melancholy was a general and abstract model which explained mental suffering; paradoxically, however, it opened the way to personal and individual forms of illness. Sorrow and desolation were experienced in an individual and private way, although they were transferences made from a global system of interpretation which gave sense to suffering and connected the disorder both to the microcosm and the macrocosm. Thus, an ancient manner of inserting the individual into society was transformed into a modern one: into that irreducible singularity of personal experience.

That melancholy has become an inseparable element in modern culture is an indisputable fact. Many of the concepts that explained the black humour have survived down to our times as powerful metaphors, thanks, among other matters, to the impulse of nineteenth-century Romanticism and to its sequels in the twentieth century. But it must be noted that, if we lay undue emphasis on the *metaphoric* nature of humoural interpretation, we run the risk of forgetting that for the physicians of the Renaissance and Baroque periods melancholy formed part of a *literal* explanation. This explanation, coherent and precise, gave unity to the notion of melancholy, regardless of the conclusions of Michel Foucault, who supposed, mistakenly, that the qualities or temperaments (heat, cold, moistness, dryness) gradually replaced the humoural substances and that, thanks to this process, the creation of an integrated idea of melancholy was achieved. In actual fact, the theory of the qualities or temperaments formed an inseparable part of the ancient humoural interpretation. The slow tendency towards abandonment of the humoural system naturally implied also the rejection of the four traditional qualities. Foucault, on the basis of a very partial and distorted reading of certain classical texts on melancholy, draws the conclusion that an advance took place, among the physicians of the seventeenth century, of interest in the qualities, thus liberating them from the need to seek substantial supports for the communication of body with soul, humour with ideas, and organs with behaviour.[5] The example of Thomas Willis is misinterpreted: in this English doctor of the seventeenth century we do indeed notice a very incipient tendency to substitute new concepts for the humoural theory; however, there is no relinquishment of interest in the substantial and organic bases of mental illnesses, but, rather, a development of explanations laying emphasis on fluid and chemical processes. This tendency was to clear the way ahead for the very gradual movement towards modern neurophysiological studies.

The abandonment of interest in the substantial and physiological supports of the mental processes was to lead the way, rather, towards what we now recognize as psychological and psychoanalytic interpretations. In this we can recognize Huarte as a pioneer, since the flight of his creative imagination leads him to adopt positions that are neither very orthodox nor particularly careful in the use of humoural theory, and to emphasize the metaphoric value of the Hippocratic system as a bridge towards the social and cultural aspects of psychological behaviour. This lack of orthodoxy, which, as we shall see, so exasperated Dr Andrés Velásquez, was a premonitory sign of the peculiar refunctionalizing of melancholy within modernity. The very capacity of melancholy to suggest links between the medical explanation and the experiences of daily life is what made possible, in modern times, the recovery of its metaphoric dimensions, in order to adapt them to the new scientific explanations. It is this same metaphoric potential that sent Foucault's analyses astray.

I should like to offer some other examples of the enormous metaphorical influence of melancholy and humouralism in our times. For Julia Kristeva, the humours are affective dispositions – such as sadness, anxiety, fear and joy – which configure fluctuating investments of energy which incorporate a number of basic homeostatic processes, prior to their codification in forms, signs or rhythms identifiable in literary mode.[6] Kristeva avails herself of the metaphorical power of melancholy: for her the semiological representation of the humour is a type of catharsis, whose efficacy is both real and imaginary, used as a means of therapy by all societies throughout the millennia.[7] A neurophysiologist, Jean-Didier Vincent, has said that 'there is reason to be sorry that the terms dopamine, serotonin, or catecholamine have not maintained the metaphoric power of the words melancholy or black bile'; and continues:

> In view of the humour's lack of material substance, we cannot fail to stress once more the intuitive power of the image and the significant coherence, to put it in a rather self-explanatory way, of the word. The suggestive power of the words black bile or melancholy confer on them a verbal reality much less open to manipulation by the Hippocratic psychotherapist than is the pedantic esotericism designated by our medicines. And while the thick black bile may have lost its substantial reality, it continues to wield its allegorical power. The lack of materiality has never lessened in the slightest the explanatory and operative power of the word. If this were not so, what would remain of the inhibitions, displacements, condensations and other manoeuvres of the unconscious of which the disciples of Freud still speak?[8]

The absence of a substantial referent has not prevented humoural theory from continuing down to our days to exercise an influence on those who study mental processes. The existence of the Hippocratic humours – with the exception of the blood – is, more than anything, metaphorical or mythical, although we may suspect that they refer to certain mucous secretions, bilious juices and excreted or vomited substances. But might we not say the same of the libido, the ego, the unconscious or repression: indispensable ideas for the Freudian explanation of melancholy? There is a curious text by Freud, the 'G manuscript', in which melancholy is explained by way of deviations, inhibitions and 'invaginations' of the fluxes of sexual tension, strange processes whose reality is surely as metaphorical as that of the classical four humours.[9] In 1994, a Harvard University psychologist insisted on a return to the theory of the temperaments, on considering that the Galenic inferences are not seriously different from contemporary speculations on whether schizophrenics have an excess of dopamine and depressives an insufficiency of norepinephrine.[10] Perhaps we are witnessing a return to humoural theory, with the discovery of the depressive effects of certain neurotransmitter substances which inhibit or stimulate the nerve cells and which flow in the brain along relatively stable paths.[11] Present-day physicians, like those of medieval and Renaissance times, use a variety of pharmaceutical products to regulate the disequilibria between neurotransmitter substances; in the past hellebore was used, nowadays fluoxetine hydrochloride for example, better known under the trade-name Prozac. Another example is the use of hypericum (or St John's wort) as an antidepressant, a wild plant that increases the presence of serotonin, norepinephrine and dopamine.[12]

I have mentioned a few examples of the modern 'appropriation' of ancient ideas about melancholy in order to indicate the existence of a fascinating process. The old texts are taken as a metaphor for certain mental situations; it is assumed that if we study the metaphor we may come to understand certain aspects of the functioning of the mind, and in some authors we can observe a substitution: by turning to the analysis of such metaphors they save themselves the trouble of studying organs and substances; it is enough to interpret the texts in order to penetrate the mysteries of the mind. It even came to be believed that, in fact, it was not possible to study the mind directly, but only the semiotics of the texts and discourse that emanate from it. Curiously, this way of observing melancholy is similar to that of the medieval and Renaissance doctors, who preferred to interpret the ancient

Hippocratic texts and the writings of Aristotle, Aretæus or Galen, rather than to practise anatomies and carry out direct observation of the sick. They were convinced that the texts enshrined original truths that had been the fruit of the ancient investigations of their authors. This of course is not the case with the modern studies; why, then, do we appreciate the metaphorical value of the texts on melancholy? Drs Juan Huarte and Andrés Velásquez firmly believed that the texts of Galen were the results of experience that had born fruit in the form of real empirical data: their interpretation of the texts of the Hippocratic tradition recognized the literal value, and not only the metaphoric dimension of humoural theory.

I have already stated that humoural theory lacks an empirical referent. But it could perhaps be argued that melancholy – even though a dark corporeal juice corresponding to the concept did not actually exist – does refer to real forms of suffering, to feelings of anguish accompanied by self-destructive types of behaviour which effectively manifest themselves in people's lives. What is of interest here, however, is not the question of whether or not concrete forms of suffering existed – it is obvious that they exist – but the real, explanatory and significative presence of a coherent set of symptoms and causes which, since ancient times, were classified under the unifying notion of melancholy.[13] It would then seem to have been a kind of inspired intuition, almost a divine spark, which implanted in the minds of men the revealing idea of melancholy. The problem which this interpretation leaves unresolved is that precisely the nucleus of what we today consider 'scientific' in the idea of melancholy (or depression) is what has least continuity: it could be said that the permanence of the external form of the idea can be evidenced and traced down through the millennia, but not its explanatory contents, which began to vary considerably, above all with the influence of the modern scientific revolution. A psychiatrist has written an important history of melancholy, assuming, at the outset, that at stake are a set of closely related clinical syndromes.[14] However, it is by no means certain that the melancholy syndrome corresponds to a single pathology; the history of the ancient relation between mania and melancholy – which ended up generating the unified notion of the manic-depressive dementia – is a demonstration of the enormous difficulties surrounding the establishment of a clinical syndrome for disturbances whose aetiology is still not well understood. The complex interrelation of hereditary genetic factors with the functions of neurotransmitter substances has enormously complicated the investigation of the depressions and manias.[15] While we may be sure that neurology will continue to clarify many areas of ignorance, the history of melancholy may also shed light on the cultural processes that ensure the continuity of certain symbolic structures. Even supposing the existence of a melancholic syndrome, this is not sufficient to explain the extraordinary stability with which the paradigm of melancholy continued to reproduce itself with very few modifications down to the time of the Spanish physicians whom I am considering in this book. Its metaphoric power is undeniable, as I have pointed out, but not so very great as to explain the way in which the canon was replicated faithfully throughout diverse periods and geographical regions through history.

2. Myth and evolution

There is another explanation that may help us to understand the survival of the canon of melancholy. We may suppose that, despite the fact that melancholia is a diagnosis enshrined in scientific traditions, it is also a symbolic structure having the characteristics of a myth: immense metaphoric power, mediating functions, long duration, capacity to generate replicas faithful to an original canon, connection with magical and diabolic rituals, etc. The metaphoric power of melancholy as a myth could be an example of what the British biologist Richard Dawkins has called *memes,* or 'new replicators', to describe the cultural equivalents of biological genes: these are units of cultural transmission which survive over long periods thanks to their capacity for self-replication as living structures, and which obey the laws of natural selection.[16] For Dawkins a meme can be practically anything: ideas, tunes, fashions, set phrases, ways of making pots or techniques for constructing arches. Every entity that has 'survival value' – such as God or a funny joke – is a meme capable of making copies of itself by means of imitation, and of transmitting itself from one brain to another. It has to be admitted that the universalizing aspiration of Dawkins's thesis limits its interest to a great extent, since not every relatively long-lived cultural element behaves like an algorithm proper to natural selection. The major defect of this theory lies, however, in its failing to provide the necessary conceptual tools to define the meme as an observable unit. If absolutely any 'good' idea that happens also to be endowed with 'great psychological appeal' is a meme,[17] we fall into a quagmire of indefinability and, I fear, the banality of stating the obvious: that there are ideas that are imitated and transmitted.

However, despite the imprudence with which some biologists trespass upon the fields of culture, one should resist the temptation to trash evolutionist interpretations of cultural phenomena. We may find good examples of replicators in the history of myths, where certain structures (which have been called *mythemes*) are comparable to the memes. The myth of the wild man, which I have studied in detail, can be explained from an evolutionist perspective.[18] The same can be done, it seems to me, with the highly canonized structure of the myth of melancholy. A follower of the theories of Dawkins has adopted a critical approach to the problem of the survival of religious elements posed by Walter Burkert in his exploration of biological influences in ancient religions.[19] Daniel Dennett maintains, against Burkert's opinions, that the survival of religious values is not necessarily based on their fulfilling certain basic functions, but on the fact the religious memes themselves use human beings to reproduce and duplicate themselves, even when they are not good for society. The memes, for Dennett,

> are complex ideas in the sense of something that one can patent or for which a *copyright* can be registered, and not in the sense of an element of experience. The idea of the wheel is a *meme*, just as is the idea of hijacking aircraft, since a *meme* tends to reproduce itself even when it is not good for people.[20]

The religious memes that have most success survive, according to this explanation, not on account of their becoming vehicles of social interests or functions, but on account of possessing certain characteristics that enable them to persist in human environments, thanks to a Darwinian type of selection process. Burkert explores the possibility that biological and genetic structures may exercise an influence on cultural behaviour; Dawkins and Dennett, on the other hand, consider that the transmission of cultural structures functions in the same way as the genetic transmission of information. They are obsessed by the following question: whose interests are served by replication? Those of the meme itself, they answer, which is 'selfish' and 'wishes' to reproduce itself, even at the cost of human beings. For the meme is an algorithm which has its own logic (and syntax) and whose ultimate aim is its own perpetuation through the process of making copies of itself. Continuing in the vein of the old joke which affirms that a hen is merely an egg's way of making another egg, Dennett has introduced the same type of game into culture: a researcher is nothing more than a library's way of generating new libraries. Thus, in the same way that a gene leaps from body to body thanks to sperm or eggs, memes as units of cultural imitation propagate themselves by leaping from brain to brain. A cultural feature evolved in a certain way simply because it was advantageous for itself.[21]

One of the most important elements in this process is to be seen in the high fidelity of the copy. Of course, this is not a characteristic of many forms of cultural transmission. But the history of the transmission of the canon of melancholy does adapt, up to a certain point, to this basic demand of every evolutionary process of Darwinian type, as do many mythic structures. However, it is difficult to believe that melancholy, seen as a meme, evolves and reproduces itself due solely to its being most advantageous for itself. Stephen Jay Gould has criticized this theory, observing that in biology the unit of selection is the individual, not the gene,[22] and that in culture the process of transmission is governed by a process that is Lamarckian, rather than Darwinian; in other words, culture evolves on the basis of the inheritance of acquired characteristics.[23]

Doubtless, we must beware of what Gould has called ultra-Darwinian fundamentalism, especially when we try to give a universal explanation applicable to the majority of cultural phenomena.[24] Nevertheless, we do not gain very much by interpreting myths in Lamarckian terms, repeating with biological metaphors well-known facts. What we must determine is whether or not, in certain cultural spheres, processes of mimetic transmission of a Darwinian type exist, which imply the selection and mutation of symbolic structures. I am convinced that there are many mythological structures whose long evolution may be explained within an evolutionist perspective; and I also believe that the canon of melancholy is home to one such structure. This does not mean that we can put aside the social, political and cultural function of melancholy in precise historical contexts. This function is precisely what guarantees the survival of the canon of melancholy: society selects the canons most suitable for fulfilling particular necessary tasks. But the functions of a myth such as melancholy may be highly varied and different; what we observe is the continuity and survival of a symbolic structure and not the permanence of a single unchanging set of functions: the functions and meanings of melancholy are very different, let us say, in the Greece of Galen, the Middle Ages of Hildegard von Bingen, the Renaissance of Ficino, the Baroque Spain of Huarte or the Romantic period of Nerval, even though the structure of the myth is similar in each of these historical periods. What we see here is a process of transmission which, viewed in the long term, is relatively blind – although not indifferent – to the changing functions of the myth of melancholy as it passes through different historical moments. It is a blind process because we are in the presence of a multifunctional mythical structure capable of adapting itself to different conditions: but these same conditions are those which gradually configure or guide, so to speak, the blind logic of the long evolution of a myth. Melancholy makes its way blindly along the path of its own mimetic reproduction, but it is not deaf to the suffering of the men and women who partake of it during each stage of the journey.

It is interesting to note that, from a very different point of view, the German philosopher Hans Blumenberg has also arrived at a Darwinian interpretation of myths. For Blumenberg the 'iconic constancy' of myths, manifested in their durability and dissemination, is a prolonged process of selection, a genuine secular process of refinement or depuration of Darwinian type.[25] The persistence of myths, according to Blumenberg, is due to the fundamental fact that the human species suffers from a peculiar anxiety, as a result of not having a precise biological niche; this unadaptedness has led to a deficit of instincts of adaptation. The function of myths consists in overcoming the anxiety produced by what Blumenberg calls the 'absolutism of reality' (biological unadaptedness), displacing this towards specific and concrete fears. The myths that survive have been subjected to a long 'work' of selection in which the fittest are those which harden and survive.

The example of melancholy is highly illustrative: I have described it as a translating and mediating apparatus, a symbolic system, a metaphor or mnemonic unit of transmission. We are faced with a complex process that codifies suffering, provides a model linking scientific explanations with the experiences of daily life. With the passing of the centuries it has acquired a functional capacity and an adaptability proper to myths. In this sense, as I stated at the outset of this essay, melancholy takes on the appearance of a cybernetic device capable of translating the most remote expressions of extraterrestrial otherness. The mental experiment discharges, however, into a paradoxical situation: a functional communication conceals a fundamental disconnection. The philosopher John Searle has proposed a similar experiment: let us suppose we are shut up in a room in which we have at our disposal a number of boxes full of Chinese ideograms (the database), and a book of rules (the program); we do not understand Chinese, but from outside, in the form of questions, little groups of Chinese symbols arrive, to which we apply the program; this in turn produces other little heaps of symbols, which are sent out as answers. Searle's conclusion is that, since we cannot be said to understand Chinese simply because we apply a program for translation, in the same way a digital computer cannot be said to understand Chinese, no matter how sophisticated the program it uses, since none of these machines have anything that we ourselves do not have. This mental experiment shows that the programs have a *syntactic* character, while our minds have a *semantic* one. Syntax is not the same as semantics, nor is it fully able to replace it. By means of this mental experiment, Searle proved that artificial intelligence is not an adequate model to represent the functioning of the mind and the brain.[26] Can we equally conclude that the canon of melancholy is an artificial apparatus endowed with complex syntactic mechanisms, but which lacks a semantic system (or has only a weakened one)?

Of course, the artificiality of the mythical canon does not have the same characteristics as that of a computer program. The logic of a myth does not obey a prior will nor is it subject to a precise aim; its crystallization has required a slow process of decantation through history. Nevertheless, it seems to me that we can locate certain mythological structures whose solid 'syntax' permits a high degree of multifunctionality and great semantic plasticity. I believe that the myth of melancholy, as I have already said, is a good example of this type of structure, endowed with a system of reproduction very similar to the algorithms that explain natural selection. It should be noted that the presence of evolutionary selection mechanisms does not explain all the cultural processes; it is necessary, in this regard, to lay aside all kinds of fundamentalism. But in what does the investigation of such mechanisms help us?

I believe it helps us to elude teleological or metaphysical solutions to the problem of the long duration of myths and other cultural forms characterized by long continuity and persistence. If there is no perennial finality enshrined in their structure, ensuring their future, and neither do they obey the non-temporal influence of an archetype or a spiritual architecture, then we must look for the explanation in their own history. For us to see the history (and the evolution) of the myth as enshrined in a process of selection, it is necessary to introduce another aspect: that of mutations. In effect, to understand certain innovatory developments in the history of the myth, we need the appearance of new elements which will form part of the group of alternatives to be selected. With the aim of expounding this problem synthetically, I shall mention a few examples taken from the history of acedia[27] and melancholy.

At some moment between the third century before Christ and the beginning of the Christian Era two mutations took place that, with time, came to be included in the mythic canon of melancholy. The first consisted in the fact that a Greek writer of the school of Aristotle established a relation between the black humour and the exceptional personality, prophetic, heroic and talented, which was given permanent form in the *Problemata* (*XXX, 1*). This appreciation, although it is linked to humoural theory, stands apart from the medical tradition by emphasizing the non-pathological consequences of melancholy. In fact, this extraordinary appreciation was not incorporated into the canon of melancholy until the Italian Renaissance during the fifteenth century.[28] On the other hand, the Greek translators of the Hebrew text of the Old Testament – the so-called Seventy – committed an enigmatic error in their version of Psalm 90. This error – perhaps it would be better to speak of transposition or imprecision – was a mutation that had important consequences. The Hebrew text of the psalm says that there is no reason to fear the terror of the night, nor the arrow that flies by day, nor the plague that spreads in the shadows, 'nor the scourge that lays waste at midday' (90: 6). But the Greek text of the Septuagint substitutes for this last menace a noonday *daimōn*, which in turn was translated into Latin as *daemonium meridianum*. The reasons for this mutation are not clear, but it is possible that they answer to some traditions from the myth or folklore of the Middle East, which interpreted the dangers associated with the moment in which the sun stood at its zenith as malign powers.[29] This noonday demon was highly intriguing for the interpreters of the Bible. St Augustine identified the *daemonium meridianum* with the intensification of heat in the battle and in the persecution of the Christians.[30] St Jerome was not in agreement with the exegesis of St Augustine: the noontide demon is Satan disguised as an angel of light who seeks to corrupt Christian dogma; the instruments of Satan are, for Jerome, the heretics, who believe they possess the light of truth, but in fact distort with their interpretations the sense of the Holy Scriptures.[31] These interpretations were forgotten. But the mutation which interests me, and which was incorporated into our myth, was consolidated by ascetics such as John Cassianus and Evagrius Ponti, who connected the noontide demon with acedia, continuing an interpretation of Psalm 90 which Origen had already mentioned.[32] Thus it became possible to associate, in a single mythico-religious conglomerate, sadness and despondency with the Devil and sin. And since acedia – in another mutation – was associated with melancholy in the Middle Ages, a complex mythical structure was firmly established whose internal connections and external associations resulted from chance and improbable mutations.[33] There remained still what we could call the fourth mutation of the noontide demon: in the fifteenth century Ficino and Petrarch began a revaluation of melancholy and acedia, which allowed a confrontation of their positive aspects to take place and exercised a powerful influence down to our days.

In this chain of mutations there is no room for metaphysical or teleological explanations. There is nothing in any of these mutations that might be determined by a sign or a finality; each mutation is to be explained by its functions at different stages or moments of history (although in many cases no trace of these remains) and not by a pre-inscribed logic guiding the concatenation. The logic (or syntax) appears *ex post facto*, and the structural ensemble is consolidated and sedimented with the passing of the centuries. The result, to be sure, is not the same as a computer program: in fact, it is something much better, more sophisticated and more potent. Nor does it function in the same way as the individual self-reflecting consciousness based on neurophysiological processes which are still far from well understood; but millions of consciousnesses participate in the crystallization of the canon and its operation. We may wonder whether the men who use and participate in the canon of melancholy understand each other; is it not a similar case to that of the users of the Chinese room (or of the computer), who in reality do not understand the meaning of the signs they use?

To resolve such doubts perhaps it would be better to examine them from a different perspective. We can use another premise as our starting-point: without a certain degree of non-communication there would be no culture (nor language, nor science). I mean by this that at the very root and origin of culture we find what Ernest Gellner calls the 'fantastic range of genetically possible conduct'[34] and which Blumenberg defines as the human species' lack of a particular ecological niche, restricting the plurality of behaviours. This extraordinary diversity, which is expressed in an important differentiation, generates problems of communication between groups or individuals who experience forms of solitude and isolation unknown in the animal kingdom. From this condition a paradox is born: a certain disequilibrium between syntax and semantics, which weakens the latter, is found to be of use in giving impulse to communication between human beings. The suffering of loneliness accompanies and stimulates the search for means of communication. Human society exists only upon the basis of loneliness and lack of communication. Other animals are never alone and communion with their fellows is perfect. Among them communication is sure and dependable.

To illustrate this subject, and also as a mental experiment, I shall offer a similar example to that of the extraterrestrials who communicate by means of olfactory signs. But this time the example comes not from science fiction but from scientific research. The study of olfactory communication among animals has made it possible to identify semiochemical elements that enable data to be transmitted between individuals of the same species (and sometimes between different species). Ethologists have coined a new term to refer to scents with a significative function: the *pheromones*, semiochemical substances, generally glandular secretions, which are emitted as signs or signals which are recognized on being smelt (or tasted) by other members of the same species. According to Bert Hölldobler and Edmund O. Wilson, pheromones have a central function in the social organization of ants: each colony operates, according to the species, with sets of ten to twenty different categories of signals, most of which are of a chemical nature.[35] The transmission of olfactory signals allows ants to recognize the distinctive smells of each colony, establish sexual communication, mark paths and territories, and send out signals of alarm, recruitment for new colonies, warning or attraction.[36]

The presence of syntactic forms of communication among ants is open to discussion; some researchers believe that they have perceived some significative connections between, for example, certain secretions from the rectal gland and movements of the head and the mandibles, or of the whole body; such combinations might distinguish different kinds of recruitment (for purposes of collecting food or for establishing new territory). It remains to be proved that ants perceive such differences, but it seems unlikely that these stereotyped combinations are lacking in function.[37] Whatever the case, what cannot be happening here is a semantic disturbance that perturbs the meanings, since that would lead to the end of the ants' colony. Ants cannot be melancholics: if they cease to communicate, they die. Human beings, on the other hand, take advantage of melancholy and other such semantic perturbations which, as long as they do not exceed certain thresholds of tolerance, stimulate them to work out new and diversified forms of communication. This might appear to be nothing more than a 'disease of language', in the sense that Friedrich Max Müller gave the expression, but in fact it is the source of mankind's health.

This means that the discordances and incoherences that we have observed, for example, regarding the black humour, the adustion (scorching or parching) of the phlegm or the animal pneuma and its supposed somatic references are not part of the pathology proper to the formation of myths, nor of an irrationality in the structure of the canon of melancholy. On the contrary, they are part of a complex process of cultural crystallizations that came into being on the basis of the problems of communication of a humanity which is dislocated, highly differentiated and disgregated. I shall not dilate further on this problem, which extends beyond the framework of this essay, and which has formed the basis of an interpretation of myths which originates in Bernard Fontenelle and culminates in Müller.[38] The lack of correspondence between words and things would be natural to a mythopoetic era, affected by a disease of language that could be corrected through the application of comparative philology. Of course, merely setting the irrational obscurity of myth in contraposition to the light of science is not something that is likely to help us understand the survival of mythological structures. Today we know that the myths which survive at the very heart of science can be potent stimulants to rational forms of investigation. Under certain conditions, they can also become obstacles to the development of the sciences. The myth of melancholy, lodged in the very heart of medical science, has fulfilled a diversity of functions, both stimulating and holding back the study of cerebral physiology and the diseases of the mind.

The equilibrium between mystery and truth – between myth and science – has varied throughout the centuries. What makes the case of melancholy so fascinating is its double condition: besides containing the symbolic structure of a myth, it also makes reference to the tragic consequences of loneliness, lack of communication and anxiety occasioned by the ever renewed diversification of human experience. Melancholy becomes a mediating network enabling communication to take place between beings who suffer or are trying to understand loneliness and isolation, incomprehension and dislocation, transition and separation. Thus, we may suppose that those who participate in the canon of melancholy understand and fail to understand each other, communicate in solitude and codify the mystery of separation. I will take the polemic between the physicians Juan Huarte and Andrés Velásquez as an example of this paradox: two Baroque and Renaissance mentalities, anchored by rigid Galenic codes, attempted to rise above the mysteries of the mind and the brain. They, like many other physicians of their time, were witnesses to a turbulent era of change and differentiation; the discontents of men and women needed melancholy in order to express and suffer their perplexities.

3. The adust humours: an overview

Constantine the African (Constantinus Africanus) was a convert from Islam whose activity as a translator of Arabic texts into Latin during the eleventh century constituted an extraordinary contribution to the European intellectual renaissance of the High Middle Ages. His translations of medical texts were still influential in the sixteenth century, and his versions of the great Arab thinkers provided a bridge linking Christian culture with Antiquity; moreover, they made Hippocrates and Galen known through Latin translations of the Arabic versions. Constantine was admired as a kind of Prometheus who had brought to Europe the advanced medical science of Islam, and around whose life a number of legends were woven. According to one such legend he was born in Carthage and travelled widely around Mesopotamia, India, Ethiopia and Egypt; on his return to Africa, impregnated with medical wisdom, he was persecuted by the envy of his countrymen, who even tried to assassinate him. As a result he fled to Salerno, where he studied and, after converting to Christianity, sought refuge in the monastery of Montecassino, where he devoted himself to the work of translation until his death in 1087.[39] One of the numerous texts that Constantine made known is titled *De melancholia*, and in it the Galenic principles are established with clarity, as Islamic medicine interpreted them. This is in fact a translation of a treatise written by a great physician of Baghdad, Ishāq ibn Imrān (who died in 909), which alleges that melancholy may attack those who are excessively religious, those who work too much with the mind, scholars who have suddenly lost their books and people who have been bereft of a loved one.[40] For Ishāq melancholy is a black humour which causes feelings of loneliness and dejection in the soul; he upholds the classical belief in the existence of three forms of illness, which are:

(1) That produced in the brain itself, which may be of two types: one manifesting itself in either an aggressive form of behaviour, such as lycanthropy, or headaches and drowsiness (these manifestations proceed from the presence of black bile in the brain or from its corruption); and another type, caused by the combusted yellow bile and accompanied by high fever, demented actions and strange movements.
(2) The illness set off by the black bile in the whole body, which may reach the brain and which produces terror, anxiety and depression, as well as the symptoms described in the first form of the illness.
(3) The melancholy of the hypocondriac, which is produced by the extravasation of black bile in the epigastrium, and which reaches the brain as a secondary effect; it gives rise to flatulence, a feeling of heaviness, bitter vomiting and constant weeping.[41]

Arab medicine concerned itself with problems that obsessed European culture, especially in the twelfth century, when concern for the internal spaces of the soul and the definition of the ego became accentuated. A Persian physician of the tenth century, 'Ali ibn al-'Abbās, known in Europe as Haly Abbas (who died in 994), was also interested in the subject of melancholy. In his *Pategni* (*al-Kitab al-maliki*) ('The Royal Book') which had been translated into Latin by Constantine the African, there is a section devoted to the causes of melancholy, lycanthropy and lovesickness, three phenomena regarded as manifestations of the same disorder.[42] This illness is 'a certain sensation of dejection and isolation which forms in the soul due to the fact that something that the patients believe to be real is in fact unreal'.⁴³ Melancholics display different symptoms: some laugh excessively, while others cry or deny their own existence. Some patients believe themselves to be prophets able to predict the future, while others think they are animals: the variety of melancholy known as 'canine' (lycanthropy) is incurable and turns yellow the eyes of the affected, who tend to go by night to howl beside tombs.⁴⁴ Haly Abbas establishes somatic bases for a series of phenomena that in many cases were considered ills of the soul rather than of the body. This physician believed that love is a disease of the brain which, in the same way as melancholy, arises from the difficulty of obtaining an intensely desired object. In his studies of melancholy, Haly Abbas based his efforts on one of the greatest physicians of Islam, Rhazes or Ar-Razi (c.850–923), who was introduced to the Latin West thanks to the versions of Gerard of Cremona, of the famous school of translators at Toledo.⁴⁵ Rhazes defined melancholy in the traditional Galenic manner; in this illness he included love, regarded as a terrible mental disorder, and recommended several cures, among them fasting, much walking, drinking wine and frequent coitus.⁴⁶

The Galenic traditions salvaged and developed by Isḥāq ibn Imrān, Haly Abbas and Rhazes found their consolidation in the *Canon of Medicine* of Avicenna (980–1037), the great treatise on medicine which exercised a powerful influence on European scientific thought until the seventeenth century. One of the important innovations of Avicenna was the systematization of the Hippocratic theory of the humours. With regard to melancholy, Avicenna added a fourth form of this illness, with the aim of harmonizing its manifestations with the four humours of classical theory. In the Hippocratic-Galenic tradition melancholy was a sickness produced by the combustion of natural black bile, yellow bile or red bile (the blood). The adustion of these three natural humours produced the unnatural black bile or adust melancholy, whose vapours could cause damage in the brain. In order to complete the systematic framework, it was necessary to consider the combustion of the fourth natural humour, the phlegm.⁴⁷ Avicenna added a fourth type of melancholy, thus organizing a coherent system which allowed for logical combinations of the four natural humours with their respective adust, or combusted, forms; in other words, he established the possibility of four types of unhealthy black choler on the basis of the combustion of the yellow bile, the blood, the (natural) black bile and the phlegm.[48] This set of combinations enabled those clinical manifestations less obviously connected with the symptoms of sadness, loneliness and dejection – such as the manias, furies and aggressiveness – to be explained more easily. It was precisely the addition of a fourth form of black humour – on the basis of the adustion of the phlegm – that motivated the criticism of Dr Andrés Velásquez. We shall have occasion to return to this problem later.

What interests me at this point is to present a schematic diagram of the traditional baggage inherited by the Spanish medical science of the sixteenth century. A good example is provided by the Catalan doctor Arnau de Vilanova (d. c.1313), who, as was normal, assimilated melancholy with mania. In his *Practica medicinae* he devoted a chapter to both ills. Arnau had a thorough knowledge of, and admiration for, Arab medicine, and his words transmit to us the flavour of the medical descriptions of the period:

> The melancholy [i.e. the black bile] is in the animal spirit, in which it generates fear and pusillanimity or sadness: which (conditions) are in him who suffers from melancholy: sadness, fear and mutism. And its place: the middle cell or ventricle of the head, between the rational and the imaginative. For these ailments come at times from the very sickness of the brain, at times from the stomach, at times from a heavy smokiness that rises to the brain, at times from a subtle smokiness that rises to the said place, at times from other ills, sometimes from the blood, sometimes from the choler, sometimes from the phlegm, sometimes from the melancholy [i.e. the black bile] . . .[49]

In this paragraph we may appreciate the traditional problem-points: to begin with, although the same name is used for both (in the original Latin, the term *melancholy* is used irrespective of whether it is the humour or the disease that is being referred to), there is a tacit distinction between melancholy as the black humour and melancholy as an illness. Likewise, the three classical forms of the illness are mentioned here, although vaguely (of the brain, of the whole body, or the hypochondria), as well as the quadruple origin of adust melancholy, as a result of the 'cooking' or combustion of the natural humours. The classification is flexible, and permitted an adaptation of the canonical explanation to a great diversity of symptoms. Arnau de Vilanova also sought various causes that might give rise to melancholy and mania. There are foods that produce black bile, such as pepper, garlic and the strong wines that burn the humours; among these external causes he also includes the bites of venomous beasts or rabid dogs, and corrupted air. But he also mentions internal causes, and this is very important, since it opens the door to therapies of a not exclusively somatic nature:

> The passions of the soul such as rage and sudden fear: or worry due to the excess of study, the loss of something, hunger that has been undergone, excessive fasting, menstruation retained longer than what is due, or sperm that has become corrupted or retained longer than the measure, and this is something we see among monks and nuns, unmarried people, both male and female, who often retain it, converting it into poison, according to Galen.[50]

This extraordinary physician did not omit mention of erotic or love melancholy, which he refers to as 'heroic love' in his celebrated treatise, on account of the fact that the actions of lovers towards the objects of their desire are comparable to the attitudes proper to serfs towards their lords; besides, this love, which could also be termed 'aristocratic', is a sickness capable of unseating even lords.[51] This amorous melancholy was explained by the overheating of the *spiritus* which rose to the brain, to the place where the estimative or rational faculty was situated.[52]

Another brush-stroke in the painting of this historical panorama of melancholy is provided by a great physician, cited and much admired by Dr Velásquez. I refer to Jean Fernel, or Fernelius (1497–1558), a French humanist, doctor and philosopher who, besides important treatises on pathology and physiology, wrote a collection of clinical case-histories or *consilia*, as such collections of pathographical narration used to be called. From this we extract the following account, entitled 'De melancholia hypocondriaca, pro Domino de Maligny'.

> I hear that the illustrious and most prudent gentlemen Mr de Maligny is afflicted by many and various symptoms, of considerable gravity and concern; even though all of them are the manifestation of one and the same affect. All of these symptoms appeared with sudden fulminancy a few days ago, during an excessively hot high summer, although it would appear that the first rudiments of their origin are [to be sought] very much earlier. Sadness, frequent and unmotivated fear, loneliness, deep and grave meditation, sleep

turbulent and perturbed by diverse and terrible nightmares; everything indicates that this is a case of melancholy – and not primary, in which the damage is only to the brain – but of that other kind that by sympathy incites the præcordial zone and which we generally call hypochondria. A visible indication of this is the tumour that can be perceived around the spleen and the pancreas.

I do not believe that the continent cause in this case is natural melancholy, which is the faeces of the blood, but that other, roasted, which has its origin in adustion of the yellow bile and which we call by its own name, that of black bile. This, sensibly accumulated over a long period in the præcordial region, began a long time ago to become inflamed and emit malign vapours.[53]

As can be seen, Fernel uses the very ancient classificatory and explanatory system without any change: the melancholy diagnosed here is not that of the brain or that of the whole body, but that of the hypochondria. Besides, it is produced by the heating of one of the four humours, the yellow bile in this case. This is a diagnosis based on the medieval canon established by Avicenna. Another great physician, of the school of Padua, regarded as more advanced, and celebrated as the founder of modern clinical medicine, was greatly concerned with melancholy; this was Giovanni da Monte or Montanus (1498–1551), who used to deliver his classes not *ex cathedra* but by the bedsides of the sick in the hospital of St Francis. Montanus accepted the typically Renaissance convention of the close connection between genius and the Saturnine humour; he developed a therapy based on diet and studied the menstrual cycles and depressive phases.[54] One of the *consilios* or case-studies that he brought together concerns a patient diagnosed as suffering from 'natural melancholy'; this was a young man accustomed to living in a disorderly manner, who had 'had love affairs with several women, it being suspected that the women had given him love potions', and had lost a lot of money in gaming. He had fallen into a condition of anxiety, worry and delirium. The young man, who was twenty-two years old, was administered purges of hellebore and was able to evacuate only with the help of clysters, eliminating pituitous motions; but not only did he fail to get well, but his delirium actually became worse, with a constant vociferation of words without sense. He also suffered panic attacks, demanded his food with fury, and would grab it angrily from the hands of those who brought it to him; he was unable to find repose, and wished only to escape and wander from place to place. On the basis of the observed symptoms, Montanus made the following diagnosis:

> The most important symptoms displayed by this young man are two: on the one hand, melancholy and damage in the operations of the brain; and on the other, an unbounded and inopportune hunger that can in no way be satisfied . . . As for the first, which is the damage in the operation of his brain, he becomes sad without cause and suffers fits of terror, which is a sign of common melancholy. But since the types of melancholy are various, I shall not distinguish the different melancholies, according to the parts affected, by consensus [i.e. sympathy between the parts] and by essence, but by the material which produces them, which is what determines the essential differences. When we speak here of melancholy we mean an affection of the brain; it is the brain, then, that suffers, even though I may have doubts regarding the cause and in which place. I hear that this patient remembers, recognizes, knows, discourses and distinguishes correctly: when he sees a man, albeit at a distance, he recognizes him, even if he has not seen him for some time. As for the internal senses, there is no alteration and he exercises the external ones well. What is then the faculty of the brain that in this case is damaged? He is afraid of things that are not normally to be feared, he is made sad by things that should not cause sadness; it seems, then, that his discourse is not normal and that the discursive power suffers damage.[55]

Montanus's conclusion is that there is a lesion in terms of diminution of activity (*diminutio discursus*), but not as a result of corruption. Later, he wonders whether the sadness is generated by the natural black humour, by melancholy '*facta per adustionem*' or by some cold humour which rises to the brain. He decides that it is not a case of adust melancholy, since in such cases patients display symptoms of mania and frenzy or, as Avicenna notes, are 'demoniac', fleeing in search of solitude beside tombs. Finally, he observes that no heating of the humours is evident, but rather the cooling influence of the black bile and the phlegm, for which reason the prognosis is not entirely unfavourable, and he prescribes a dietetic treatment accompanied by drugs.

On examining the abundant medical literature written on melancholy in the sixteenth century, there is one aspect that seems particularly surprising: the permanence of the essential characteristics defining the illness over a period of fourteen centuries. The continuity of the syndrome of melancholy is extraordinary and brings us face to face with several problems, among which I wish to emphasize two. First, we have reason to doubt the existence, in the history of the treatment of mental illnesses, of the profound changes implied by the Renaissance in other areas of knowledge. In the second place, we may suspect that the survival of the Hippocratic-Galenic theory regarding the existence of the *atrabilis* or black bile is to be explained by its correspondence to a valid and fundamental intuition, as Jean Starobiniski suggests.[56]

It is not easy to find in the European psychiatry of the sixteenth century the humanist spirit and the restless desire to investigate on the basis of objective reality which characterizes Renaissance culture.[57] It is true that we come across some efforts to avoid non-natural explanations, but the influence of theology counterbalanced the naturalist tendencies. We do not find in the study and treatment of mental illnesses any equivalent to the extraordinary description of the physical human body executed by the Belgian anatomist Vesalius. It is also true that there is a greater emphasis on clinical observation and on the description of concrete cases,[58] but the return to the Greek and Latin sources brought about a strengthening of humoural interpretation, which served as a brake on the seeking of new manifestations and explanations of melancholy illness.

On the other hand, the persistence of a theoretical outlook based on the effects of the black humour and the malign vapours supposedly produced by the combustion of humoural substances could be explained by the great symbolic potency of the images invoked, linked to the discovery of a successful method to induce, via the administration of powerful drugs, the patient's psychological participation in a catharsis that anticipated in certain ways Freudian psychoanalytic practice. As Starobinski has stated:

> As long as science did not have at its disposal an anatomical and chemical methodology of sufficient precision to demonstrate that the *atrabilis* was a purely spiritual image, this black humour was to continue to be the most satisfactory and synthetic representation of an existence dominated by preoccupations regarding the body, charged with sadness, and with little presence of initiative and movement.[59]

I shall return to this interpretation below; and for the moment I only wish to point out that, without being completely mistaken, it may serve to deflect attention from an extraordinary phenomenon that was taking place during the Italian Renaissance and the Spanish Golden Age. The important changes are not those that occurred in the explanation of the melancholic syndrome: the structure of this syndrome does not change essentially. The great transformation is to be found in the fact that melancholy comes to be one of the fundamental axes of Renaissance culture. The novelty is not to be found in the field of explanation, which remains wound up in ancient and medieval theories, but in the irradiation by the phenomenon of melancholy of broad areas of Renaissance culture and life: this explosion of melancholy was to have important repercussions and lasting consequences in Europe.

NOTES

[1] I published this tale in a different version in 'Ludonomicon: el poder burlado'. T. S. Kuhn devotes an interesting section of his book *La estructura de las revoluciones científicas* (Mexico City: Fondo de Cultura Ecónomica, 1971) to the problem of translation (Postscript, p. 4).

[2] Ludwig von Bertalanffy, *General System Theory* (New York: Braziller, 1968).

[3] Niklas Luhmann, *Love as Passion* (Cambridge, MA: Harvard University Press, 1986), p. 10.

[4] Luhmann only mentions in passing the fact that amorous passion was regarded in the Middle Ages as an illness, in contrast with sexuality, which was seen as a normal physical behaviour (ibid., 52)

[5] Michel Foucault, *Histoire de la folie à l'âge classique* (Paris: Gallimard, 1972), p. 282. Foucault's entire interpretation of melancholy and mania, to which he devotes a section of the book (*apartado*), is vitiated by a failure to understand the humoural system and a lack of information regarding the texts of the period.

[6] Kristeva, *Soleil noir. Dépression et mélancolie* (Paris: Gallimard, 1987), pp. 32–3.

[7] Ibid., p. 35. The idea that the ancient treatment of melancholy was similar to psychoanalytic catharsis had already been expressed by Starobinski, *Histoire du traitement de la mélancolie des origines à 1900* (Basilea: J. R. Geigy, 1960), p. 44.

[8] Jean-Didier Vincent, *Biología de las pasiones* (Barcelona: Anagrama, 1987), p. 29.

[9] Sigmund Freud, 'Manuscript G' (*c.*1895). The classic Freudian text on the subject is 'Mourning and Melancholy', in *Standard Edition of the Complete Psychological Works*, XIV (Toronto: Hogarth Press, 1957). Another important treatment of the subject can be found in 'A seventeenth-century demonological neurosis'; see a commentary on

this essay below, in note 72. On the basis of Freud's thesis, the psychoanalist Pierre Fédida ('Le cannibale mélancolique') has developed a curious theory, according to which the safest means for protecting ourselves against the loss of the object of one's love is to destroy it: to devour it, in order to identify with it in the most absolute manner. According to Fédida cannibalism is the mythical expression of a melancholic state of mourning; the myth is interpreted as narrating the way in which alimentary incest is committed with the object of love (in the breast-feeding child).

10 Jerome Kagan, *Galen's Prophecy. Temperament in Human Nature* (New York: Basic Books, 1994), p. 8.

11 Simón Brailowsky, *Las sustancias de los sueños. Neuropsicofarmacología* (Mexico City: Fondo de Cultura Económica, 1995), pp. 61–95, 192–6. On the modern reverberations of the subject of melancholy, see the essay by Héctor Pérez-Rincón, 'Reflexiones melancólicas (un paseo bibliográfico)', *Ciencia y desarrollo*, 28, 105 (1992).

12 Sales of extract of *hypericum perforatum* have expanded enormously; in Germany alone over 20 million people consume it, and in 1993 it occupied the seventh place on the list of the most popular pharmaceutical products in that country, with 2.7 million prescriptions. I have found no evidence of its having been used in ancient times or in the Middle Ages as an antidepressant. Dioscorides recommends its use in the treatment of renal and pulmonary illnesses. See Gerardo Heinze and Martha Ontiveros, 'La fitofarmacología como tratamiento alterno en psiquiatría', *Salud mental*, 21, 6 (1998), pp. 35 ff.

13 The idea of melancholy as a general expression of suffering is used by Arnoldo Kraus in his excellent essay 'Suffering. a vital experience', *Journal of Clinical Rheumatology*, 4, 1 (1998).

14 Stanley W. Jackson, *Melancholia and Depression. From Hippocratic Times to Modern Times* (New Haven: Yale University Press, 1986).

15 See the fascinating book by Samuel H. Barondes, *Mood Genes: Hunting for Origins of Mania and Depression* (New York: W. H. Freeman, 1998), who – on the basis of a study of mentally ill people in Costa Rica – expounds the possibility that on the short arm of chromosome 18 there is a group of genes responsible for the manic-depressive syndrome.

16 Richard Dawkins, *The Selfish Gene* (Oxford: Oxford University Press, 1976 (rev. edn, 1989), ch. 11.

17 Ibid., pp. 192–3.

18 *The Wild Man in the Looking Glass* (Anne Arbor: Michigan University Press, 1994) and *The Artificial Savage* (Anne Arbor: Michigan University Press, 1997).

19 Walter Burkert, *Creation of the Sacred: Tracks of Biology in Early Religions* (Cambridge, MA: Harvard University Press, 1996).

20 Daniel C. Dennett, 'Appraising grace. What evolutionary good is God?', *The Sciences* (January–February 1997), p. 41.

21 Daniel Dennett developed this idea of Dawkins in his book *Darwin's Dangerous Idea. Evolution and the Meanings of Life* (New York: Simon & Schuster, 1995), p. 362.

22 Stephen Jay Gould, 'Caring groups and selfish genes', in *The Panda's Thumb* (New York: Norton, 1980). It is possible that such an unconditional affirmation ought to be qualified, as do Elliot Sober and David Sloan Wilson in *Unto Others: The Evolution and Psychology of Unselfish Behavior* (Cambridge, MA: Harvard University Press, 1998); they maintain that evolution takes place on different levels of causation, so that we may find processes of natural selection in genes, in individuals and in groups. One would need, however, to establish which of these levels is the most frequent.

23 Stephen Jay Gould, 'Evolution: the pleasures of pluralism', part 2 *New York Review of Books*, 44, 11 (26 June 1997), 47–52.

24 Stephen Jay Gould, 'Darwinian Fundamentalism', part 1 *New York Review of Books*, 44. As an example of a reckless and immoderate application of the principles of 'memetics' to culture, see Susan Blackmore's book, *The Meme Machine* (Oxford: Oxford University Press, 1999).

25 Hans Blumenberg, *Work on Myth* (Cambridge, MA: MIT Press, 1985), pp. 159 ff., 164 ff.

26 John R. Searle, 'Minds, brains and programs', *Behavioral and Brain Sciences*, 3 (1980), 417–57.

27 I use the ancient form, *acedia* (in preference to the more familiar forms, *accidia* and *accidie*), since it is closer to the original Greek and Latin expressions and, above all, because I like it better. In Spanish the modern form '*acidia*' was already recognized by Sebastián de Covarrubias in his *Tesoro de la lengua castellana o española* [1611], ed. F. C. R. Maldonado (Madrid: Castalia, 1995), matching the Italian (*accidia*). In Portuguese the form *acédia* is still in use.

28 See an extensive discussion of this subject in Klibansky, Panofsky and Saxl, *Saturne et la Mélancolie* (Paris: Gallimard, 1989), pp. 91 ff.

29 The Hellenized Jewish translators, the Seventy, established a relation between the term *yasud* (that which devastates) and the word *sedim* (lords), and interpreted the latter as demons; Pierre de Labriole ('Le «démon de midi»') explains that the two terms have in common the root *sud* (to be powerful). This association may have arisen from the popular tradition that connected a variety of calamities with noon. In Arabic, for example, *samum* is associated with the heat of midday, with the sudden hot wind that blows during the day (and at times during the night), and with the dog-days of high summer; it also refers to cold winds and the cold of winter. These scourges could have been associated with demons of the desert; a popular belief is cited from Abyssinia and Arabia regarding the noonday demon, *Ganena Qatr* (William H. Worrell, 'The demon of noonday and some related ideas'). There is a very interesting essay by Aldous Huxley on acedia, from 1923 ('Accidie', in *On the Margin* (London: Chatto & Windus, 1923)). For Huxley, the ancient noonday demon, the acedia described by Chaucer in the *Parson's Tale*, Robert Burton's melancholy, the 'spleen' of Matthew Green and the *ennui* of Charles Baudelaire form a single chain. He explains its survival into the twentieth century by the failure

of the French Revolution, the misery produced by modern industry, the growth of monstrous cities and the great catastrophe of the 1914 war.

30 *Enarrationes in psalmos*, cited by Rudolph Arbesmann, 'The "daemonium meridianum" and Greek and Latin patristic exegesis', *Traditio*, 14 (1958), pp. 20–3.

31 *Sancti Hieronymi prebyteri tractatus sive homiliae in psalmos quattuordectum*, cited by Arbesmann, ibid., pp. 25–6.

32 Origen (c.184–253) mentions the relation in a fragment: 'the demon of midday is meant to be that of acedia' (*Sel. in psalmos, Ps. XC, Patrol. gr., 12, 1551*, quoted by Pierre de Labriole in 'Le "démon de midi" ', *Bulletin du Cange*, 9 (1934), p. 50).

33 The history of acedia is expounded in greater detail in the essay 'Melancholy and Christianity: on Don Quixote's sadness', which forms ch. 3 of this book. In the other essay, 'The Golden Age of Melancholy', I explain the close relation between melancholy and the Devil, which was a commonplace of theology and Renaissance medicine. The Prince of Shadows exploited the darkness that reigned in minds invaded by the black humour, in order to exercise an influence on the behaviour of human beings. We should not be surprised at the case studied by Freud of a Bavarian painter of the seventeenth century who, tormented by melancholy, entered into a pact with the Devil in an attempt to alleviate his overwhelming sadness ('A seventeenth-century demonological neurosis'). The Devil availed himself of the melancholy condition of the artist, Haitzmann, in order to take possession of his soul. This case apparently involved a man, profoundly disturbed by the death of his father, who came to suffer visions, convulsions, pains and paralysis. It is important to note that Haitzmann's dementia adopts the cultural form established in his times, which perceived the connection between melancholy and the Devil. Freud was not concerned to unravel these cultural connections; his interpretation suggests that the melancholic depression following the death of his father brought the painter to seek in the Devil a substitute for the lost paternal figure. In a note Freud suggests a generalization: 'If we are bold enough to apply this idea of the Devil as a father-substitute to cultural history, we may also be able to see the witch-trials of the Middle Ages in a new light' (p. 87, n. 1). Might it be possible to recognize a neurosis in the witches of either sex who were persecuted, and who paid by means of torments, and even death at the stake, for the unconscious substitution of Devil for father? This interpretation does not seem to me very useful, but it is revealing of the renewed modern approach to the canon of melancholy.

34 Ernest Gellner, 'Origins of society', in *Anthropology and Politics. Revolutions in the Sacred Grove* (Oxford: Blackwell, 1995), p. 31.

35 Bert Hölldobler and Edmund O. Wilson, *The Ants* (Cambridge, MA: Harvard University Press, 1990), p. 227.

36 In these cases the chemical signal is an active space defined by the relation between the quantity of pheromone emitted and the threshold of concentration above which the receiving animal responds.

Unlike vocal and visual forms, communication by means of pheromones has the disadvantage that emissions take time to disappear, which interferes with the succession and substitution of signals; this property, on the other hand, may be utilized to advantage to create compound messages or sequences of signals by means of graduated concentrations of the same substance or mixtures of different secretions. Ibid., p. 246.

37 Ibid., p. 252.
38 Bernard Fontenelle, *De l'origine des fables [1724]*, ed. J.-R. Carré (Paris: Félix Alcan, 1932), and Friedrich Max Müller, *Comparative Mythology [1856]*, ed. A. S. Palmer (New York: Dutton, 1909).
39 Mary F. Wack, *Lovesickness in the Middle Ages. The Viaticum and its Commentaries* (Philadelphia: University of Pennsylvania Press, 1990), pp. 32–4.
40 Ibid., p. 40.
41 Cited in M. Ullman, *Islamic Medicine* (Edinburgh: Edinburgh University Press, 1978), pp. 72–9. Commented on by Donald A. Beecher and Massimo Ciavollela in the introduction to their excellent critical edition and translation of the book by Jacques Ferrand, *De la maladie d'Amour, ou mélancolie érotique, discours curieux qui enseigne à cognoistre l'essence, les causes, les signes, et les remèdes de ce mal fantastique* (Paris: Denis Moreau, 1623), pp. 64–5. Also commented upon by Jackson, *Melancholia and Depression. From Hippocratic Times to Modern Times* (New Haven: Yale University Press, 1986), p. 57. The version by Constantine the African is slightly different. The first type of melancholy is linked to the 'frenetics'; his variant without fever is called 'leonine', due to the fact that those suffering from it are as strong as lions. The second type, the melancholy affecting the whole body, may, according to Constantine, produce patients who are bad, astute, audacious and arrogant. The third type, the hypochondriac, is very harmful, generating sadness of the heart, terror, fear of death and unfounded suspicions (bilingual Latin–Italian version by M. T. Malato and V. de Martini, *Della melancolia* (Roma: Istituto di Storia della Medicina dell'Università di Roma, 1959), ch. 4, pp. 100–5).
42 Haly Abbas (Albohazen o Alí ibn al-abbas), 'De malincolia et canina et amore causisque eorum et signis', treatise 9 of ch. 7 of *al-Kitāb al-malikī*, in *Liber totius medicinæ* (Lugduni: J. Myt, 1523), cited in the critical edition of Jacques Ferrand, *A Treatise on Lovesickness*, p. 63. An example of the enormous influence of Islamic medicine on European culture may perhaps be found in the very likely Arabic origin of the Portuguese word *saudade*, which has been regarded as one of the pillars of the Lusitanian national identity. It seems likely to me that Portuguese Jewish doctors may have frequently used Arabic terms to refer to sicknesses associated with sadness: *saudā'*, for example, referred to a sickness of the heart which revealed itself in bitter sadness and melancholy. An Arab physician contemporary with Rhazes, Najab ud-din Unhammad, defined a sickness caused by the excess of love for philosophy and law as '*murrae saudā'*', and another febrile delirium was '*saudá a tabee*' (Gregory Zilboorg, *A History of Medical Psychology*,

pp. 123–4, quoting an 1878 article by J. G. Balfour). To be sure, a derivation of *saudade* from the Latin word *solitates* is not very plausible. While the loss of the intervocalic /l/, and the reduction of medial consonants, which pass from voiceless plosives [t] to voiced spirants [đ], may be explained by normal phonological processes, the tendency in Portuguese is to form decreasing diphthongs (ou → oi); and here we would be seeing the inverse process, which is rare: i.e. that [oi] should produce [ou] (taken from Carolina Michëlis de Vasconcellos, *A Saudade Portuguesa. Divagações Filológicas e Literar-Históricas em Volta de Inês de Castro e do cantar Velho 'Saudade Minha – ¿Quando te veria?'*, pp. 55–69). The Arabic origin of the word *saudade* has been proposed by João Ribeiro, *Curiosidades verbais*, p. 201, and by Karl Vossler, *La poesía de la soledad en España*. The Arabic root *s-w-d* is used in words that refer to the black bile, sadness and melancholy.

43 Haby Abbas, 'De malincolia et canina', p. 63.
44 E. Ruth Harvey, *The Inward Wits. Psychological Theory in the Middle Ages and the Renaissance*, p. 20.
45 Rhazes (Abū Bakr Muhammad ibn Zakariyā al-Razi), *Liber ad Almansorem decem tractatus continens (Kitab al-Mansuri)*.
46 Jacques Ferrand, *A Treatise on Lovesickness*, tr., ed. and critical introduction by Donald A. Beecher and Massimo Ciavollela (Syracuse, NY: Syracuse University Press, 1990), pp. 62 and 128.
47 As Klibansky, Panofsky and Saxl have explained in their classic study on melancholy. I use the French edition of 1989 revised by Klibansky, *Saturne et la Mélancolie*, p. 150.
48 See the *Canon of Medicine*, book I, fen 1, thesis 4, in Oskar Cameron Gruner, *A Treatise on the Canon of Medicine of Avicenna, Incorporating a Translation of the First Book* (London: Luzac, 1930), pp. 84–7. See also Nancy G. Siraisi, *Avicenna in Renaissance Italy. The Canon and Medical Teaching in Italian Universities after 1500* (Princeton: Princeton University Press, 1987).
49 ['La bilis negra está en el espíritu animal, en el que genera temor y pusilanimidad o tristeza: los cuales están en quien padece melancolía: tristeza, temor y mutismo. Y su lugar: la celdilla media de la cabeza, entre la racional y la imaginativa. Pues estos padecimientos vienen a veces del mismo padecimiento del cerebro, a veces del estómago, a veces de una gruesa fumosidad que sube al cerebro, a veces de una sutil fumosidad que sube al predicho lugar, a veces de otros males, a veces de la sangre, a veces de la cólera, otras de la flema, otras de la bilis negra . . .' (tr. Bartra)]; Arnau de Vilanova, *Practica medicinae*, book I, ch. 26, quoted by J. B. Ullersperger, *La historia de la psicología y de la psiquiatría en España desde los más remotos tiempos hasta la actualidad* (Madrid: Editorial Alhambra, 1954), p. 52. Regarding the historical context in which this Catalan physician worked, see Antoni Cardoner i Planas, *História de la medicina a la corona d'Aragó (1162–1479)* (Barcelona: Scientia, 1973).
50 Arnau de Vilanova, *Practica Medicinae*, book I, ch. 26, in Ullersperger, *La historia de la psicología*, p. 52.
51 Wack, *Lovesickness in the Middle Ages*, p. 151. See also Danielle Jacquart

and Claude Thomasset, 'L'amour "héroïque" à travers le traité d'Arnaud de Villeneuve', in Jean Céard (ed.), *La folie et le corps* (Paris: Presses de l'École Normale Supérieure, 1985). On the subject dealt with by Cervantes, see Yvonne David-Peyre, 'Deux examples du mal d'amour dit "héroïque" chez Cervantès. Du langage médical a la transcription rhétorique', *Bulletin de l'Association Guillaume Budé*, 4 (1982).

[52] Ullersperger, *La historia de la psicología y de la psiquiatría en España*, 63.

[53] Jean Fernel, *Consiliorum medicinalium liber* (Paris, 1582), ed. Julián Palmario. Consilio 45, trans. Pedro Laín Entralgo in *La historia clínica, Historia y teoría del relato patográfico* (Barcelona: Salvat, 1961), pp. 92–3. Dr Velásquez also quotes, on several occasions the Portuguese Pedro Váez, who belonged to an illustrious family of physicians, and who studied medicine at Salamanca, practising at Avila and Barcelona; there is a section devoted to melancholy in his work *Petri Vaezi, excellentissimi principis ducis Machedae et pro regis Cathaloniae medici*. In Spain and Portugal, hypochondriacal melancholy used to be called 'merarchia', as can be seen for example in the book by Alonso López de Hinojosos, *Suma y recopilación de cirugía, con un arte para sangrar muy útil y provechosa*, in chapter LVIII, which deals with 'merarchia y tristeças'. The term comes from the Arabic marâqq, which means belly or hypochondrium. Amato Lusitano devotes cure 54 of the fourth *centuria* to 'flatulent, hypochondriacal or precordial melancholy, which the Arabs call myrachial' (*Centúrias de curas medicinais*, III, pp. 98–103). Regarding this subject see the study by Germán Franco Toriz, 'Una singular aportación indiana al tema de la melancolía: la cura de la «merarquía» por cauterios', in Roger Bartra, *El Siglo de Oro de la melancolía. Textos españoles y novohispanos sobre las enfermedades del alma* (Mexico City: Universidad Iberoamericana, Departamento de Historia, 1998). On the use of the term 'melarchía' in Góngora, see note 233, p. 156 below.

[54] Luciano Bonuzzi, 'Il contributo dei ricercatori padovani allo studio della «melancholia» nel '500', *Acta Medicae Historiae Patavina*, 15 (1968–9).

[55] Giovanni da Monte, 'De melancholia et appetentia canina', consilium 26, in *Consultationes medicae*, Bononiae, 1586, trans. Pedro Laín Entralgo in *La historia clínica. Historia y teoría del relato patográfico*, pp. 89–90.

[56] Starobinski, *Histoire du traitement de la mélancolie des origines à 1900*, p. 44.

[57] See Luciano Bonuzzi, 'Il contributo dei ricercatori padovani allo studio della «melancholia» nel '500', p. 36.

[58] Pedro Laín Entralgo, *La historia clínica. Historia y teoría del relato patográfico*, pp. 82–6.

[59] Starobinski, *Histoire du traitement de la mélancolie des origines à 1900*, p. 44.

Chapter 2

The Golden Age of Melancholy: A Sixteenth-Century Physician at the Frontiers of Madness

For Josefina, who wished for this essay

1. A Baroque physician explores the house of the soul

Within the framework of humanism, melancholy is the best example of the extraordinary metaphorical power of the marvellous Hippocratic-Galenic mediating system. This metaphorical power expanded considerably during the sixteenth century, as may be ascertained from Huarte's *Examen de ingenios*, a book which, while admittedly abandoning some points of Galenic orthodoxy, uses traditional humoural theory as the basis of a wide-ranging application to customs, vocations, trades and education. Nevertheless, the coherence of the Galenic *corpus* was jealously guarded, since on this depended its mediating efficiency. Thus Andrés Velásquez, in his *Libro de la melancolía* of 1585, criticizes Huarte openly. It seems to me interesting to pay close attention to Velásquez's recriminations, not only in order to introduce readers to a typical and Baroque argument between physicians of Spain's Golden Age, but also in order to identify some of the aspects that made of humouralism such a long-lasting and influential mediating system.

Velásquez's criticism of Huarte centres on four problems: the physiological functioning of the brain, the natural instincts, the causes of laughter and the extraordinary capacities of melancholics. Let us look briefly at each aspect.

Huarte maintains that the function of the fourth ventricle of the brain – situated in the back of the head – is to 'cook and alter the vital spirits and convert them into animal spirits'.[1] Velásquez, on the other hand, believed that in this ventricle, the smallest, little 'cooking' of spiritous material takes place; it is nevertheless the most important, since it contains a major concentration of nerves which connect it with the whole body.[2] Elsewhere, Velásquez reproaches Huarte for assigning precise cerebral instruments to the imaginative, rational and memorative faculties,[3] a criticism that is unfounded, since the *Examen de ingenios* expressly rejects the ancient idea according to which the imagination, the understanding and the memory have as their dwelling-places the pair of frontal ventricles, the central ventricle and the posterior ventricle, respectively: 'in each ventricle are all three powers, since as the result of a lesion to one of them, all three powers are damaged.'[4] On this point, Huarte and Velásquez follow the Galenic text. It has been mistakenly believed that Galen assigned specific functions to each cerebral ventricle. This is in fact a medieval tradition that goes back to Nemesius, bishop of Emesa, who laid down that the *phantasia* – sensations and imagination – was to be found in the two frontal ventricles of the brain and the reason in the central ventricle, while memory inhabited the posterior ventricle.[5] St Augustine, on the other hand, located the sensations, the memory and the power of movement in the anterior, central and posterior ventricles, respectively: thus sensation did not directly and necessarily give rise to movement, but did so by mediation of the memory (and forgetting). This controversy reminds us of the problems that are being investigated today regarding the spatial localization of the mental or emotional functions and cerebral plasticity.

I should like to emphasize at this point the ancient image of the mental functions as substances that are cooked inside cavities subject to intense internal heat. On reading Velásquez we can imagine the ventricles as cauldrons in the brain's kitchen, where the spirits are cooked as a result of the natural heat that emanates from the heart. These spirits are, if not the soul itself, its instruments,[6] and operate in the brain, which is defined as the most important instrument of all those that make up the body. The brain as described by Velásquez is an organ that palpitates in a slight movement of dilation and compression, full of 'animal liquids' (that is, the animal spirits) in constant flux from one ventricle to another, where the actions of cooking and reasoning are not mutually exclusive, since what takes place is a very gentle 'spiritous cooking', above all in the frontal ventricles, the middle and posterior serving more for 'reasoning and philosophizing'. Other physicians, apart from the culinary images, refer to processes of fermentation and putrefaction.[7] We know that the cerebral processes, in the mentality of Renaissance man, were related to the mysteries of the macrocosm; but they were also conceived in terms of everyday experiences, in which they could recognize activities similar to the concoction, fluxes, impressions and reflections that occurred within the head.

In the brain not only is there a culinary activity: its moist and soft matter receives and retains the impressions that come from the external senses. Here a problem arises: the nerves are not hollow conduits permitting the movement in circulation of the spiritous liquids that are cooked in the ventricles; in reality, Velásquez explains, interpreting Galen, the animal impulses (animal virtues) communicate (with each other) by 'illustration' or 'irradiation';[8] in other words, via processes of optical or luminous transmission. It must be stressed that Velásquez's posture, when he maintains that the nerves are not hollow, and that consequently no spiritous substances flow along them, is very advanced; apart from seeking support in Galen, Velásquez upholds his position on his own experience and on the many anatomies he has seen, especially of the optical nerves.[9] We would do well to remember that as late as the eighteenth century doctors such as Thomas Willis speak of 'nervous liquors', although there is a tendency, under the influence of Newton, to think of nervous fluid as ethereal, or as the transmission of impulses by means of mechanisms of an oscillatory, vibratory or electrical nature. Nonetheless, the great English doctor Richard Mead (1673–1754) was still unsure whether the nerves were solid or hollow.[10]

Velásquez's discussion of the causes of laughter is in itself highly amusing because of the solemn, doctoral manner he brings to bear on a problem whose complex psychophysiological dynamics are still not completely understood. His principal argument is that laughter is not only produced by the cerebral spiritual functions (especially the imagination, as Huarte says).[11] It is necessary for a vital force to intervene in the process, apart from the spiritual force, since the imaginative function lacks in itself the power to move muscles. Thus laughter is caused by a combination of wonder with enjoyment: the former is a passion characteristic of the brain, from which the animal faculty flows, while the latter is one proper to the heart, from which the vital force emanates which moves the muscles of the chest and causes the transverse septum to vibrate. The imaginative faculty, on being surprised, stimulates the contentment or joy of the heart. What is really at stake here is the relation between thought and emotion. Velásquez points out that Huarte was wrong when he said that natural melancholy made men prone to laughter;[12] the black humour does not produce that effect, although he acknowledges that if a melancholic becomes 'fatuous', he will readily be moved to wonder and thus to laughter.[13] Whatever the case, for Velásquez laughter is associated primarily with the sanguine humour. Tickling is an additional proof that laughter requires, as well as the intellectual functions, a vital force that emanates from the heart: on touching certain parts of the body a delight is produced that reaches the heart, especially if there is a degree of surprise involved.[14] Huarte, on the other hand, believed that laughter was related only to the imaginative functions of the brain (or, rather, to a lack of imagination), although he agreed with Velásquez in associating it with the sanguine humour.[15] The dispute regarding laughter enables us to have an idea of the difficulty that physicians faced in trying to understand the relation between the forces which Velásquez refers to as the 'vital virtue' and the 'animal virtue', in other words, between the natural emotional forces sustained by food (by means of the stomach, the intestines, the liver, the spleen and the heart) and the mental forces that give breath to thought, and which are lodged in the cerebral ventricles. The origin of the controversy lies in the relation between the psychic or animal pneuma (associated with the brain) and the vital pneuma (connected with the heart), spirits which in the Galenic system were used to explain thought, sensations, impulses and movements. This polemic surprises us today by what we might call its modernity, which in fact is a measure of our own backwardness.[16]

It is remarkable that Velásquez should have devoted an entire chapter of his *Libro de la melancolía* to the subject of laughter, since physicians generally were more interested in other affective situation – such as love, anger and fear – to which they accorded greater importance, due to the potential seriousness of their consequences. Nevertheless, since Aristotle, laughter had been an subject of interest and reflection. Let us recall that Descartes, in his treatise of 1649, *Les passions de l'âme*, devoted an important section to laughter and pointed to its relation to the fluidity and subtleness of the blood (since, when the blood is heavy and thick, this is a cause of sadness). In this little book Descartes takes a physician's approach to the problems of ethics, on the basis of his reflections on the interaction between the soul and the body, a relation which is articulated in the pineal gland, situated at the base of the brain. I should like to stress the fact that the medical study of laughter also made reference to everyday concerns and curiosities which intrigued many people, and established a comprehensible link between the mysterious ventricular activity of the brain and the open manifestations of merriment and gaiety.

It must be stated that Velásquez recognized the importance of the imagination. Elsewhere in his polemic with Huarte he offers an example of the force of imagination in the apparently instinctive and natural behaviour of a certain part of the body. I have already referred at some length to this subject,[17] so at this point I shall only make a brief reference. Velásquez observes that Huarte does not do justice to Galen in his exposition of the natural instincts; however, he allows himself in turn to criticize the Greek physician, who had concluded that the behaviour of the penis is similar to the natural abilities of new-born kid goats who, without having been taught, are attracted by certain herbs; the penis would have an erection, just as the greyhound by instinct pursues its prey. Velásquez maintains, however, that it is the power of the imagination that guides and lifts the male sexual organ. This is, of course, one more example of the interaction between the mind and the body that could be understood and discussed by anybody on the basis of his own personal experiences in the conjugal bed or during amorous flirtations. But here, unlike his explanation of laughter, Velásquez emphasizes the importance of mental activities in the process of sexual excitation.

Finally, Dr Velásquez comes to the most important matter: melancholy. He had also approached this aspect of the discussion before;[18] Velásquez refused to accept that melancholics possessed extraordinary qualities – such as the gift of foretelling the future or knowing languages or sciences without having previously learned them – [19] and insistently maintains that the black humour is the cause of the most terrible ravages of illness. It is evident, however, that melancholy presents an extraordinary clinical range of symptoms and conditions, including some which Velásquez terms *preternatural*: exceptional and dislocated states, not natural, whose causes, nevertheless, are not to be sought in the supernatural. Melancholics suffer a miserable illness that extends far beyond sadness and fear: they believe, for instance – and he gives the most widely known examples – that the sky is about to fall upon their heads; they shake their arms and crow like cocks; they become extravagantly prodigal or avaricious, or flee from water for fear of dissolving, as if they were clods of clay or mud bricks. The cases are innumerable, and all of them horrendous:

> Of how many do we read that they met with untimely deaths. Some hanging themselves, others throwing themselves from precipices, yet others consuming themselves in fires, and in such miserable manners ending their lives; what could be more dreadful or more worthy of tears, than to see the powers in a man afflicted with this disease all so ravaged, ruined and lost? For such a man may be likened more to a wild and raging beast than to a rational man, such is the force of this fearsome malady.[20]

In his explication of the melancholy illness Velásquez defends the idea that its causes lie principally in the humours and not so much in the temperaments.[21] Distemper damages the activities of the brain in different ways: cold principally impairs the memory, while heat affects more the imaginative and rational functions. Cold tends to diminish the faculties, while heat contributes more to their 'depravation' or degeneration. Damage resulting from the body's distemper leads to partial or total loss of memory, mental confusion, fatuity, and weakening of the reason and the imagination.[22] The relation between the three great cerebral functions – *phantasia, ratio* and *memoria* – and certain illnesses is very confused and imprecise in the texts of Galen, as Jackie Pigeaud has observed.[23] It is worth noting that, without having set any precedent in the medical tradition, Isidoro de Sevilla established a precise relation between the cerebral functions and three very well-known diseases: he linked epilepsy with fantasy, melancholy with reason, and mania with memory, but he did not locate them in any cerebral ventricle.[24] During the Middle Ages and the Renaissance physicians continued to discover a variety of relations between the parts of the brain, the functions and mental illnesses.

Andrés Velásquez explains that if fear and sadness appear during an extended period of time, we find ourselves in the presence of the symptoms of a melancholy, whose cause is not distemper, but rather 'the dark and black colour of the atrabilious humour'.[25] This emphasis on the dark colour was, it cannot be doubted, a powerful symbol that facilitated the translation of the specialized language of the physician into everyday expressions; it was important, besides, since according to Velásquez it was precisely the opaque colour of the black humour that prevented the healthy functioning of nervous and cerebral communication, which was based on the luminous transmission of the animal and vital spirits. More than the dense, compact or thick nature proper to the combusted humours, what prevented the black humour from adequately reflecting spiritous activity was its opacity: like fog, which is tenuous in comparison with glass, although the latter, in spite of its hardness, allows the free passage of light.[26] Mental lucidity was an expression of the adequate transparency of the channels of nervous communication.

Dr Velásquez was perfectly familiar with the Aristotelian theory regarding the relation between wit and melancholy, enshrined in *Problem XXX, I*, and he even cites it as an example in his discussion of the influence of temperaments on illness. He adds that Galen found that the causes of prudence were to be attributed to dryness, one of the temperaments proper to melancholics; he quotes Galen in that curious affirmation that the resplendent stars are prudent due to their dryness: the fact that old people, who are dry, become demented in old age, is due not to the lack of moisture but to the excess of coldness in their constitution.[27] Velásquez's foremost concern is to underscore the fact that the heightened abilities of some men find their principal cause in the good qualities of the four temperaments, and cites in support of this Marsilio Ficino, François Valleriola and Jason Pratensis.[28] It is probable that Juan Huarte would have known Velásquez's book, and it is possible that in the emendations to the expurgated edition of 1594 he may have added some allusion to the criticism of the Andalusian physician. For example, in a long added section Huarte refers to the problem of the dryness of old people and the stars:

> Some natural philosophers would like to feel that the incorruptibility of the heavens, and that diaphanous and transparent [character] that they have, and the great resplendence of the stars, were born of

the extreme dryness that there was in their composition. Old people, for this same reason, discourse so well and sleep so badly: because of the exceeding dryness of their brains they have everything clear and transparent; and, since dryness hardens the substance of the brain, they take so badly to memory.[29]

It might be thought that in this passage Huarte is replying to Velásquez without mentioning him, in order to emphasize the positive side of dryness and, in consequence, of melancholy. He also reaffirms the ancient idea of the close relationship between the microcosm of the cerebral temperaments and the stellar and celestial macrocosm.

I have paused to expound Andrés Velásquez's criticism of Juan Huarte in order to use a concrete example in the interpretation of a problem proper to what has been called the 'history of mentalities'.[30] It also seems to me stimulating to penetrate the strange circle formed by the Baroque mentality when it discusses the human mind.[31] Of course, as G. Jahoda has said, collectives do not think, only human beings do.[32] Nor does a mediating apparatus – such as the humoural system – think, although it is intelligent: but, rather it serves to make individuals think along predetermined lines. In this sense, a mediating or translating system may give us clues to understand the mentality of an era. Moreover, and this is what is most important, it helps us to understand the processes by means of which mentalities – or fragments of them – remain functioning with such efficiency throughout different periods.

The Velásquez–Huarte polemic on melancholy shows, above all, the presence of an almost completely closed self-referring system. The supreme proof of the arguments is sought in the Galenic texts and almost never in direct medical experience. An important physician of the period, Alfonso de Santa Cruz, expresses it clearly: he refers to Galen as the 'almost divine cultivator of our art'.[33] In Velásquez's little book on melancholy Galen is named once per page on average, more than 170 times in all. The typical Baroque obsession with trying to understand the origins of prudence and wit is brought by the physicians face to face with the overwhelming Galenic apparatus of interpretation of the mental functions, which in some way reflects the image of a society plagued by all kinds of evils, madnesses and other illnesses, as was the Spain of the Golden Age. Within this Galenic apparatus Lady Melancholy reigns with an unrivalled power: not only does she cast a gloomy shadow over humanity, but she is also transformed into a hope – dangerous but alluring – for a way to attain prudence and wit or wisdom. Dr Velásquez, sensible and pedestrian, did not trust melancholy, while the more inquiring mind of Huarte felt the attraction of a light to be sought in the lugubrious darkness of the black humour.

Before proceeding further I should like briefly to point out that humoural theory, despite the overwhelming hegemony it exercised, was not the only available explanation. Ancient medical sceptical traditions which rejected the existence of non-observable entities and causes survived down to the Renaissance. For example, we have the edition printed in the sixteenth century of the versions by Cælius Aurelianus of the texts of Soranus of Ephesus.[34] Soranus was a physician of the 'methodist' school who studied at Alexandria and practised in Rome during the period of Trajan and Hadrian. One of his texts, translated by Cælius Aurelianus (who is thought to have lived in the fifth century AD), was the *Tardarum passionum* ('On Chronic Diseases') – part of *De morbis acutis et chronicis* ('Concerning Acute and Chronic Diseases') – in which there is a chapter on melancholy. This text lays down that the name of this illness is derived from the fact that the patient vomits black bile, but that this humour is neither the cause nor the origin of the morbid condition. To think that the black humour is the cause of this illness would be the kind of conclusion drawn by those who work by guesswork instead of by the empirical observation of reality. Melancholy is characterized by anxiety, dejection, taciturnity, suspicion, fits of weeping without cause alternating with joviality, and a desire to live, accompanied by suicidal tendencies. Soranus also describes other physical symptoms which, together with mental disturbances, make up the classical and well-known clinical description of melancholy. On the other hand, his description of the causes of this disorder makes no reference to humoural theory:

> The illness is more prevalent among men, especially those of middle age; it rarely affects women and is not common at other ages. Its antecedent causes are the following: indigestion, habitual vomiting after meals, ingestion of poisons, bitter food, affliction and other matters that may influence.[35]

Methodist medicine understands diseases as the effect of abnormal conditions of the body, which may be of contraction (*strictura, stegyobis*), of relaxation (*solutio, rybis*) or a mixture of the two (*complexio, etitlokê*). Melancholy, according to the version of Cælius

Aurelianus, is principally a state of contraction, and at times a mixed condition. Nonetheless, this theory – lacking the powerful metaphoric ingredient of the black humour – was of scant influence during the Middle Ages and the Renaissance: theology preferred well-established dogmas and did not look kindly on doubt regarding the existence of the black bile, a scepticism which characterized methodist medicine.

Humoural theory, in contrast, offers a marvellous landscape, both coherent and replete with attractive imagery and metaphors. The mental and cerebral system in which the vapours of melancholy find their abode functions as a *combinatoria* of mechanical processes, optical reflections, pneumatic transmissions and chemical concoctions. Images and sensations move forces in the mental machine and print marks in the cerebral substance, similar to those made by a potter on clay. Besides such impressions, cerebral messages are disseminated by illustration, and the light of ideas expands or is blocked in intercalated series of transparencies and opacities, of vapourous veils and ramifying networks of crystalline nerves, of sombre ashes and celestial flashes. The brain is also a pneumatic apparatus of interconnected bladders, of sensual transmissions of vapourous fluids driven by the slow and almost imperceptible pulsations of the cells or ventricles. Furthermore, the house of the soul is like a series of chambers articulated around the kitchen: there, boilings and fermentations of moist and warm substances take place. Frequently, the steam and the smoke come to fumigate the whole house and the fluids dry up and are combusted; afterwards a sediment of hard and dry ashes remains, the walls coated with a patina of smoke from the combustion of humours, deposited by draughts of pneuma blackened and denatured by adustion. This complex cerebral universe was, nonetheless, understandable and intimate: tragically close to the concerns of everyday life, but also connected to the secrets of astrology and the mysteries of theology. It was not easy to orient oneself in this mental and cerebral labyrinth of temperaments, fluids, emanations, spirits, lights and impressions. Yet this notion of an internal labyrinth was of great importance, since it left a space open for a number of options: despite the influence of the stars, humours and temperaments, the cerebral machine must be flexible, since free will was enclosed up there in the chest of the cranium and its movements introduced a certain degree of disorder in the house of the soul.

The nature – at once intimate and mysterious, comprehensible but encoded – of the activity of the cerebral organ of the human body was an attraction for poets, who availed themselves of the metaphoric power of medicine in a similar way to the evocation of mythological images. A beautiful example of this translation of humouralism into the poetic description of the flight of the soul, which takes off from the corporeal earth, is to be found in the poem *El sueño* (*The Dream*) by Sor Juana Inés de la Cruz.[36] The soul avails itself of the sleep of the body to undertake its journey. Sleep transforms the body into 'a corpse endowed with life, / dead to life and unto death alive' (202–3).[37] Sor Juana offers us a vision of the way in which the flesh gradually succumbs to sleep: the 'temperate bonfire of human heat' (253)[38] sends to the brain the moist and clear 'vapours of the attempered four humours' (256),[39] with which the images become steamed up and the fantasy is unleashed; an 'invisible paintbrush' (282) draws mental figures of sublunary creatures and of ideas that are not seen. Heats, winds, moistures and vital spirits permeate a body dominated by the heart, the 'reigning member' (210), assisted by the pulmonary bellows, 'magnet of the wind' (213), and heated up in the alembic that digests the food (243). When the soul returns, its Platonic journey over, to the bodily house, Sor Juana describes once again the somatic functioning: 'that which boiling came to be ebullient / of the union between the moist and ardent' (840–1)[40] comes to an end; and thus the soporific vapours that overcharged the 'rational throne' cease to emanate and, little by little, the limbs, the nerves, the senses and the bones abandon the nocturnal rest of sleep:

> And from the brain, now unoccupied,
> the phantoms fled,
> and – as of light vapour formed –
> in facile fumes, in wind converted,
> their form resolved. (868–72)[41]

The oneiric phantasies dissolve and the images projected by the 'magic lantern' (873) on the white wall of the brain vanish. The 'black vapours' (8) of the night withdraw before the arrival of the sun which awakens the world. Octavio Paz viewed the soul that journeys in *El sueño* as feeling the same anguished bewilderment, on being unable to transform the contemplation of the cosmos into form or idea, that was felt by the angel etched by Dürer in his engraving *Melencolia I*. The journey of the soul in Sor Juana's poetic dream would be analogous to the melancholic flight of Dürer's angel.[42] Frances Yates, however, has noted that the Angel of Melancholy does not appear to be in a state of depressive paralysis, but rather is in a visionary trance;[43] this interpretation is better adapted – as Jorge Alcázar points out – to Sor Juana's poem.[44] Actually, the soul of Sor Juana's poem undertakes a genuine scientific journey – as Elías Trabulse has suggested – with the aid of the hermetic theories of Athanasius Kircher and, I would add, of Galen.[45] The nocturnal intellectual flight of the soul avails itself of the pyramidal, baneful shadow which emanates from the silent earth, and which rises as if intending to reach the stars, given impulse by the black humours of a war waged within the body. The mind avails itself of dark melancholy in order to rise up, like the luminous pyramids, towards the heavens. But the contemplation of cosmic chaos blinds the soul, which is forced to withdraw to the shadows and, following the advice of Galen, takes a small measure of the poison that clouds the eyes in order to make them better able to see, from within the darkness, the great chain of being: an impossible dream, since the body awakens and the journeying soul must return home without having reached its goal.

2. The Little Book of Melancholy

It may seem strange that an Andalusian physician of the sixteenth century should have decided to write a treatise on melancholy. When Doctor Andrés Velásquez published his *Libro de la melancolía* in Seville in 1585,[46] he was a man of some fifty years of age who probably already felt himself to be getting old. We do not know whether he had ever been a victim of the black humour, but it seems likely that this may have been the case. He lived and exercised his profession in the little town of Arcos de la Frontera, which lies to the south of Seville and not far from the port of Cadiz. He was a respected man – married and father of at least four children – who enjoyed a comfortable economic position. Dr Velásquez himself states in his book that one of the principal causes that led him to write was the considerable variety of opinions on a subject 'of such importance for health and the public good'. He was especially irritated to see how ordinary, uneducated people honoured the detractors of the sciences, and how uninformed gossipmongering and quackery set obstacles in the way of the truths established by the 'best ancient and modern authors'. One of the so-called detractors, in Dr Velásquez's eyes, was the celebrated doctor Juan Huarte de San Juan, who wrote one of the most influential essays of the period, the *Examen de ingenios* (*The Examination* or *Tryal of Wits*, as it was variously translated into English),[47] published in 1575 and prohibited shortly afterwards by the Inquisition.[48] Nonetheless, Dr Velásquez does not seem concerned to refute Huarte's book as a whole, but only those ideas regarding melancholy that stray from the established Galenic canon.

It seems doubtful that the physician of Arcos would have attended more cases of melancholy than of bubonic plague or syphilis. During the very years in which Andrés Velásquez was writing his book, the plague reached the town, acquiring a high degree of virulence in 1584; that same year a new hospital was set up in Arcos. The fear of epidemics was so great that the town imposed on all non-residents arriving there the obligation to spend forty days in the so-called *cotarro de los viandantes* (traveller's night-shelter), a small, damp cave that was in front of the hospital of San Sebastián.[49] We also know that the town had been paying Dr Velásquez since 1571 an annual salary of 5,000 *maravedís* for the medical care of the prostitutes of Arcos, who surely must have suffered more from the physical ravages of venereal diseases than from the spiritual effects of the combusted or 'adust' black bile. The book written by the physician of Arcos does, however, reflect the anxieties of a period immersed in a particular obsession with madness.

In his *Libro de la melancolía*, Dr Velásquez mentions at the outset another factor that motivated him to write his treatise: the exorcists of the Catholic Church needed to learn to distinguish between melancholy and demonic possession. To this end Velásquez sets about solving a problem that worried many people of his time: was it possible that a rustic ploughman, as a result of suffering from melancholy, might be able to speak Latin or discuss philosophy without ever having been to school? This brought him face to face with a burning and practical issue of the times, since at a period when witch-hunts were taking place all over Europe, exorcists sometimes had recourse to medicine in order to identify signs of Satanism in those affected by symptoms that might in fact have been produced by melancholy illness. The problem thus raised was also clearly connected with the ancient Aristotelian idea of the relationship between genius and melancholy, which contributed to giving it an aura of extraordinary, though mysterious, attraction.

Andrés Velásquez's *Libro de la melancolía* cannot be described as a great book, either in terms of physical size or of intellectual substance, and yet it confronts us with problems that are by no means insignificant ones. In the same way that the circumstances and motives behind its publication remain obscure, the fact of melancholy having become one of the principal cultural axes of the Renaissance is also a mystery that has yet to be accounted for satisfactorily. From Marsilio Ficino and the 'Angel of Melancholy' engraved by Dürer, to the figures of Don Quixote, Hamlet and the Segismundo of Calderón's *Life is a Dream*, the theme of melancholy is deeply etched into the European culture of the Renaissance. It seems to me that a study of the little book written by Andrés Velásquez – precisely because its mediocrity goes hand in hand with its striving towards the *aurea mediocritas*, the golden mean – offers interesting clues and significant connections. The life and work of this provincial doctor are situated at a fundamental point of intersection of the Spanish Golden Age: between village and court, in daily contact with the misery of the sick but protected by the shadow of the rich, oscillating in response to the dogmas of the Church and the appetite of the aristocracy, exercising an ancient wisdom in a context of suspicion, violence and religious tensions.

The religious tensions in question were not only those that set medical science against theology. For centuries, medical knowledge had been associated with the Jews and, following their expulsion, the *conversos*.[50] Besides, the medicine of the sixteenth century depended almost entirely on Hippocratic or Galenic sources and the interpretations of these made by the great medieval Arab thinkers. Medicine was impregnated with non-Christian forms of thought, whether Gentile, Jewish or Arab. The following burlesque verses written by a famous physician give an idea of this:

Galen and Hippocrates
Gentiles were, as is well known;
and a million of mankind
or more have perished with their aid.

Avicenna was a Moor,
Isaac and Rabbi Moisés
are by kind of Jewish race,
and so in consequence thereof
their writings have been spared the flames.[51]

We might add that even as late as the beginning of Philip IV's reign, the authors of a petition to reform the practice of investigating 'purity of blood' wondered why a sword-maker was automatically regarded as 'clean', while a doctor was invariably classified as a Jew.[52] The problem is a pertinent one, since melancholy was traditionally regarded as a Jewish illness. Marcel Bataillon has wondered whether the roots of Spanish melancholy are to be found in the Renaissance or whether they have a Jewish origin.[53] Was Dr Velásquez's interest in melancholy due to his being himself of Jewish origin? We have no information that allows us to affirm that the physician of Arcos was indeed a descendant of Jews; however, the matter cannot have been without interest to him, since the suspicion surrounded all those who exercised his profession.

Dr Velásquez, as I have already mentioned, believed that his treatise on melancholy was of the greatest importance 'for the public good'. His text does not clarify exactly to what he was referring here; the claim does, however, point towards one of the most fiercely debated problems in the history of Spain: that regarding the causes of imperial decline. This is a question that has given rise to considerable controversy and many explanations of doubtful value; nevertheless, it is worth bringing a variety of perspectives to bear upon the problem, since it is an incontestable fact that Golden Age Spain was undergoing far-reaching and crucial changes which were to determine its subsequent evolution and were already making a deep impression on its character. One such effect was the prevalence of melancholy, which could be seen by Spaniards of the sixteenth century as a harbinger of the gradual decline upon which their powerful empire was about to embark. I believe that such a notion is a simplification, but it does direct our attention to an aspect which is worth meditating upon and investigating: the idea of melancholy formed a fundamental part of a dense cultural and sentimental texture that spread throughout Europe during the Renaissance. The peculiarities of this texture may help to explain the great transformations undergone by the continent as a whole at the dawn of modernity.

In fact, the Spaniards of the Golden Age were the first to concern themselves with ways in which the temperaments and the humours might come to affect society and the body politic. Greek humoural theory passed from medicine into political treatises;[54]

Huarte's book, criticized by Dr Velásquez, is itself a creative application of medical science to the problems of the social constitution of knowledge.

In a certain way, Andrés Velásquez's little book is an authentic microcosm in itself that puts us in contact with a wide diversity of topics; I shall attempt to follow some of the tracks offered by its reading. The *Libro de la melancolía* is in all dimensions small: it is a volume in octavo which fits in the palm of one's hand, consisting of ten folded sheets giving eighty pages. It was printed in Hernando Díaz's printing shop at the expense of a publisher, the bookseller Alonso de Mata. The licence for its publication was granted in the name of King Philip II on 18 May 1585. Its pocket-book format and the fact that it was not written in Latin, but in Spanish, are an indication of its author's, and the Sevillian publisher's, intentions: it was not aimed at specialists, but rather at a broader public interested in the melancholic forms of madness and in the functioning of the brain, the nature of consciousness, and cognitive activity. It does not offer remedies for the ills it describes, since, as the author tells us, he is writing a gloss on these elsewhere, in the form of explanatory notes to the famous *Liber ad Almansorem* (*Kitab al-Mansuri*) of Rhazes, a great Persian physician of the Middle Ages.[55] What Velásquez offers us is a description of the brain and its functions, in order then to discuss their influence on the capacity for studying the sciences, the wits (*ingenios*), the emotions or passions (*afectos*) and the reason. Later he refers to a number of matters relating to the imagination, laughter and tickling, in order to demonstrate how the brain operates. All this serves as the introduction and basis for an explanation, which takes up the following three chapters, of the causes and effects of melancholy. The book concludes with a chapter on the much debated problem of whether melancholy can endow totally uneducated peasants with the power to speak Latin, philosophize, discuss matters of astrology, or even predict the future.

With the unadorned style of a provincial doctor – although not lacking in erudition – this little book speaks to us of the way in which Spaniards of the sixteenth century regarded diseases of the soul. Dr Velásquez, on studying the mysteries of the mind, opens for us a little door on to the history of mentalities. He also invites us to unveil another mystery: who was the physician of Arcos, and why was he so interested in madness and melancholy? Why did Dr Velásquez find in the study of unreason a reason, as it were, for his own existence?

Dr Velásquez's book, like all medieval and Renaissance medicine, is traversed by a long suture: one that unites in a single fabric the powerful Galenic tradition and Christian Scholastic thought. This suture had been so well sewn, and had lasted for so long, that it was only with great difficulty that modern medical science was able to open a way through it to allow its own development. Hippocratic medicine, by way of Galen, had established itself in the West with extraordinary solidity, and had been firmly stitched to Scholastic philosophy, thanks to the resistant threads spun by Averroes, Avicenna and Rhazes.[56] In the same way that dissection of the human body was frowned upon, it was likewise intolerable that thinkers and physicians should try to unstitch the Galenic-Scholastic suture in order to anatomize the contradictions sewn into it. The *Libro de la melancolía* describes in an orthodox manner the cerebral functions and, in the name of Christianity, constructs its thesis with the help of the overburdening weight of numerous quotations from Galen, occasionally supported by references to Arab medicine. The classic texts of Gentiles and Moors form the basis that enables Dr Velásquez to explain how the fluids that set off the functions of recordatory, ratiocinative and imaginative functions, to use Velásquez's expressions, are cooked or 'concocted' in the ventricles of the brain.

During the Renaissance melancholy disseminated itself as a key idea, as a dense emotional texture and, above all, as a myth, thanks to this long and sinuous suture which united classical thought to Christian humanism.[57] In the Spain of the sixteenth century there was another suture that united (and separated) what remained of Iberian medieval Islam with the kingdom of Castile. The *Reconquista* – the gradual incorporation through warfare of the Moorish-ruled zones into Christian Spain – had resulted in a violent stitching of the lands of the Moors to the Christian kingdoms, but had done nothing to hold back the enormous influence of Islamic thought in medicine and other branches of knowledge, nor had it made the Muslim population of Andalusia disappear. The small town of Arcos, where Dr Velásquez lived, was situated right on the suture and owed its name precisely to that fact: during the Middle Ages it had been set up to guard the frontier between Castile and the Islamic emirates; it was known as Medina Arkosh to the Arabs, until it was captured by the Castilians in the mid thirteenth century. The life of Arcos had been for centuries a frontier life, and to a certain extent its inhabitants in the sixteenth century continued to live a frontier existence. Of the ancient mosque of Arcos only the *mihrāb* remained, still pointing toward Mecca, hidden behind the reredos to the high altar of St Mary's church; but the Muslim population of Andalusia was much more visible than the niche blocked off by the altarpiece.

It has been said that Spain was living at that period a general obsession with frontiers, stimulated originally by the dangerous and conflictive proximity of the Islamic emirates.[58] Arcos is a good example of this obsession that had become an element ingrained within the conquering spirit of the Castilians; at the beginning of the sixteenth century the small town was little more than a military post in conquered Arab territory. The troops of Arcos had participated actively and had distinguished themselves in the war against the Moriscos[59] of Granada, who rose in 1499 against the aggressive campaign of forced baptisms led by Cardinal Jiménez de Cisneros. King Ferdinand in person organized the repression, ordering the troops at Arcos to begin the difficult assault on the mountainous region of Lanjarón in the Alpujarras. The following year, the men of Arcos went to repress the rising of the Moors at Ronda; nearby, in the Sierra Bermeja, on being surrounded by the Moriscos, several important persons from the town were killed.[60] By 1535, possibly the year of Dr Velásquez's birth, the warrior spirit of the *Arcenses* had already subsided a little and the town had ceased to be a military camp. Its residents set about financing the construction of sumptuous chapels for the Gothic churches of St Mary and St Peter; they also undertook the foundation of monasteries, such as that dedicated to St Francis, as well as hospitals and the lay societies known as *cofradías*. But what most engaged the energies of the bellicose residents of Arcos was an internal vendetta: in 1530 the citizens filed a lawsuit against Duke Cristóbal Ponce de León for depredation and dispossession, and began a process which terminated in 1544 with a compromise agreement, which represented the defeat of the citizens before the voracity of the Duke of Arcos. A total of 1,988 residents turned up to sign the document which concluded the settlement; among them were only two Moriscos, in a region that must surely have been densely populated by people of Muslim origin.[61]

A quarter of a century later, in 1569, the same duke who had despoiled the citizens of Arcos led the armed and mounted men of the town on a new persecution of Moors in the mountains of the Serranía de Ronda. The same year, another resident of the town commanded a company of harquebusiers which was sent to Granada to put down the great Morisco uprising, which spread rapidly and caused such consternation in Spain as it reached its climax in the autumn of 1570.[62] Fernand Braudel has devoted some memorable pages to this war, and his investigations led him to discover the importance of the revolt by ten thousand indigenous Moriscos, vassals of the Dukes of Arcos and Medina Sidonia, who rebelled in protest against the Castilians, who were abducting them and enslaving them in order to sell them as alleged booty of war, and thus despoil them of their women and possessions. The feudal lords put down the rebellion and prevented those in revolt from joining forces with those who had already taken refuge in the mountains.[63]

In those turbulent years Dr Velásquez, having finished his studies, was already comfortably installed in Arcos de la Frontera exercising his profession. Little is known about his life, but we do know that on 27 November 1568 he had his son Juan baptized in St Mary's church.[64] At that time Velásquez was a young doctor of little more than thirty, married to Doña Ana de Vargas Rubiales; he had at least three other children (two female and one male), but we know nothing of his forebears or their origin. It is to be supposed that he was born in Arcos, but in the parish records of the period there is no information on the matter and the surname appears very infrequently.[65] It is possible that the family may have been of Jewish origin or *conversos* arrived from Portugal, but this is no more than a speculation. The one thing for which we have evidence is that he enjoyed a good economic situation: we know that he had several slaves at his service, which was common to all comfortably off Andalusian families. In 1568, the same year in which he baptized his son in the parish church of St Mary, a little girl named Jerónima was also christened there: she was the daughter of two slaves of Dr Velásquez, Alonso and Catalina, who figure under the physician's surname.[66] During the following years, between 1580 and 1602, nine other children were baptized, all of them born to three slaves of Dr Velásquez, called Jerónima, Josefa and Teresa; the latter had two boys and five girls christened. Only in the 1568 register was mention made of the father; the rest mention the mother by her first name, followed by the reference 'Slave of Dr Velásquez'.[67] Who was the father of these children? Could it have been the doctor himself? Another revealing piece of information is provided by a letter of attorney granted by Andrés Velásquez in 1587, two years after publishing his *Libro de la melancolía*, to sell his slave Catalina 'of black countenance, who would be aged about twenty-eight or very close thereto'. The letter of attorney assures that the said slave 'is of neither a thieving, nor a drunken character, nor given to flight, nor afflicted with the gout, nor the falling sickness (*mal de corazón*), nor with whiteness of the eyes or lack of sight'; it states that she is not married, and guarantees that should she prove to have any one of the above-mentioned faults the buyer shall be entitled to return her and recover the sum in *maravedís* paid for her.[68] It leaves the price of the slave open for agreement with the buyer; in accordance with the valuations of the period, she could have been sold for 80 or 90 ducats.[69] What we shall never know is the reason for selling the black slave: did Dr Velásquez prefer the slave Teresa, who had nine children baptized without mention of the father? Or was it his wife Ana who, out of jealousy, wished to have her separated from the family? Or did they regard her as past her best? Or did they simply need the money for the purchase of the organ that Dr Velásquez presented to the Augustine friars that same year, and which cost him 180 ducats? Nor shall we know whether, at the moment of granting the power of attorney, it crossed his mind that his black slave Catalina might possibly suffer the effects of melancholy as a result of the change of master. These scanty data may serve to remind us of the existence of an internal frontier which is often forgotten: that which segregated a numerous group of people who had lost their liberty. In Andalusia the majority of these were black, but there were also many 'white slaves', less highly appreciated, generally Berbers or Moors. In Seville in 1565 there were more than 6,000 slaves in a total population of 85,000 inhabitants (seven per cent, compared with nine per cent in the case of Lisbon).[70]

We may well imagine that Dr Velásquez, like all the residents of Arcos, felt uneasy at the ever more alarming news of the bloody conflict taking place in Granada. In the same way as the difficult relation with the Moriscos no doubt agitated the spirits, the problem of the Arab tradition in medicine had also become a delicate matter. Dr Velásquez had learnt much from Avicenna and, although he criticized him, he also praised him for 'his good letters and wit' along with other 'serious authors', such as Paul de Ægina and Alexander of Tralles,[71] whom he mentions immediately after the three incomparable authorities of the ancient world, Aristotle, Hippocrates and Galen; he also makes reference to Aëtius and Aretæus of Cappadocia.

He quotes Avicenna several times, almost always in order to criticize him. He reproaches him, for example, for exaggerating the power of the imagination, since the Arab physician believed that this 'directing power' was so strong that it could alter the elements and engender rain.[72] He condemns Avicenna, and Averroes too, for accepting that the sadness and fear associated with melancholy could be produced by a cold and dry distemper of the brain without the presence of the black humour; Dr Velásquez maintains, following Galen, that the melancholy sadness is caused by the black colour of a humour that darkness the spirit, shrouding it in shadows, as the 'learned Doctor Vallés' had shown.[73] Francisco Vallés was one of the most influential celebrities of Spanish medicine, a leading light in a powerful movement seeking to de-Arabize Galenic thought. The basis of Arabized Galenism was the scholastic commentary of the *Qānūn* of Avicenna, which had been disseminated thanks to the Latin version of Gerard of Cremona. The *Libro de la melancolía* reflects this Renaissance and humanist tendency in Spanish medicine, which proposes a return to the original purity of the Hippocratic and Galenic texts, rejecting the versions and commentaries of the Arab physicians, who were seen as symbols of backwardness. The movement in which Dr Vallés was involved was successful in eliminating the teaching of the *Qānūn* and the Arabic language from medical curricula in the universities.[74]

Thus, a relation was established between the persecution of the Moors and the de-Arabization of Galenic medicine. For many surgeons, the indigenous Moriscos who lived in Andalusia were as backward as their illustrious forefathers. Andrés Velásquez, on rejecting the thesis of Averroes on the existence of melancholy generated by combusted phlegm or pituita, stated that this was an opinion adhered to by 'all the common school of barbarians'.[75] Nonetheless, Dr Velásquez did not totally reject 'barbarian', medicine: not only is the influence of the Arab canon on the interpretation of the melancholy disease clear throughout the text, but it is also manifest that he excepted Rhazes from his critique; not only does he avoid condemning him, but he tells us that he is writing the scholia to the ninth book of the great Muslim physician's *Ad Almansorem*. Thus, Dr Velásquez was at the same time a cultivator of Arabizing scholasticism and a critic of the deviations he considered the Arab physicians had made from the original Hippocratic and Galenic corpus. Velásquez's contradictions are those of his time, the contradictions of a society which expelled and persecuted those it exploited and on whom it depended.[76]

The shock-waves of the war against the Moriscos reached every corner of Andalusia. In Arcos de la Frontera, during the bloody year of 1569, the effects of the struggle were felt with such force that one can hardly doubt that the surgeon's hand of Andrés Velásquez must have trembled if he ever had to treat a neighbour of Moorish origin. There existed, outside the city walls, a quarter known as the *barrio de los gomeles*, inhabited by a population whose origins could be traced back to the ancient Berber mercenaries who dispersed among many towns and villages of Andalusia after the fall of Granada in 1492. The 'Gomeles' became part of the daily life of Arcos, working mainly as masons.[77] The story of a Morisco from Arcos, known as Juan Grande, has survived: Grande was accused of professing the Islamic faith, and so the Inquisition began proceedings against him. Juan Grande had refused some eggs fried in pork fat and 'said certain words such as the Moors are accustomed to pronounce' on beginning his work (doubtless he would have spoken the word *bismillah*).[78] How many of Dr Velásquez's neighbours could have been accused of adherence to Islam, simply on the basis of their dietary and religious habits and their use of their own language? One can hardly doubt that the answer would have been 'many' – especially in the surrounding rural areas. And there must have been many thousands more like them in Spain: a whole people for whom forced conversion to Christianity had produced as few beneficial effects as the de-Arabization of Galenism had in the field of medicine. Just as the obstacles to the development of medicine were to be found, not in the influence of the Arabs, but in its Galenism, in the same way the Morisco problem did not lie in the Islamicism of the Morisco population, but in the way in which the powerful Christian culture of Castile reacted to the indigenous Muslim population whose territories it had conquered and colonized.

The subject chosen by the physician of Arcos de la Frontera for his book – apparently the only one he published in his life – placed it at the centre of a great controversy. Melancholy was also a fashionable subject, much commented on not only by physicians but also by theologians and other writers.[79] It seems to me that one of the keys that permits us to glimpse the great importance of the problem taken up by Andrés Velásquez in his book may be found in the very name of the city where he wrote it. Melancholy was a frontier disorder, an illness of transition and upheaval; a sickness of displaced peoples, migrants, associated with the fragile lives of people who had undergone forced conversions and had faced the threat of great reforms and mutations of the religious and moral principles that guided them; an affliction which attacks those who have lost something or have failed to find what they were seeking, and in this sense a malaise which affects both the vanquished and their conquerors, both fugitives and new arrivals. Melancholy was liable to unbalance those who crossed forbidden frontiers, invaded sinful spaces and fed dangerous desires.

3. The courtly sickness

During the Spanish Golden Age melancholy was a fundamental idea whose influence greatly exceeded the limits of medicine to permeate culture, and even politics.[80] This idea was so important that, for example, many believed that Philip II himself ended his days as a melancholy king shut away in El Escorial. It has been said that *El melancólico*, the famous play by Tirso de Molina, took the King of Spain himself as a model for its protagonist, Rogerio, a wise and studious man who finds himself obliged to govern against his will; as a result, he loses his beloved Leonisa and spends his life sunk in melancholy, married for convenience to his cousin, a woman he does not love.[81] We cannot be sure that the character in Tirso's play was really a representation of the 'prudent king',[82] but it no doubt reflects the ancient and widely accepted idea that life at court was a source of melancholy and sadness.[83] In a different way, a comedy attributed to Lope de Vega, *El príncipe melancólico*, had already described the simulated melancholy of a character as part of a skein of courtly pretence.

The case of Dom Duarte, sad and ephemeral king of Portugal in the fifteenth century, is an exemplary precedent. The king himself acknowledged his own melancholy and wrote a number of counsels to prepare the members of his court to deal with it. Dom Duarte was invaded by this condition from his youth, when his father, King

John I, loaded him with administrative duties to the extent that he had no time for social life or for hunting. To make matters worse, many of the young Prince Duarte's friends were wiped out in a great plague, which instilled in him a terror of death and an intense preoccupation with the brevity of life. One part of his *Leal conselheiro*, a notable philosophical and autobiographical text which he completed around 1435, is devoted to commenting on the sadness and melancholy that he himself suffered. The melancholy of Dom Duarte, in some measure, proceeds from the problems typical of the court: dishonour, cruelty, unsatisfied desires, imprisonment. To these causes was added the fear of death, spiritual suffering, the melancholic humour and *suydade*, as he calls what was to become the famous *saudade* of the Portuguese.[84]

It is worth observing that in the twelfth century, Maimonides had already noted a relation between melancholy and kings. In a text on the causes of disease symptoms, the Jewish philosopher of Córdoba describes treatments he applied to the Sultan, who suffered from a rather hot temperament, with 'generation of vapours caused by the black bile, which is occasioned by the chronic combustion of the phlegm'.[85] He recommends, following the customs of old people versed in the ancient wisdom of Andalusia, the use of the cortex of the root of bugloss (or ox-tongue), and not its leaves (as used among the Syrians and Egyptians), 'because it has the virtue of dilating the spirit, eliminating the black humour and eradicating its consequences'.[86] Maimonides's conclusion is interesting:

> I have already treated some who follow the same course as the kings afflicted with melancholy, a disorder that tends towards mania, in other words towards a savage madness [rage or fury]. In these cases I have added to the moderate prescription the weight of a dram of hyacinth well pulverized, of an exquisite garnet colour, and they have been very much benefited by it after their desperate condition.[87]

In Spain, the feeling that life at court could be a cause of melancholy was a preoccupation that frequently reflected a powerful resentment against the court on the part of different groups who found themselves marginalized in view of the increasing power of the absolute monarchy. In this respect, Fray Antonio de Guevara's *Menosprecio de corte y alabanza de aldea* (1539), is a surprising book that reflects the immense discomfort of provincial hidalgos and other wealthy inhabitants of the villages in the face of the new tendencies that excluded them from power. Guevara laments the years wasted in the court:

> My life has been nothing but a prolonged death; my living has been not living but a long drawn-out dying; my days have been not days but deepest shadows; my years not years but troublesome dreams; my pleasures not pleasures but merely frantic amusements that left me embittered without touching me; my youth no youth but a dream I dreamt and an undefinable something that I saw; finally, I say that my prosperity was not prosperity, but a decoy of feathers and a treasure of alchemist's gold.[88]

The inhabitants of the small town of Arcos de la Frontera, at the time when Andrés Velásquez was a child, almost certainly bore considerable resentment towards the court. They had to suffer the mean aggressions of the Duke of Arcos, one of the powerful men of Spain, who usurped the extensive outlying lands of the town and levied numerous taxes and feudal dues on the peasantry who traditionally cultivated them and grazed their animals there in common. Since the period of Alfonso el Sabio, the local hidalgos had enjoyed the usufruct of Arcos and its limits, and these rights were protected by the *fueros* of Toledo and Seville, until the arrival of Duke Rodrigo Ponce de León, who overruled the privileges enjoyed by the local notables of Arcos in the form of usufructs, exemptions and other rights.[89]

It should not surprise us if the residents of Arcos, in common with broad sectors of Spanish society, saw the court as a source of calamities and illness. Fray Antonio de Guevara reproached himself for the years spent in the court, which had sown his head with white hairs, troubled his feet with gout, deprived his mouth of teeth, filled his kidneys with stones, charged his estate with debts and his heart with cares. 'And the worst of all', he wrote, 'is that nowhere now may I find pleasure and most of all am I discontented of myself.'[90] The village, on the other hand, was the utopian image of well-being and the natural domain of liberty, the place where the vanities and banalities of everyday life became meaningless, opening the way to the stoic ideals that saw in rural life a path to happiness and salvation that prepared men for a good death. Village life, in a certain way, seemed an excellent antidote to the melancholy that emanated from the court and centralized power. But was not Arcos in any case a good enough refuge to escape courtly melancholy? Arcos, as the visitor sees it today, is one of the most beautiful white towns of Andalusia, with its limewashed houses and its streets winding steeply along a promontory which is surrounded on three sides by the river Guadalete. In Dr Velásquez's times the little white town lived enclosed within the high promontory, and its village life was in a way a microcosm reflecting the tensions affecting the whole of Spain. Dr Velásquez had his house in a lane situated exactly behind St Mary's church.[91] In order to leave Arcos, the physician would have had to choose one of the three gates, since the town was completely surrounded by walls and precipices; he would almost certainly have used only the Belén gate, which opened its great façade on to a grove of chestnut trees and the road to Jerez; this was the principal gate, by way of which the nobles and prelates would enter, and which received visiting dignitaries and messengers bringing news or documents. The physician would have passed through this gate on his way to visit an oil press, which he owned, and which was situated beyond the bridge.[92] Returning home must have been fairly arduous, on account of the steep slope of Belén, where he would surely have paused at the Hospital of St John of God (San Juan de Dios), in order to visit a sick person or to contemplate, while recovering his breath, the Gothic façade or the Mudéjar *ajimez* of the sumptuous house of the Espinosas. In the Calle Corredera he would perhaps have watched the improvised jousting of bulls with canes that took place there.

At the opposite end of town, towards the east, was the Matrera gate, transited by the soldiers who kept watch over the *sierra*; after the wars against the Moors began to lose intensity it was little used by the residents. In the vicinity of this gate there were few houses, but Dr Velásquez would have gone there often in order to visit his friends at the Monastery of St Augustine. On his return he could have chosen two roads. One of these climbed the steep slope known as the Socorro, where there was a hermitage, and arrived at the church of St Peter, rival of St Mary's (of whose congregation the doctor was a member). The bitter rivalry between the flocks of the two parishes was of an intensity that lasted for several centuries without abating. On occasions Dr Velásquez, after attending mass with the Augustine monks, would have deviated towards the north by another road, in order to visit the prostitutes whose health had been entrusted to him by the town administration. This road would have taken him dangerously close to the third entrance to Arcos, the Carmona gate, transited by muleteers, gypsies, *pícaros*, servants, pedlars and other wanderers of doubtful lawfulness. This gate was not much guarded, and beside it was the low-class *barrio* of Zarahonda, little frequented by well-off people such as Dr Velásquez. Just outside the Carmona gate the gypsies used to camp, devoting themselves to smithying and basket-making.

But the peaceful image of village life in Arcos de la Frontera did not correspond to a reality charged with threats and conflicts, such as the dispossession suffered by its residents, who in around 1530 began a legal process against Duke Ponce de León. He had appropriated lands, enclosed pasturage and other property deriving from royal grants and belonging to the town council, and had, furthermore, usurped the rights of inspection of weights and measures, the rents of a slaughterhouse and other privileges. The citizens also complained of having lost exemptions enjoyed since time immemorial and of having to pay the Duke of Arcos taxes on the wheat bought by the muleteers, on livestock, cloth and clothing sold, as well as on oil and wine.[93]

The litigation extended over many years, until in 1544 a conciliation agreement was entered into between the citizens of Arcos and their Duke. The young Andrés Velásquez – if he did indeed live in Arcos at that time – must have grown up in a climate of upheaval, tension and the dire consequences of this legal battle that overshadowed the daily life of the town. Formally, the citizens of Arcos had obtained two judgments in their favour, but the duke had used his powerful influence to drag out the process of reaching a definitive resolution, by appealing – as was said at those times – 'with the one thousand, five hundred *doblas*', which meant depositing the said coins for their sharing-out among the judges.[94]

The inhabitants of Arcos were obliged to come to an agreement. Thus, on 4 September 1544, the entire population, both men and women, were summoned by town crier and the ringing of bells to a meeting in the atrium of St Peter's church. It is possible that the child Andrés Velásquez, who would have been at most ten years old, would have been present to hear the town clerk read aloud the thirty-five articles of an agreement which eventually awarded the Duke of Arcos full dominion over the property he had usurped, in exchange for some minor concessions.[95] The deed testifying to the settlement was signed by 1,988 citizens, including 30 muleteers, 25 clergymen, 22 shepherds, 18 tailors, 17 carpenters, 17 millers, a schoolmaster and a doctor. The majority did not state their occupation but almost certainly were landowners, peasant farmers and stock-breeders.[96]

Ten years after these events at Arcos, we find Andrés Velásquez living as a student in another small town in Andalusia. It was at Osuna – to the east of Seville – that he graduated, with the degree of *bachiller*, on 24 February 1554, in a new and modest university that had been founded only four years earlier. The University of Osuna was one of the few institutions of higher education in Spain founded by the lay aristocracy, the immense majority of universities and colleges of higher education being in the hands of the Church. That of Osuna was regarded as a lesser university, in which there were few Chairs and not very many students. Of course, the rich families of Seville did not send their sons to Osuna, but preferred Alcalá or Salamanca.[97] Dating from shortly afterwards, in 1555, the same year in which Philip II succeeded the Emperor Charles V, there is evidence of the *bachiller* Velásquez's having attended a course in medicine at the same university. In the book of degrees it is stated that the student was a 'native of Arcos', which is the only datum that allows us to suppose that Velásquez was actually born in the same town where he exercised his profession during half a century.[98] Andrés Velásquez must have obtained his *licencia* to teach and practise medicine at Osuna, since he appears in the archives of the parish of St Mary, Arcos, as *licenciado* Velásquez, when he acted as godfather at the baptism of a little girl in October 1557.[99] Apparently, Andrés Velásquez continued his medical studies at the University of Alcalá, where he was perhaps a fellow student of Huarte de San Juan, who had finished his studies there in 1559.[100] The same year, following the death of his wife Mary Tudor, Philip II returned from England in order to re-establish himself in Spain, and some time later, in 1561, he set up his court in Madrid. We have no further records of Andrés Velásquez until 1568, when we find him already established in Arcos de la Frontera and christening his son Juan.

What relation did Dr Velásquez have with the world of the court? We do not know, but we may well imagine that the tensions of power made themselves felt strongly in Alcalá, whose university was attended by large numbers of students, among them some of few resources, with the aspiration of obtaining posts in the ramified and growing government and ecclesiastical bureaucracy. There is an ironic episode invented by Francisco de Quevedo to describe the scarcely courtly manner in which the new students were received at Alcalá. Quevedo, in his picaresque novel *Historia de la vida del Buscón*, narrates how, the moment his hero sets foot in the courtyard of the University, the students greet him as 'new', anointing the young *pícaro* with such a quantity of spittle that they leave him 'rendered a spittoon full of old and pure saliva'.[101] This type of behaviour, which Castiglione would have considered wild and boorish or rustic (*selvatico, contadinesco*, in the terms of his influential manual on good manners), was to be sieved out in the filter of rigid and complicated rules of behaviour that were designed to prevent people devouring each other in the court.[102] Perhaps the Spanish students, through such repugnant and aggressive behaviour, were preparing themselves to resist their future immersion in one of the most complex mazes of courtly protocol in the whole of Europe in the sixteenth century.

The court despised by Guevara also took a toll of its victims, of course, among the aristocrats and hidalgos who found themselves trapped in its ceremonial labyrinth. Wolf Lepenies has observed, closely following the interpretations of Norbert Elias, that the complicated rules of etiquette were a way of passing time, in the absence of which the aristocracy might have become overconscious of the wasting of time and the dramatic fact that they had absolutely nothing to do, since absolutism did not permit them to do anything. Courtesy and good manners were a formal power that compensated for the gradual loss of real power they had undergone. Lepenies's reflections refer to seventeenth-century France, but they could equally apply to sixteenth-century Spain: a courtly society in which it was becoming ever more important to find a dignified way of killing time, of killing the time in which there was no longer anything important to be done. Likewise, it was essential that boredom be repressed at court, since otherwise it could easily overflow into dangerous attacks of melancholy.[103] Guevara confirms this peculiar tension, when he sums up his experience at court:

> Solitude brought me sadness, and the excess of company importunity. Excess of exercise tired me while idleness harmed me. When I was healthy, cares tormented me, and when I was sick the doctors put me to trial by ordeal. Finally I say and do affirm that often I found myself so bored in the court and so disgusted with myself that I dared not seek even death, nor did I take pleasure in life.[104]

Guevara reveals clearly the cause of his desperation: 'the King did not give me what I wished for, and the favourite refused to open the door to me.'[105] This attitude reflected not only the annoyance of provincial hidalgos at the hostility of the court, but the malaise that affected the nobility as a whole.

It has been pointed out that Guevara's criticism of courtly customs is also an expression of the difficulties of a court which, in the mid sixteenth century, was saturated by the flocking to the cities of hidalgos and low-income farmers, who sought there an improvement in their economic position. This migration from the village to the court strengthened mercantile activities and lessened the strength of the traditional nobility, who sought a way to convince the hidalgos to remain on their lands, in the depopulated rural areas whose population had, besides, already been decimated by epidemics.[106] To be sure, Antonio de Guevara did not criticize the court as such, but rather defended it from modern corruption and the novelties that were destabilizing it; Guevara himself wrote a manual for guiding the behaviour of favourites and courtiers with regard to princes.[107]

Another humanist who took refuge in a village in order to write, Cristóbal de Villalón, has left us an archetypal picture of the image of melancholy and acedia. In the curious dialogues between a poor shoemaker and his cockerel, to be found in *El Crotalón* (written in the mid sixteenth century), there is a section or canto narrating the descent into hell, in imitation of the *Necromantia* of Lucian. The first infernal figure he describes is Melancholy in the form of a woman, an allegory that was made famous by Dürer in his engraving *Melencolia I*. Cristóbal de Villalón describes her thus:

> we saw seated in a corner a very dishevelled and ragged woman. She was [all] weeping and miserable sorrow, she was seated on the ground with her elbow on her knees, the hand under the chin and cheek. We saw her very pensive and miserable for a long time without moving, and as if at the movement of our feet she looked up, [and] I chanced to see a yellowish, thin and unhappy visage: the eyes deep-sunken and cheeks that made the nose [seem] longer, and from time to time gave a sigh from the depths of her heart, with such force and affliction that it seemed to be done on purpose just to torment souls by driving them to sorrow. This moaning is of such effect that it transfixes and wounds the soul entering in it, and with such force that it brings it every moment to the point of desperation; and this is the first misery that torments and wounds the souls of the

damned and is such a great evil that without any other was enough to avenge the justice of God.[108]

For many hidalgos the court must have seemed a hell, and melancholy a diabolic sickness that attacked the worshipers of worldly powers and pleasures.

4. The Devil's bath

Melancholy was often associated with the ability to foresee the future, and this made the mentally ill liable to suspicion of satanic possession. Dr Velásquez relates a story in order to prevent his readers from jumping to conclusions regarding the prophetic power of certain persons affected by melancholy or frenzy, a power which could be explained only by the intervention of the Devil. On one occasion, as our physician was travelling in the company of an illustrious gentleman of the city of Zafra, together with other hidalgos and a number of servants, among whom there was a mulatto called Juanico, the group – which was on its way towards Jerez de los Caballeros – stopped at an inn in Burguillos, a village that still has its castle, built by the Templars at the top of a hill surrounded by woods of holm and cork oaks during the *Reconquista*. The mulatto, who was a servant of Don Fernando de Bazán, the gentleman from Zafra, started joking with the waitress while dinner was being served, already late in the evening, and pestered her repeating time and time again: 'Confess, old woman, for you are to die before midnight.' The waitress, who was well-known to the mulatto, told him he was drunk; but shortly afterwards the old woman, seeing that more water was needed at the table, took a bucket and went to an excellent well that was next to the hamlet. While she was raising water, she fell into the well and drowned. The hidalgos came to the defence of Juanico, who had immediately fallen under suspicion, and begged those present not to make an indictment against him, for they were all witnesses – including the waitress's husband – that the mulatto had not left the inn at any moment, that he had only been joking with her, and had spoken those words that had turned out to be prophetic without being prompted to do so.[109]

This tale relates to a person who was not sick, but whose condition as a person of mixed race automatically aroused suspicion; Velásquez makes use of it to criticize Juan Huarte who, in his

Examen de ingenios, tells the story of a barber who was bleeding a frenetic woman; while the treatment was in progress the patient warned him that he had very few days left to live, even notifying him of the name of the man who was to marry his wife: 'the prophecy was so true to the mark', says Huarte, 'that before even six months were out, it was fulfilled.'[110] Huarte concluded that it was possible, without demoniac intervention, for those affected by melancholy, frenzy or mania, to foretell the future. One of the arguments he adduces is the following: if the demons are able to conjecture and discourse on the basis of certain signs and thus reach into the future, in the same way the rational soul may achieve similar feats. This natural capacity for imagining what is yet to come is made more acute by the degree of heat proper to a disease that comes about as a result of the adustion of the humours, and which often also predisposes a person to considerable eloquence.[111] Note that Huarte does not reject the idea that the Devil may imagine the future; he believes, however, that cases of natural prophecy may exist independently of satanic influence.[112] He considers that, if the Devil is able to prophesy, with all the more reason the same process may occur as a result of natural causes. Andrés Velásquez, on the other hand, refuses to accept the existence of prophetic phenomena caused by natural causes. It is possible that he strongly doubted the intervention of the Devil in cases of prophecy and other apparently supernatural phenomena, as in the case of the rustics who suddenly start to speak Latin or to philosophize without ever having studied previously. But he does not wish (or does not dare) to cast doubt on the effects of the action of the Devil: what he suspects is that such cases of prediction of the future do not exist, that at the most they would be – as in the case of the mulatto – mere coincidences. Velásquez's book concludes by saying that such effects belong to the world of the marvellous and that 'they do not come about by the strength of a humour, nor by the influence of the stars, but by the activity of the Devil', the latter statement being in Latin, and – against his custom – Velásquez does not translate it.[113]

This discussion was of extraordinary importance and did not merely refer to theoretical problems of interpretation: it took place at a period in which an appalling craze for witch-hunting was going on all over Europe, costing many thousands of lives. Physicians and theologians who saw in the symptoms of melancholy the long arm of the Devil condemned many mentally ill people to withstand inquisitorial trials, which began with torture and often ended with the condemned victims being burnt at the stake. Shortly after the publication of Velásquez's book, the work *De la démonomanie des sorciers* (1580) by Jean Bodin appeared in Paris; this was a terrible manual for witch-hunters and a brutal refutation of the more flexible, though contradictory, ideas that Jean Wier (Johan Weyer) had developed in his influential book *De praestigiis daemonum* published in Basle in 1563.[114] Bodin's text was a secular version of the *Malleus maleficarum*, which was used in ecclesiastical trials.[115] Bodin refused outright to accept that the natural phenomena attributed to witches were an illusion produced by melancholy. For the reputed French jurist, women in general and witches in particular could not be affected by this disorder:

> never has any woman died of melancholy, nor any man of joy; on the contrary, rather, many women die of extreme joy, and since Wier is a physician he cannot be ignorant of the fact that women's humour is directly contrary to the adust melancholy that produces mania, whether it proceed from the *bile flava adusta aut a succo melancholico*, as the doctors agree, since both one and the other come from excessive heat and dryness, as Galen states in his book *De atra bile*. But women are naturally cold and damp, as the same author explains, and all the Greek, Latin and Arabic authors agree on this point.[116]

Bodin also cites the traditional idea according to which melancholy makes men wise and contemplative, which he regards as something incompatible with the nature of the female sex. Melancholy does not attack women, Bodin believes, on account of their menstruation; but, as Sydney Anglo points out, he fails to explain what happens when women cease to menstruate, a condition which would be frequent among those accused of witchcraft, a large proportion of whom were of advanced age.[117] Neither does Bodin accept that certain powerful ointments have hallucinatory properties that induce some women to soporific states in which they dream they are flying. This is what Wier had affirmed, citing the Neapolitan physician Giovanni Battista della Porta in his *Magia naturalis* of 1558, and the great mathematician and physician Girolamo Cardano in his *De subtilitate rerum* of 1552.[118]

The association between witchcraft and melancholy had been stressed by the Protestant physician Jean Wier in his famous book

De praestigiis daemonum. Christopher Baxter has clearly demonstrated that Wier was not a lucid and tolerant spirit of the Erasmian school but, rather, a dogmatic, severe and confused Lutheran who used belief in witchcraft as a stick for beating Catholics, whom he saw as practitioners of a diabolic magic similar to that of the infamous sorcerers whom it was necessary to persecute. Despite calling for a certain tolerance in the treatment of witches, who were mere tools in the hands of the Devil, he demanded the repression of sorcerers, who manipulated the Devil.[119]

As Sydney Anglo has pointed out, Wier's prestige as an opponent of witch-hunts is ill-founded and has overshadowed the much greater importance of the sceptical view of Reginald Scot, who, in his *Discoverie of Witchcraft* of 1584, opens up a fundamental critical path.[120] Wier believed that women are very liable to suffer from melancholic vapours, a fact of which the demons availed themselves in order to manipulate them. But the supposedly supernatural phenomena – such as flying through the air, the witches' sabbaths, copulation with the Devil – are in reality, for this physician, a fruit of the depraved imagination induced by the Devil but made possible by the black bile. 'The Devil, a cunning, astute and cautious enemy', says Wier,

> easily induces the female sex, which as a result of its complexion, is inconstant, of easy beliefs, malicious, impatient, and melancholic as a consequence of its being unable to control its affections; and especially [vulnerable are] the old women, weak: stupid and of hesitant spirit.'[121]

Elsewhere he states that the Devil 'mixes very easily with the melancholy humour, finding it an extremely apt and convenient vehicle for the execution of his impostures, for which reason St Jerome was very much to the point when he described melancholy as the Devil's bath'.[122] Wier did not believe, however, that all melancholics are tormented by the Devil, although he does establish that all 'demoniacs' (i.e. those possessed by the Devil) become melancholics due to the severe illnesses and cruel pains that they must bear, and cites as an example a woman from a place called Buderic who, at Whitsuntide, would usually set up camp for long periods beside the tombs in the cemeteries.[123]

The idea that the demons take advantage of the humours, especially of the atrabile, in order to cause illnesses or visions in people was very common among physicians in the sixteenth century. Two important medical authorities, cited by Andrés Velásquez, were of this opinion. Jason Pratz believed that demons hid in the viscera to produce terrifying dreams and general discomfort.[124] Francisco Vallés who, as I mentioned above, led the de-Arabization of Galenism in Spain, stated in his *De sacra philosophia* that the Devil was not born in the body itself, but rather penetrated it from outside in order to excite the melancholy, transporting black vapours, causing the atrabilious fluids to increase by fomenting adustion or by avoiding the evacuation of the natural black humour.[125]

This question was the subject of considerable discussion in sixteenth-century Spain, although it has been little commented upon. Some doctors adopted a defence of natural philosophy and of more flexible and advanced somatic explanations than those of Jean Wier. I have already mentioned how Huarte and Velásquez themselves adopted a sceptical and cautious attitude to the problem. I should now like to cite another Spanish physician, Pedro de Mercado, who included in his *Diálogos de filosofía natural y moral* (1558) a discussion between a melancholic, a theologian and a physician; this dialogue constitutes a representative example of the tensions that traversed the period.

Pedro de Mercado was, like Velásquez, an Andalusian, and held a Chair at the University of Granada, the city of which he was a native. The sixth dialogue of his work, 'De melancolía', is an agile exposition of the confrontation between Christian morals and natural science in the treatment of this sickness.[126] The melancholic (whom he calls Antonio) succeeds in bringing together the theologian and the physician in order for them to explain to him the nature of his illness, but from the outset the two experts throw this hot potato from one to the other, each one insisting that the problem is not of his competence. The physician (Joanicio) maintains that melancholy is a matter of conscience and scruples that must be attended to by theology, while the theologian (Basilio) insists that it is a disease of the body which it is the job of the physicians to cure. Nevertheless, each agrees to discuss his conception of the melancholy disease: the doctor defines it as 'a shifting of the imagination from its natural course towards fear and sadness, effected by the shadows and darkness of the clear spirits of the brain'.[127] Melancholics are always discontented, suspicious of everything, on the run even though there is nothing to escape from; he describes them by recourse to a popular expression: 'it's a fight against the *duende*',[128] in allusion to the fact that the struggle in which they are engaged is an intense and wholly internal one in which they alone judge, question, answer, condemn or absolve. For the theologian, on the other hand, it is the Devil who prevents the sick from

> making good use of their time (holding them as it were in suspense, in vain and sad imaginings), or persuades them to abhor themselves, tormenting them with a thousand kinds of desperation, proposing means for them to put the desperate intention into effect, without leaving them in peace for one moment.[129]

Throughout the dialogue, during which a description of melancholy gradually unfolds, the point of view of the author is expressed through the words spoken by Joanicio, whose name is almost certainly a reference to the Arab physician known in Europe as Johannitius or simply Physicus (Hunayn ibn Ishaq, 808–73). At a certain point, a fourth interlocutor (Damián), whose function is to lead the dialogue forward and mediate between the other characters, takes up the argument:

> Señor Joanicio, you as a doctor must attribute all the effects of our bodies to the humours; but Señor Basilio and the theologians will say otherwise. For I have heard them tell that the bad thoughts and imaginings that we have are prompted in us by the Devil in order to disturb us and tempt us therewith [. . .] Señor Joanicio puts the cause of them within us and the theologians outside us.

The theologian, however, warns that 'many bad things may be imagined by men of themselves, without there being need for the Devil to have a hand in the matter',[130] a fundamental statement that opens a way for the free will, since men are tempted not only by the Devil but also by their own greed. How, then, are we to distinguish between our own greed and the prompting of the Devil? By the great fear and turmoil suffered by the soul when it is affected by the Devil. But here a new doubt arises: how can the corporeal medicines prescribed by Joanicio cure what is a spiritual disease? The doctor answers: 'Although the soul is spiritual, so long as it is incarcerated in our bodies it may not function without corporeal instruments.' Nonetheless, the doctor admits that there is an extra-somatic dimension, for he states that melancholy may also be cured by the advice of wise people, to which the theologian retorts with the complaint that melancholics often take no notice of their confessors, insisting in interpreting everything to their own prejudice.[131]

I should like to offer another Spanish example, earlier than the work of Mercado, which shows the incredulity of certain doctors with regard to the powers attributed to witches. The example comes from a very famous and beautifully illustrated pharmacopoeia, which offers a translation and commentary of the *Materia medica* of Dioscorides. This book is also known for its having been despised by the melancholic Don Quixote when, beaten and faint with hunger after his imaginary battle with two armies (in reality flocks of sheep), he responds to Sancho's invitation to search for curative herbs in the meadows: 'I would rather have now a quarter of a loaf, or a cake, and two pilchards' heads, than all the herbs that Dioscorides describeth, although they came glossed by Doctor Laguna himself.'[132] Dr Andrés Laguna (1499–1563) – who possibly came from a family of Jewish *conversos* from Segovia – was educated in Salamanca, Paris and Toledo; he lived for several years in Metz and, in 1545, accompanied the Emperor to Rome, where he established himself for a period of twelve years as physician to Popes Paul III and Julius III; in 1557 he returned to Segovia, where he died six years later. In his marvellously illustrated version of the text of Dioscorides, he recounts a highly significant story from his personal experience.[133] Describing the herb *solanum*, 'which engenders madness and is known commonly as black nightshade', Dr Laguna explains that this plant produces 'vain, though very pleasant, imaginings', for which reason the ointments with which witches smear themselves must surely contain this herb, which 'tenaciously imprints within their brains a thousand deceptions and vanities, such that after awakening they confess to things they have never done, for the confirmation of which I wish to tell you a story'.[134] And he goes on to describe how, in 1545, when he was called on to attend the Duke of Lorena who was taken ill at Nancy, a pair of solitary witches, husband and wife, were accused and, under torture, confessed that not only had they caused the Duke's sickness, but that also by devilish arts they had brought about the death of his father. The whole affair had been started by the Duke himself, who failed to include the old witch among the twelve poor men whose feet he traditionally washed on Maundy Thursday; this drove the old man into a profound melancholy, which was exploited by the Devil, who persuaded him to cast a spell on the

Duke. The pair of elderly hermits were condemned to die at the stake, but only the woman was actually burned, since the husband obtained the Duke's pardon by means of a promise to cure him by a secret remedy; however, the old man was found dead of asphyxiation the next morning, and the Duke died shortly afterwards. Dr Laguna learned that in the hermitage where the two witches lived a pot had been found containing a green ointment 'which gave off such an intense and fetid aroma that it was deemed to be composed of herbs, cold and soporiferous in the highest degree, which are: hemlock (also known as cicuta or conium), black nightshade, henbane and mandrake'. Through the offices of his friend, the constable, Laguna obtained a tub of the ointment, which he took with him to Metz, the city where he was working. There he engaged in a genuine scientific experiment, whose development is the substance of the whole story:

> I had the hangman's wife anointed from head to toe, who – out of jealousy of her husband – had completely lost the ability to sleep, even becoming as it were half-frenetic, and [I did so] both on account of the subject's being highly suitable – one on whom one could carry out such experiments – , [and] because I had tried out an infinity of other remedies in vain; and it seemed to me that this came very much to the occasion; it was something I could not fail to take advantage of, to infer from its colour and smell. She – immediately upon being so anointed, with her eyes open like a rabbit, and looking moreover somewhat like a cooked hare – fell into such a deep sleep that I thought I should never be able to waken her. Whence, with strong ligatures and frications of the extremities, with perfusions of costus oil and oil of euphorbium, with fumigations of incense and smoke to the nostrils and finally, with cupping glasses, I gave her such vexation that after thirty-six hours I restored her to her wits and senses, although the first words she spoke were: 'In God's name why did you have to wake me when I was in the midst of all the pleasures and delights of the world?', and turning her eyes toward her husband, she said to him smiling: 'Old miser, I'll have you know that I have just put the horns on your head, and with a fine fellow younger and more lusty than yourself.' And saying many other and very strange things she importuned us to leave her alone, and so we let her return to her sweet dreams whence little by little we led her apart, although she did always retain henceforth certain vain opinions in her head.[135]

We may well appreciate how it was that scientific minds who wished to understand the natural causes of many strange phenomena found themselves faced with a disquieting dilemma. Many authors, such as Wier, resorted to natural explanations while at the same time trying to show how the Devil took advantage of the functioning of bodily fluids – by means of mimetic processes, for example – to induce certain morbose spiritual states, such as melancholy. Another approach, which was that of Velásquez, consisted in looking for natural explanations and, in the case of not finding them in the established scientific canon, leaving the terrain to the Devil and his marvellous, supernatural activities, extraneous to the logic of humoural theory. This position, taken to its extreme, was what led Bodin to suggest that the acts of the Devil were totally irreconcilable with the laws of nature. Contrary to what has been commonly supposed, in the sixteenth century there was still no clearly articulated opposition between the naturalist point of view and the perspective of demonology; in reality, natural scientific explanations often complemented and were even used to uphold the demonological practices of the exorcists.[136] The idea that Satan, when interfering with natural events, ought to respect the general laws of nature was shared by many specialists in demonology. The criterion for identifying the presence of satanic effects was generally sought in their exceptional and unusual nature, and not in supernatural or miraculous causes; at times the term *preternatural* was used to refer to the phenomena inspired by the Devil.[137] In this sense the explanation given by Dr Andrés Laguna for the erotic activity of witches is an expression typical of its period, and an important precedent for the thesis of Wier:[138]

> We may conjecture that everything the unfortunate witches say is a dream, caused by potions and cold ointments, which so corrupt their memories and fantasies, that they imagine themselves afflicted and even most firmly believe themselves to have been awake when they were asleep dreaming.
>
> To all the above a by no means insignificant argument may be added, which is that in the same way she [i.e. the hangman's wife], like all those who in such infamous exercises were until now convinced, with a single voice confessed (as is set forth in the accounts of their trials) that they had many times known the Devil in the flesh; and asked in particular whether they had felt notable pleasure in their congress with him they responded each time that they had not, this being on account of the unbearable coldness that they felt in the diabolical parts: from which also, so it seems, there flowed through them a humour as cold as ice, like a hail falling within their entrails.

> Which accidents cannot proceed from any other cause but the excessive coldness of the unguent, which invades them utterly, entering even into the marrow of their bones. Thus, it being granted that such persons are shameful and worthy of exemplary punishment for making pacts with the Devil, nevertheless, the greater part of what they say is delirium; since neither in the spirit, nor in the body, do they ever go apart from the place where they are overcome by sleep, and this is the opinion of the majority of theologians, approved, besides, by the decrees of certain Holy Synods which it is opportune to mention: viz. that the Devil cannot work other than through natural causes, applying *activa passivis*; and that this being so, by his surpassing wisdom and astuteness, knowing the virtue of such unguents, he shows them to the vain witches, in order to make them dream and believe infinite deceptions and vanities.[139]

With prudence, Dr Laguna adds that, against his own conjecture, 'certain Pious Lords hold it to be true that the Devil can transform [witches] into a myriad phantasms and transport them in body and soul through the air',[140] and he declares that he rests his opinion on that of the Church in Rome.

The subject continued to worry Spanish doctors until well into the seventeenth century. For example, Thomás Murillo, in a book published in Zaragoza in 1672, writes that 'certain authors say that the Devil delights in the melancholy humour', but that 'although the Devil may cause innumerable illnesses, the Doctor, with the instrument of Divine Justice, or any other man of irreproachable life, pious and devout, may drive away the Devil'.[141] A much more interesting essay is that written by the personal physician of the Archbishop of Toledo, Dr Alonso de Freylas, an Andalusian like Andrés Velásquez, published in 1605 and entitled *Whether Melancholics may Know what is to Come, or Divine the Good or Evil Outcome of the Future, through the Strength of their Genius, or by Dreaming.*[142] Freylas takes as his starting-point the distinction between the melancholy humour that produces such good temper as that possessed by Plato, Socrates, Empedocles and Hercules, and the 'black melancholy caused by adustion and burning up of choler', which 'causes the most tremendous illnesses, such as madnesses, strange melancholies, depraved imaginings, and various furies and maniacal thoughts'.[143] He is interested in the first condition, in which men acquire a natural strength of the wit and a profound imagination: could it be that the souls of these melancholics – when in a state of concentration, withdrawing to dark places, or when they go to sleep with a calm mind – might be able to foretell the future?[144] The great danger, of course, is that the Devil may take advantage of their melancholy state:

> without fault of their own, nor having made any pact with the Devil, they are deceived and, the Devil availing himself of the black humour moving in the body, and representing thereby in the imagination certain things under the appearance of good, with a resplendence that seems celestial: so to make believe that what is seen is a revelation from Heaven.[145]

This first category of divining, with its characteristic hallucinations, is false, vain and diabolic. A second type is of divine nature, such as that of the holy prophets, and is the true kind. The third category, according to Freylas, is natural divining, which is neither true nor perfect, but which has a worrying similitude to prediction of the future:

> I believe that with the strength of the melancholy humour, aided by conjectures or by some natural internal cause which moves us . . . it might be possible in some way to say something regarding what is to come . . . And the melancholy humour, although it disposes, is not the cause, except in so far as those who have it in abundance have a profound imagination and a hot brain; and with this heat they tend to discourse much and talk much and thus they come to be right in something or another.[146]

According to Freylas, it is not only the Devil who respects and avails himself of natural and organic conditions. In many cases where what appears to be natural foretelling takes place, it is God himself who is the 'effective beginning of true inspiration', and 'disposes things with his infinite goodness so gently, that even in supernatural and miraculous things he often allows the natural order to be maintained'.[147] This kind of prophesying is related to that field of unknown and mysterious phenomena – hidden from the scientific gaze – but which it was believed were not of diabolic inspiration: this was the so-called natural magic, the same that had been studied by Giovanni Battista della Porta.

It is important to stress a paradoxical fact: the most coherent and solid criticism of demonology did not grow out of ideas that established that the Devil acted by means of natural causes. On the contrary, in many cases the medical ideas that provided scientific arguments in support of the actions of the Devil and witches ended up legitimizing demonology and strengthening the practice of witch-hunts. It has been stated that the new tendencies in European medicine – more rigorous and scientific – began gradually eroding medieval ideas and increasing the experimental attitudes of doctors, who started to observe more and more the specific symptoms of each patient ('cases') and paying correspondingly less attention to the Galenic texts and such matters as the positions of the stars. This resulted in an increasing number of strange or unusual cases escaping diagnosis and treatment, which meant that many doctors – as we have seen in the text of Pedro de Mercado – sent the most peculiar patients – many of them melancholics – to confessors and exorcists in order for them to be released from the clutches of the Devil.[148] Also, the changes in orientation of medicine contributed to the expansion of witch-hunting in another way perhaps even more important: the expansion and reinforcing of scientific explanations invaded demonology, but did not weaken it; to the contrary, it was the close collaboration between physicians and theologians that put demonology on a more solid footing: for the fact that the flights of witches or their copulations with the Devil at their sabbaths might really have been occasioned by black humours or green ointments did not exclude the possibility that behind all that lay satanic influences or pacts. In Spain a good example of the close connection between science and demonology can be seen in the theologian Pedro Ciruelo (1470–1560), a scholar highly versed in mathematics and astronomy, who wrote the influential 'Treaty on Superstitions' (*Tratado de las supersticiones*, 1541). There, for example, we find the marvellous capacities of demons for understanding secret things explained as a consequence of their having fallen from Heaven, losing grace and glory, but without 'losing their faculties of good wits, nor the sciences that they attain by their natural wit . . . And thus they have knowledge of the whole order of the Corporeal world, and of all the course of nature'. Ciruelo describes the demons as extraordinary scientists: 'They know astrology, philosophy and medicine better and more perfectly than all the philosophers and wise men of the world that are or have been among men.'[149] Thus, the demons were able to manipulate the physical world with much greater ability than the most learned doctors.

The keenest criticism against demonology arose from within attitudes that, in some way, could be described as less scientific and more medieval. I refer to those ideas that were radically opposed to the medical interpretations of diabolical phenomena. Thus, the aggressive demonology of Jean Bodin was defeated on its own ground: Reginald Scot, who was not a physician, also set out from the idea that the natural explanation strictly ruled out supernatural influence. Since demonology had adopted a natural basis, the alternative that Scot hit upon was to deny the Devil all capacity for manipulation of natural causes for his malign ends: 'divels are spirits', he wrote, 'and no bodies. For (as Peter Martyr saith) spirits and bodies are by antithesis opposed one to another: so as a bodie is no spirit, nor a spirit a bodie.'[150] Scot reduced the influences of the Devil to a metaphysical incorporeal statute, from which he was incapable of exercising his forces upon corporeal nature.[151] Scot denied any possibility of the demons or spirits interfering in human affairs, and practically declared nonexistent such unearthly beings, which he suspects would be visions set off by mental disorders, effects of physical disease or even metaphysical expressions of mysteries that men may not fully understand.[152]

For these reasons the position adopted by Dr Andrés Velásquez of refusing to admit the presence of the Devil in his interpretations of melancholy is an attitude at once advanced and old-fashioned. It is advanced because, as I have already mentioned, in order to stop the persecutory proliferation of the demonologists, it was necessary also to establish the territory of nature as a domain inaccessible to the demoniac powers. But it was also a backward and medieval outlook, to the extent that it accepted the existence of a fantastic dimension which could be explained only by supernatural causes.

5. The dark night of melancholy

Dr Andrés Velásquez lived in a small town with an intense religious life. Sacred activities centred around two imposing churches, St Mary's and St Peter's, and their many sumptuous chapels. The rich families traditionally paid for the construction and maintenance of these chapels, as well as for the upkeep and running costs of the hermitages, monasteries and hospitals. On days sacred to the patron saints or other religious advocations of the hermitages, especially that of the Christ of the Rosemary (*Cristo del Romeral*) and that of Fuen Santa (the Holy Well), great pilgrimages were organized, dances were held, music was played and bullfights were arranged. These fiestas were still very much alive in the mid nineteenth century.[153] Even more important was the feast of Corpus Christi, financed by the town council, during which the religious plays known as *autos sacramentales* were performed and dances were held. Famous companies of players or comics were hired, and 'gypsies or new Christians of both sexes' were invited, as the local historian tells us, 'and paid considerable sums to dance in the procession and on the days of the *Octava*'.[154] However, in 1587 the city of Arcos decided to expel all the gypsies to be found there, giving them two days' grace to abandon the town, subject to a fine of 600 *maravedís*.[155] All those groups whose blood was considered to be 'unclean' were appreciated as part of the spectacle; on the other hand, coexistence with them was not easily tolerated. The threat of a fine that did not even amount to two ducats was sufficient to drive away the gypsies. In contrast, in the same year in which the gypsies were expelled from Arcos Dr Velásquez showed his religious devotion, donating to the monastery of St Augustine an organ that cost 180 ducats. The Augustinian friars had just moved into a building that belonged to a convent of the nuns of St John Lateran, founded in 1539; the nuns in question had joined the convent of the Incarnation, not far from St Mary's church, and abandoned the cramped building that was close to the city wall and the Matrera gate. The rich residents offered substantial alms for the extension of the building, now occupied by the Augustinians; a large cloister was built, with twenty-eight columns of black jasper, a retable was constructed for the main chapel and other works taken in hand for the extension of the church. The organ donated by Dr Velásquez was built by the organist of Seville cathedral.[156]

I cannot help wondering whether the monks who received Dr Velásquez's organ were also presented with his *Libro de la melancolía*, published two years earlier. Melancholy was an illness well known in monasteries, where it frequently shadowed the souls of those who strove to come closer to the divine light. In the European religious consciousness the ancient Hippocratic idea of melancholy had come close to the dangerous and mortal sin of acedia which used to lie in wait for solitary monks, and which was regarded by St John Cassian as one of the eight capital vices (later, in the Gregorian tradition, these were reduced to seven, acedia being assimilated to *pigritia/desidia*, sloth). The terrible paralysis of the soul that threatened those afflicted with acedia does not come from their having forgotten the divine object of their contemplation, but from the very fact that they can see the object of their longing but do not know how to attain it, since an immense abyss lies in between. This situation leads to *tristitia* (sadness), *desidia* and the *tædium vitæ* proper to both acedia and melancholy. In a beautiful essay, Giorgio Agamben has pointed out that the shrinking of the will that is experienced with acedia or melancholy does not arise from the insufficiency or weakness of desire, but, on the contrary, from such a lively exacerbation of love for the Godhead that the object becomes inaccessible.[157] It should be added that, in a perverse dialectic, the distancing of the object of love becomes so great that it finally extinguishes the desire itself, and consequently a profound indifference arises.[158]

We should not be surprised that the mystics were so concerned that the intense inward experience of those devoted to the religious life might be confused with the symptoms of melancholy, since they realized that the same road that brought them into communication with God could also lead them to a morbid delirium. St Teresa of Avila (santa Teresa de Jesús) feared that her ecstasy, which was a desire that burned like a fire within, could be confused with melancholy or with a deceit of the Devil. So strong was her 'delightful inflammation' that she defines it with metaphors that could lead one to think of illness: delightful pain, delicious tempest, metaphors that link quietude with pain; but 'to be melancholy', the saint wrote, 'leads nowhere; because melancholy does not make and fabricate its objects of desire anywhere except in the imagination; this other comes from within the soul.'[159] Nevertheless, people often believe they hear God speaking to their souls, when in reality 'it may be a mere fancy, especially in persons of weak imagination or melancholics, I mean of notable melancholy'; it is no use explaining to these sick souls that their imaginings are the product of melancholy or the Devil, for they will always swear that they see and hear God.[160] Further on she compares the delicious pain of her ecstasy with inebriation or melancholy, though she apologizes for this crude comparison.[161] Along similar lines perhaps, to an Italian of the seventeenth century, the ecstasy of St Teresa, as represented in the famous sculpture by Bernini, would have seemed a symptom of erotic melancholy or the expression of an orgasmic rapture.

It is very likely that the fear of the deceptions produced by the melancholy delirium proceeded from Teresa of Avila's own personal experience; during her youth the saint suffered a strange illness as a result of the extreme penitences she imposed on herself, which left her prostrated for a long time, sunk in a profound sadness, suffering fainting fits, epilepsy, fevers and pains.[162] St Teresa lived through a dramatic interior struggle until she achieved a spectacular mystical conversion, when she was almost forty years old, which liberated her from the prolonged suffering which had been her life up to that moment: 'I longed to live – for I well understood that I was not living, but rather wrestling with a shadow of death – and that there was no one who might give me life, and I could not reach out to take it myself.'[163] St Teresa delighted in immersing herself in her interior world in search of God, and tried to understand what was happening to her inside her head, where she heard the 'turmoil of her thought', which came – so she believed – from her imagination and not from her understanding.[164] The fact of not understanding that there is an interior world here within, produced internal conflicts and melancholies;[165] St Teresa heard a great noise inside her head:

> It seems only as if there are inside it many tumultuous rivers and that somewhere else the same waters are falling in cascades, and many little birds and much whistling, and not in the ears, but in the upper part of the head, where they say the superior part of the soul is.[166]

But the saint assures us that her soul remains undisturbed by this din of thoughts that agitates within her imagination, and which comes from the Devil or from the residual misery of Adam's sin.[167]

Although the saint of Avila may have recognized in her own interior life the symptoms of melancholy, she made a determined recommendation that nunneries should not open their doors to women prone to that illness. Yet melancholy made its appearance with great frequency among nuns, causing enormous upsets. In order not to fall into the snares of the Devil, St Teresa said that it was necessary to overcome melancholy with fear, for the delirium of a single nun could unsettle a whole convent: 'If words are not enough, then let punishments be given: if small punishments do not suffice, let great ones be administered; if one month of imprisonment is not enough, let it be four months, for no greater good may be done to their souls.'[168]

The logic of repression is based on the consideration that in melancholics there is guilt, since what is involved is not madness but an irrational attitude that makes nuns anxious as a result of exercising their will and their liberty without restraint. 'I fear', writes St Teresa, 'that the Devil, behind the banner of this humour . . ., hopes to win many souls; for now it is the custom much more than is normal, and the fact is that all [kinds of] self will and liberty now go by the name of melancholy.'[169] However, the saint recommends not only submission to a strict regime of obedience, but also tender words, occupation in handicrafts, a limited time for prayer, eating little fish and not being subjected to excessive fasting. Melancholy was a growing cause of concern in Spanish monasteries; a proof of this is the ironic text of a follower of St Teresa, Fray Jerónimo Gracián, the *Constituciones del Cerro* (1582), whose exhortation is made in the name of a certain 'Fray Melanco Cerruno, provincial of all melancholics, all those [who are] sad and bitter of heart, angry, restless and anxious, tormented by doubt, choleric, insufferable and uneasy'.[170]

St Teresa knew very well that the journey through her inward spaces implied moments of great spiritual drought, at times produced by the intensity of prayer; and this drought produced intolerable 'inward travails', conflicts proper to melancholy and other illnesses.[171] These rigorous inward travails were also well known to St John of the Cross, one of St Teresa's disciples, who explained the difficulties of the high road of the soul through the dark night in search of the divine light; it is a 'path of obscure contemplation and drought' in which the soul believes itself to be lost in view of so many travails, hardships and temptations, above all when people tell him 'that it is melancholy, or dejection, or his nature (*condición*), or that it could be some hidden malice of one's own'.[172] St John, from the outset, was concerned to define the dark night that accompanies the loving soul on its way towards the high beloved, and to 'know whether it is melancholy or some other imperfection regarding the sense or the spirit'.[173] He longs fervently to immerse himself in the dark night because he believes that only thus will he be able to reach the highest degree of perfection:

> O night that guided!
> O night more beloved than the dawn;
> O night that brought together
> Lover with beloved,
> Beloved into Lover transformed![174]

There is a very precise moment at which it is advisable for a person devoted to the religious life to abandon meditation in order to pass into a state of contemplation. St John notes the existence of three signs which enable us to understand that the time for contemplation has arrived: what he describes as dryness or drought in the imagination, an unwillingness or inability to concentrate on anything in particular, and a liking for solitude. Pondering and meditating no longer produce useful results: now a general loving attention is sought and a longing to be alone with God is experienced. It is necessary to exercise much care to perceive this moment and to see that none of the three signs is missing, for it is easy to confuse the pre-contemplative state with a melancholic condition:

> for although it is seen that one cannot ponder nor think about the things of God and that neither does one feel drawn to think about other things, this could proceed from melancholy or from some other humoural juice situated in the brain or the heart, that often cause a certain clouding over [*empapamiento*] and suspension in the sense which cause one to think of nothing, nor wish nor feel inclined to think anything, but to be in that pleasant enchantment [*embelesamiento*].[175]

In this melancholic state, which may be very attractive, one essential condition is lacking: the longing to be in amorous solitude with God. The imaginative dryness of a soul that wanders without resting is not enough: contemplation also needs the immersion in an obscure and strange accompanied solitude. In the 'dark night of the soul', St John of the Cross describes once again, but in different terms, the signs that allow one to discern the moment of contemplation and differentiate it from a dangerous melancholic state. The process is described here in a stronger form, as a horrendous purgation of the soul, consisting in a terrible blocking of the capacity for meditation, a distaste for everything worldly and a bitter sense of shame at not being able to serve God.[176] Of course, St John of the Cross offers a poetical play of imagery which leads the reader to feel the religious experience in his or her own flesh, as both a delightful eroticism and at the same time as pain or sickness. He utilizes amorous and pathological metaphors to bring us very close to both sexual pleasure and mental disorder, and in so doing to express his mystical purpose in a vivid and heart-rending way.

One is tempted to wonder whether St John's 'dark night' is something more than a powerful metaphor. According to the psychiatrist Javier Álvarez, the great mystical poet suffered from an endogenous depression, whose symptoms are reflected in his description of the dark night.[177] It seems to me beyond doubt that St John took from his own and other people's experiences, as well as from the medical culture of his period, the ideas which he used to depict the painful road of the spirit in its search for God. But the psychiatric study does not take sufficiently into account the saint's concern to differentiate the sickness from the mystical suffering proper. There is also a fundamental fact that this approach overlooks: John of the Cross, besides employing for expressive purposes the symptomatology of the melancholy disease, also makes metaphorical use of the painful process of healing recommended by physicians since ancient times: catharsis, or the purging of the bad humours. The terrible dryness linked to melancholy could be remedied by means of mild methods of humectation (diets based on soft foods, baths). But when melancholy persisted, violent remedies were turned to, which caused the expulsion or evacuation of the superfluous humours and vapours; severe methods were applied, which could cause a multitude of sufferings and discomforts: emetics, laxatives, irritants, diuretics, sternutatories, bleedings and cauterizations. For this purpose, drugs, infusions, clysters, frications, sections of the veins, leeches, hot irons or trepannings were used, with the aim of cleansing the body and expelling impurities. It is understandable that St John – who may have undergone some of these remedies himself – should seek a parallel between the healing of the body and that of the soul, which also must undergo an extremely painful purgative contemplation. The soul must be purified, must evacuate all the powers of the soul and the affections, purge the senses and passions, put out the fires of sensuality and pleasure, empty the memory and the understanding, expel ignorance and imperfections. The metaphor is obvious: 'This divine purge sets about removing all the bad and vicious humours, which since they are deeply rooted and seated in the soul, the soul itself was unable to see them and was thus unaware that she had in her so much evil.'[178] The soul is able to see the corrupt humours only in the shadows of the purgation, illuminated by the obscure light of divine contemplation. For St John of the Cross the dark night is not only illness, but above all the painful application of the cure and the dolorous road of the soul's healing.[179]

Another great poet of the period, one who did not form part of the mystical school of poets as properly understood, also refers to melancholy; this was Fray Luis de León, who was consulted – in connection with a celebrated case of prophetic dreams – by one of those involved in the inquisitorial proceedings against Lucrecia de León, in order to find out his opinion regarding this strange prophetess and her divining powers. Luis de León was of the opinion, as he wrote to Alonso de Mendoza in 1588, that this was not a case of 'melancholy or illusion', and ended his statement of opinion by saying: 'If I had power over that person [Lucrecia de León] I would exorcize her as an energumen without her being aware of what was being done, and it might be that in that way the dreams would go away in which she, apparently, is innocent.'[180] Some years later the same defender of Lucrecia, Alonso de Mendoza, was himself incarcerated in the secret prisons of the Inquisition and diagnosed as a mad melancholic.[181] Fray Luis de León had also experienced those prisons and had raised suspicions himself as a descendant of Jews.

The connection between dreams and melancholy had already claimed the attention of Luis de León. In his beautiful *Exposición del Libro de Job* he interprets the nocturnal visions of Eliphaz as caused by melancholy (Job 4:13); the revelation occurs in a nightmare, during profound sleep, at the darkest moment of the night:

> when the thick shadows and solitude born of the silence of everything cause horror in the spirit, and when all that is seen and imagined to be seen, as it is not descried, causes amazement that sets the hairs on end; and when the melancholy humour, which, heated with sleep and forced with the distancing of the sun, moves in the body, and with the fumes that it sends forth, pressing upon the heart and blackening the imagination and sense, breeds heavy and horrible dreams.[182]

According to Luis de León, Job himself suffered from melancholy; depicting the long-suffering man prostrated by illness (Job 7:13), he imagines the bed like a hot oven:

> because the infirmities of [the] melancholy humour, of which this was [an example], acquire strength with the darkness, which is the very time when the melancholy boils and smokes; so that, if one lies awake, the bed burns with black flames, and if one sleeps . . . the black humour, moved with sleep, stirs up in the imagination the species [or forms] and tinges them with its bad colour, from which arise horrid figures that terrify and inspire awe in the spirit of him who sleeps.[183]

The dark night of the soul of Luis de León is not the same as that imagined by St John of the Cross. In his attitude to the darkness of the night, Fray Luis is closer to Teresa, since, like her, he appreciates the dazzling solitude of which Américo Castro speaks.[184]

The black flames of melancholy are a terrible illness that covers the body with abscesses and sores and produces incredible onsets of sadness and mistrust.[185] In his diagnosis, Luis de León is very orthodox in applying his knowledge of medicine, citing Galen and Aëtius:

> the father of physicians says, as is well-known, that 'melancholy makes those it vexes sad, exceedingly fearful, and of low spirit'. And another very famous doctor has stated that 'Some fear their friends; others are frightened of any man they happen to see: this one dare not go out into the light; that one seeks the darkness and murkiness; another fears it and flees from it; some are afraid of wine and water and everything that is liquid; and as melancholy is of many different kinds, but all have in common the general [effect of] producing sadness and fear; that all melancholics are seen to be frowning and sad, and can give no reason for their sorrow, and almost all of them fear and mistrust what does not merit being [feared or] mistrusted.'[186]

The diagnosis of the illness of Job serves Luis de León also as a means of explaining the cause which motivates him to offend God by wishing to take his own life (Job 7:15). It is not the will guided by reason that inspires in Job suicidal impulses: it is his sickness, the quality of the humour that,

> on the one hand, blackens the light, and thus blots out all that is joy, and for the same reason represents life as a dark and very sad thing; and on the other, the terror of the visions that the same humour brings in its train makes [life] odious and abhorrent. And thus as a natural consequence those affected with this calamity long to leave this life immediately, and in any way possible; and it is a sign of this desire what happens in fact with many of these who put [the desire] into effect, and throw themselves off cliffs or drown themselves.[187]

One should also mention that Luis de León himself suffered from melancholy, and that, therefore, when he refers to the ravages of the black humour, he knew from his own experience what it felt like. A variety of evidence has been found to the effect that the Augustinian friar was melancholic, but there is one fact that is truly revelatory. When he was imprisoned in 1572, accused of having translated and dedicated to a nun who was a friend of his the Song of Songs of Solomon, Fray Luis requested of the court of the Inquisition leave to have sent to him by a nun at the convent of Madrigal 'a box with some powders she used to make and supply to me for my melancholies and passions of the heart and which she alone knows how to make, for I never had greater need of them than now'.[188] Mystical visions do not attract him, and he gladly uses drugs to avoid the fits of melancholy that torment him in prison and to drive away nocturnal and terrestrial dreams. If there is an ecstasy in Luis de León, it is expressed in his calm, stoic wisdom, in face of the obscurity of the body in which the soul is incarcerated.

The relation between mystical ecstasy and melancholy was something more than a powerful Baroque figure of speech used by the poets of the day. It was a real threat that assailed men and women who sought intensely to follow a direct way of their own towards God. Jakob Böhme, in the same period, expressed a similar concern: he confessed the anxiety produced in him by the incongruity he perceived between the distant blue circumference of heaven, where the wise supposed that God had his kingdom, and the ever-present contradictory world full of misery and goodness, of living and inert beings, of rage and love. This gave rise to violent shocks in him until, as he described in *Aurora*:

> In the end I fell into a profound melancholy and sadness on contemplating the great abyss of this world; on seeing the sun and the stars, as well as the clouds, the rain and the snow; on considering in my spirit the whole creation of this world. Since in all things I found good and evil, rage and love, both in inanimate creatures such as wood, stones, the earth and the elements, and in man and beasts.

Böhme could not bear the vertigo he felt before the abyss in which good and evil coexist; he wondered what possible value there could be for God in the little spark that was man, lost in the immense fabric of heaven and earth:

> I was thereupon very melancholy, perplexed and exceedingly troubled; none of the Scriptures could comfort or satisfy me, though I was very well acquainted with them, and versed therein; at which time the Devil would by no means stand idle, but was often beating into me many heathenish thoughts, of which I will here be silent.[189]

The problem seemed to Böhme so important that he devoted a little book to the subject, *For the Melancholy*, written with the purpose of showing those whose spirits were afflicted the origin of their sadness, and the way to resist it and remedy their dejection and temptation.[190] If the soul is dressed in this complexion, being nourished by it, says Böhme, its fire burns with extreme darkness, and the Devil takes advantage of this in order to assault it. Nevertheless, not all temptations come from the Devil: in melancholics, the afflicting sadness which falls so heavy upon them comes from the imagination of the soul. He warns melancholics against drunkenness and inflaming themselves with anger, lest the fire of the imagination be lit or the wheel of nature begin to turn madly, with a tumultuous noise, in the inward void, in such a way as to prevent the thoughts from concentrating, and causing the outward members of the body also to turn, impelled by the inward wheel.[191] Could this noisy tumult be the same that St Teresa heard inside her head?

Alexandre Koyré, in his excellent essay on Böhme's philosophy, has shown how the melancholic's internal disorder and lack of harmony manifest, in the final instant, a lack of harmony between the spirit and the flesh.[192] This is not, as in the case of St Teresa (or Luther, according to Koyré), a matter of the overwhelming weight of sin: it is the contemplation of a world impenetrable to the understanding, a universe that seems to lack sense or meaning. Böhme's melancholy comes from the contemplation of a world without God or, as Koyré points out, where the divinity is present only as a result of the devastating effects of his choler. The meaningless mixture of men, beasts, stones and stars – in which goodness and evil, love and hate, consort – represented for Böhme a world with no exit that might afford a genuine means of escape, even with the help of the holy scriptures.

But where Böhme saw the dangers of the *Ungrund* and the *Abgrund*; where St Teresa felt an inward inflammation and imaginary fancies; where St John of the Cross suffered the dark and dry purgation of the soul; where the mystics found themselves caught between the abyss of the black humour and the road of the dark night, pedestrian and sensible doctors like Andrés Velásquez saw the shadowy influence of a dark bile that submerged the brain in the shadows of fear, sadness and the most corrupt imaginings. In these conditions, and under the influence of the black humour, the world appears to melancholics as menacing, overwhelming and devoid of meaning. For Dr Velásquez, who follows Galen in this respect, the sickness is due to the 'shadowy and black colour of the atrabilious humour' and not to the 'distemper of the qualities', as Avicenna and Averroes had supposed.[193] This means that fear and sadness are produced by the lack of light and natural clarity in the spirits that flow to the brain, and not only by the fact that the instruments of the soul dry up and grow cold. In the same way as almost all men fear the shadows, the black humour which darkens the brain frightens melancholics and, in extreme cases, drives them beyond fear:

> there are many of these melancholics who in such a degree come to lose their sense and reason, and remain so terrified, crazed and perplexed, that they remain ignorant of all things and, then distempered and forgetful of themselves, lead and pass their lives in the manner of beasts'.[194]

For Dr Velásquez, the obscurity was not to be found in the external world, but in the brain of the melancholic.

For this reason, many physicians looked with suspicion on the mystical flights or ecstasies of some members of religious orders. Dr Alonso de Freylas, whom I have already mentioned above, believed that the Devil at times brought a deceiving light to people sunk in the obscurity of the black humour, and advised

> melancholic people who live in withdrawal from the world, who are of profound imagination and prone to fasting and watching, not to give easy credit to their melancholy visions, revelations, raptures, but to humble themselves there and then, recognizing their misery and lowliness, and to consult a wise, prudent and devout confessor experienced in such matters.[195]

Freylas adds that the Devil adopts the figure of an angel of light, causing in melancholics 'great ruptures in their raptures and ecstasies'. In this way the black humour threatened those dedicated to the monastic life not only in the form of acedia, that terrible torpor of the soul, but also in the form of onsets of counterfeit mysticism. In fact, as I have already pointed out, acedia and melancholy can be seen as, or confused with, a path towards mystical ecstasy. In contrast with Freylas's thesis, it is interesting to cite the opinions of a Jesuit of Irish origin, Miguel Godínez (1591–1644), who devoted a chapter of his *Práctica de la teología mística* to the humours; while stressing the perils of adust melancholy, which is derived from the faeces of the blood, and which 'makes men mad, furious, treacherous, bold, cruel and extremely bad in their inclinations', he pointed out that there is another melancholy, 'which is made from the flower of the blood', and which 'causes a moderate sadness, repose in actions, profundity in discourse, weight and maturity in judgement'. Miguel Godínez, who was educated at Salamanca and was a missionary in New Spain, resumes the ancient Aristotelian tradition regarding the relation between genius and melancholy, and applies it to the practice of mystical spirituality:

> There is no great, prudent and wise man, who has not something of this melancholy. those who were choleric in their youth have in their old age this melancholy. Those who have this humour are good for government, great counsellors, profoundly learned people; and if they chance to be spiritual, they are good as spiritual masters, being generally prudent and discreet.[196]

These ideas were not shared, as may be understood, by those theologians in Spain who delivered an aggressive opposition against the mystics and all those who sought divine illumination to lighten the obscurity of the world. Melchor Cano, bishop of the Canaries and one of the fiercest opponents of illuminism and the mystics, wrote that acedia founded on the melancholy humour could drive the soul towards desperation, 'when fear, whether of death or of hell, or of not succeeding in achieving virtue' lies in wait for believers.[197] To Melchor Cano it seemed that acedia went beyond an excess of the black humour (an excess which could be treated by a physician of the body) and could come to constitute a horrible mortal sin. For him who, 'having already left behind the transitory delights of the flesh, feels in the spirit the wound which sin has left behind', he recommended as remedies penitence, exercise, prayer and submission to another's will, and rejected pastimes and recreations which, far from consoling, served only to increase affliction. Darkness, from the point of view of Fray Melchor Cano, was not to be found in an incomprehensible and strange world, but in the deliberate sinful choices of persons who abhor godly things, reject salvation and neglect their Christian duties.[198]

Religious ecstasy, which, for mystics, was a light in the dark world, was seen by many physicians as a morbid effect of the black humour, and was feared by hard and ascetic temperaments as a shadowy sin towards which the sins of the flesh paved the way. Here we find three very different ways of regarding existential contradictions: as cosmic darkness, as blackness of the cerebral fluids, or as sinful shadows of the pleasures of the flesh.

6. Love sickness

The erotic expressions of the melancholy illness were an extraordinary laboratory for testing and discussing the relations between the soul and the body. The potentially devastating consequences of love – both in the body politic and in the physical constitution of individual human beings – had received extensive discussion since ancient times and had given rise to the most diverse interpretations. The famous stories of King Perdiccas and Antiochus – who both fell in love with their stepmothers – were much commented upon, especially on account of the action supposedly taken by their doctors, Hippocrates and Erasistratus, who had discovered the erotic cause of illness by means of 'taking the pulse'. Likewise, Galen, when he treated the wife of Justus, who was suffering from insomnia without fever, felt that her pulse accelerated and became irregular in the presence of the dancer Pylades, thanks to which he discovered in this secret passion the cause of the illness.[199] The incestuous love of Amnon for his sister Tamar, recounted in the Old Testament – which displays a remarkable dialectic interlacing genuine sickness, pretended illness, love and hate – also served as an exemplum stimulating reflection on the disastrous consequences of the amorous passions, which represented a threat to customs and caused physical and spiritual damage to those possessed by them.[200] Tirso de Molina referred to the pathology of love in his play *El amor médico*, and summed up in a few lines the most discussed problems of the period:

> Love, too, is a disease,
> even though affection 'tis
> Of th' soul, whose subject is, my lord,
> the will; and since by instruments
> of th' body love doth work and is
> a passion which in th' heart doth dwell,
> in experience we find

our medicines do work their cure,
for though 'tis true that soul pure spirit-
substance is – being held within
the mortal field a prisoner –
it ever in the body's presence
laboureth. You have a lover's pulse.[201]

On the other hand, the Aristotelian tradition which begins with Problem XXX, 1, established a relation between melancholy and lasciviousness, since in the same way as wine, the black bile incites to love, for which reason 'most melancholics are obsessed by sex'.[202] This is so because the black bile – like wine – contains wind, and this windy nature, as well as producing diseases of the hypochondria, makes the penis swell; it is thanks to these pneumatic processes that the ejaculation and spilling of sperm takes place.

We can understand that for physicians it was important to define in physical terms the relations between the psychic and organic functions. The internal winds fulfilled this mediating function, and it was precisely that tenuous and subtle substance called pneuma or spirit which enabled the interaction between the soul and the organic functions to be explained. The circulation of spirits in the organism set both senses and passions, both thoughts and the functions of the different parts of the body, both faculties and perturbations in movement. The Galenic system, such as it had been codified by the medieval Arab physicians, supposed the existence of three spirits: the psychic or animal pneuma, which is found in the brain and is related to the nerves that conduct the sensations and the voluntary impulses; the vital pneuma, which has its origin in the heart and is found in the arteries, is responsible for nourishing the psychic pneuma and regulating body heat; the natural pneuma is related to the liver and with the veins that depart from this organ. The texts of Galen are not very clear with regard to the three spirits (he is precise only regarding the psychic or animal pneuma), but the Alexandrian physicians and their Syrian and Arab successors codified the system of the three spirits.[203]

In his disputation with Huarte de San Juan, Dr Velásquez uses an example which illustrates the way in which the prudent good sense of this Andalusian physician enabled him to approach sexuality and the relations between thought and the organism at one and the same time. Following Galen closely, Velásquez describes the difference between the natural instinct and the temperaments in the determining of the different abilities and skills (*ingenios*). He explains that the instinct of nature determines that, without exception, all infants know how to suck, all kid goats eat grass and all greyhounds pursue game. On the other hand, it is the nature or quality of the temperament which makes some greyhounds particularly light-footed or lively and others less so in their various actions. He expresses annoyance at the fact that on this matter Huarte criticizes Galen since, he says, 'I take it for a very dishonest way of seeking personal advantage, this wishing to bite serious authors in order to gain more honour for oneself'; nevertheless, after this declaration of orthodoxy, Velásquez advances the view that, if Galen is to be criticized, it would be more appropriate to level such criticism at another matter, which, 'although ... of a somewhat lascivious nature, it would be well to deal with it [albeit] in a summary fashion and with the greatest brevity'.[204] This is the old problem of the erection of the penis, which according to Galen occurs by natural instinct, since the genital parts rise by their own 'virtue' or power. Velásquez states on the contrary that:

> if what Galen says were true, it would seem that the imagination and the contemplation of venereal acts were of no effect for the dilatation and erection of the genital members: and [yet] we see that such contemplations do, more than any other thing, serve to raise them.[205]

He thus concludes that the erection does not occur by an instinct of nature: it is the vital spirits, instruments of the soul, that on imagining the sexual and libidinous act move towards the genital parts, causing them to swell:

> From whence it follows logically that these [the vital spirits] going to that fistulous member and running to it, it rises, and not as Galen said: that by its own altering and rising *ex naturae instincto*, the movement of the spirits follows, but that this happens by the going there of the spirits in accordance with the movement of the imagination, and thus the genital members rise.[206]

In a certain manner, what we are seeing here is a discussion to determine whether the organ makes the function or the function makes the organ: which comes first, the desire or the instrument; the contemplation of the act or the act of erection; the habit or the organ? It is not a matter of seeing Velásquez as a Lamarckian *avant-la-lettre*, but of observing his position within a broader polemic; many theologians could be made to fit on the head of a penis, so to speak, ready to discuss the transcendence of the instrument of sex. St Augustine had already established the impossibility of escape, by means of the power of the will, from the consequences of original sin, as had been proved by the fact that a man could not control his erection at his own free will.[207]

But from the point of view of a Renaissance physician interested in exploring the powers of the imagination, the Galenic and Augustinian theses were unacceptable. Moreover, they were unacceptable from the Spanish Counter-reformation point of view, which exalted the free will, even in view of the dilatations of the virile reproductive organ. Of course, when the Devil got mixed up in the controversy, things got even more complicated, as can be seen in the *Malleus maleficarum* of Kramer and Sprenger, which offers the test proposed by Henricus de Seguisa to determine the influence of curses/spells/maleficiation on the abnormal pneumatic behaviour of the penis: 'when the verge does not move at all and can never have knowledge, this is a sign of impotence; but when it moves, becomes erect, and cannot finish, this is a sign of maleficiation.'[208] It seems likely to me that Dr Velásquez was inspired, in this 'somewhat lascivious' question, by an unusual gargoyle that existed in the narrow street called Callejón de las Monjas (literally, Nun's Lane), to one side of St Mary's church, a few steps from his house. This gargoyle, a Gothic carving by the local artist Juan García Combado, represented the torso and buttocks of a man projecting from the upper part of the wall, in a defecating position; the spout that carried the water shed from the roof passed through the figure's anus. The physician of Arcos must surely have passed every day beneath the gargoyle, which – for the greater amusement of the Arcenses – displayed for all to see a set of pendant genitalia of exaggerated proportions. The gargoyle can still be seen today, although the sexual parts are missing; it appears that in 1939 the parish priest of St Mary's ordered the outsized symbols of original sin (and of free will) to be cut off, after having been on view for so many centuries.[209]

Renaissance medicine did not only take upon its shoulders the problems passed on to it by demonology; it also inherited the responsibility for determining the morbid consequences of love. The moralizing tendencies that vigorously opposed the increasing popularity of courtly and worldly love made their influence felt on many physicians of the late medieval and Renaissance periods, some of whom chose to define love as a dangerous disease and to study its causes and possible cures. It is interesting to note that, since ancient times, one of the remedies against love melancholy recommended by doctors was coitus, which enabled the excess humours to be expelled, eliminating fixed ideas and, according to Rufus of Ephesus, 'to dissolve love'.[210] It has been remarked that here we face an unresolvable contradiction between theological psychopathology, which enjoined pious abstinence as a way of combating the acedia of the ascetic, and medical psychopathology, which recommended sexual relations as a way of remedying melancholy.[211] Most doctors, nonetheless, do not seem to have been over-concerned by this contradiction, and continued to uphold the tradition regarding the therapeutic nature of coitus alongside the idea (supported by the theologians) that the amorous passion was an illness. The example of Petrus Hispanus (Peter of Spain), a great Portuguese physician of the thirteenth century, is symptomatic: in his *Cuestiones sobre el Viaticum*, he establishes that love is a disease of the brain – and not of the testicles – which affects the estimative faculty, and he quotes Avicenna, who said that the best cure was to go to bed with the object of desire.[212] In another text, *Thesaurus pauperum* ('Treasury of the poor'), a brief treaty that was highly popular, Petrus Hispanus brings together a number of prescriptions both for 'exciting the coitus' and for 'suffocating erotic desire', which demonstrate the physician's willingness to manipulate sexual relations with remedies in one direction or the other, with the aim of curing a variety of problems. For the purpose of inciting to coitus he recommends smearing the testicles and the area over the kidneys with a substance prepared from laurel berries and the juice of dogstones or a similar salep-yielding orchid, or alternatively a mixture of moss and wine; he also recommends ingesting an ounce of leopard's medula, badger's testicles or, with water, fox's testicles. Stag's or bull's testicles or the point of a fox's tail excite women, who obtain delight – says Petrus Hispanus – if the man's penis is anointed with the bile of a domestic or wild boar. If someone is suffering from a 'maleficiation' or evil spell which makes him or her to be excessively in love with a man or a woman, the lover should anoint his or her right foot in the morning with the fresh faeces of the beloved before putting on his or her shoes: after smelling the odour, the bewitchment will disappear. He offers around thirty prescriptions in a similar vein; he also lists over a score of remedies for suffocating the libido: if nine ants boiled in juice of southernwort are given to someone to drink, he will have no sexual potency in all the days of his life; another prescription, equally radical, consists of a plaster of hemlock on the testicles; the same effect is obtained with an ointment containing opium, henbane and mandragora, or an unguent of juices of black nightshade and of houseleek mixed with vinegar. If vervain is carried on the person or drunk, the erection of the penis will be impeded, and if the member is anointed with cedar rosin it will contract to such a degree that it becomes useless for coitus and engendering.[213] The prescriptions and opinions of Petrus Hispanus are interesting because he was not only one of the greatest physicians of the thirteenth century, but also an important theologian, with a copious output in the fields of logic, psychology, ancient and scholastic philosophy. He was born in Lisbon and studied in Paris. In 1272 Pope Gregory X appointed him court physician at Vitterbo, and in 1276 he became Pope, under the name of John XXI. He died the following year, crushed under the collapsing roof of the new papal palace.

As Mary Wack points out, therapeutic coitus does not seem to have presented too many ethical dilemmas, because a man's extramarital sexual relations, especially with prostitutes, did not constitute a threat to family order or to the purity of the line of descent; besides, the easy access to prostitutes in many cities allows us to suppose that coitus as a remedy did not present too many practical difficulties. As has been mentioned above, Dr Velásquez himself had been appointed by the Arcos authorities to look after the health of the prostitutes.[214] This tolerant attitude will be better understood if we take into consideration the fact that Arcos was an active military centre, where the prostitutes doubtless helped to dissipate the bad humours of the soldiery and tranquillize the high spirits of the male population, which was passing through a turbulent era in a region plagued by tensions. At a meeting of the Arcos town council held in 1571, the *regidores*, Rodrigo de Tobar and Baltasar de Gamaza, were entrusted with the function of 'choosing and tasting' the women that were to give service as prostitutes, at the same time as Dr Velásquez was awarded a salary for overseeing their hygiene. There were brothels for payment and also free or 'charity' brothels, the latter being subsidized by the city for the needy; in some towns or villages the brothels were monopolized by a powerful local grandee, but it is not known whether the Duke of Arcos had any part in this business.[215] It must be underlined, besides, that sexual relations were not regarded as morbid, in contrast with love, which was indeed seen as an illness requiring the attention of doctors and confessors. Thus, the contradiction between the condemnation of worldly love and the acceptance of coitus as part of the therapy is not as profound as it seems at first sight.

There is a text that has been seen, rightly, as the first great Spanish literary expression of the reaction against love and the cult of woman. This is the *Corbacho*, an acute, colloquial and dogmatic treatise written by the Archpriest of Talavera, Alfonso Martínez de Toledo (1398–1468), with the intention of reproving love and identifying women – together with the menaces of the Devil and the world – as the worst enemies of men.[216] The vigorous denunciation by the Archpriest of Talavera is symptomatic, since he brings to his aid the theory of the humours in order to explain the misfortunes that may be caused by 'mad love'. Besides the vices of the 'perverse women' who originate the terrible malaise of love, each of the four humours – he calls them '*complisiones*' (complexions) – exacerbates in a different way the catastrophic effects of the erotic passion. He describes each of the humoural complexions according to its qualities and relations with the elements, the parts of the body, the temperaments, the planets, the cardinal-compass points and the signs of the zodiac. The best complexion is the sanguine, and it is followed in decreasing order by the choleric, the phlegmatic and the melancholic; melancholy men are the worst, since, as well as being sad and pensive, they can be aggressive and prone to anger: 'They are violent, and then, [given to] throwing punches [*luego las puñadas en la mano*], obstinate, mendacious, deceitful . . . they are corrupted, spitting frequently, given to anger, and cruel.' The three astrological signs corresponding to them are feminine (Taurus, Virgo and Capricorn), and these are related to the planets Venus, Mercury and Saturn respectively.[217] He examines the dispositions and conditions of each complexion for loving and being loved, with the aim of showing that even the good qualities (especially those of the sanguine type) are suffocated by the perverse influence of love and women. But melancholy men are so abominable that not even women – so despised by the Archpriest of Talavera – can put up with them.[218] *El Corbacho* forms part of an anti-feminist and anti-erotic current linked to the resurgence of Platonism and the critiques of courtly love so well expressed since the twelfth century by Andreas Capellanus, whose book *De amore* is one of the principal sources used by Martínez de Toledo.[219]

The Golden Age of Melancholy

This anti-erotic and misogynous vein culminated in *La Celestina* by Fernando de Rojas, the extraordinary 'tragicomedy of Calisto and Melibea, composed in reprehension of those madly in love who, vanquished in their uncontrolled appetite, call their lovers their God, and insist that they are so'.[220] It is clear in *La Celestina* that the love of Calisto for Melibea is presented as a disease which it is necessary to cure;[221] it is the typical erotic or love melancholy caused by the senses (above all, by the contemplation of a woman).[222] The drama begins with the entrance of Calisto, in pursuit of his falcon, in the orchard of Melibea; there begins the inexorable chain of cause and effect: 'the entry, the cause of seeing her and speaking with her; speaking engendered love; love gave birth to your pain and sorrow; pain and sorrow will cause you to lose your body, your soul and your estate.'[223] Thus, with implacable logic, the senses, pain and sorrow, the flesh, the mind, and even the economy, are linked together as in a chain. The same malign process that Calisto sets off by chance constitutes a kind of chain-reaction which is also doomed to become set in motion in Melibea, but here it is through the artifices of the old Celestina, who calls on the powers of hell, though not without the wise manipulation of anger, which burns the damsel's blood.[224] The dangerous adustion of the humours has the effect expected by the procuress: Melibea in turn falls sick with love, loses appetite and sleep, is consumed by sadness: 'it is a hidden fire, a pleasing wound, a delicious poison, a sweet bitterness, a delectable sickness, a gay torment, a wound both fierce and sweet, a soft death.'[225] Behind the apparent condemnation there is an invitation to experience erotic pleasure, to taste mad love. José Ramón Enríquez has pointed out that Rojas is practising with intelligence the *taqqīya* of the Moorish *conversos*, who knew 'how to deceive with the truth, in order to sow another truth by means of this deceit'.[226]

We see in the *Corbacho* and in *La Celestina* the fascinating phenomenon by means of which Renaissance culture – in this case literature – took as its point of departure, or rather, as its texture, medical studies on melancholy: the black humour made it possible to weave a sentimental fabric in order to test erotic emotions. La Celestina is clearly a woman who parodies the profession of the doctor, and treats the illness of Calisto, as if she were Avicenna, by bringing about his carnal relationship with Melibea; her knowledge of pharmacy, her alchemical apparatus, the use of medicinal herbs, her equipment for baths and her surgical abilities might have been the envy of many physician of her period, and we may suppose that her prescriptions would not have been very different from those of Petrus Hispanus.[227] Medicine added 'natural' arguments to the traditional theological critique of worldly love: to the moral horrors of sin were added the terrible consequences of melancholy, a dreadful illness that could lead to death via a path of unspeakable carnal sufferings. There is a curious and symptomatic example of the use of medicine to denounce the ravages of love sickness ('el mal de amores'). In a pastoral narration by Antonio de Villegas, which celebrates worldly love, although diluted in melancholy Neoplatonic terms, there is included the song of a woman whose love has been rejected:

> Love is born in Heaven of that
> divine Idea; and thence engendered
> created 'tis anew, and so
> like rain upon the ground doth fall.
> The creatures then receive it and
> each one another one doth cherish;
> so it is that, without love,
> they die, and by its means they live.

These lines from *Ausencia y soledad de amor* ('Absence and solitude of love') were published in 1565; but in the second edition, of 1577, the verse quoted above was replaced by another very different one, in which one is tempted to see the influence of some doctor-turned-theologian who counselled the change:

> Love and all its passions dire
> are naught but rabid care and travail.
> Love's a cancer in disguise
> which doth consume the hearts of men.
> Those who're enter'd in its books
> like vassals of an ancient line,
> we may in reason call them sad,
> whate'er the pleasures they receive.[228]

The divinity of earthly love is brutally ousted by the idea of a devouring cancer: this is how the opposition between natural worldly love and sacred love directed toward God is expressed. Many physicians who offered anti-erotic arguments were actually making opportunistic concessions to ecclesiastical pressures. The Spanish doctor Juan de Barrios, who published a voluminous treatise on medicine in Mexico City in 1607, offers an example of this duplicity; following a chapter on melancholy, he includes another on love, where he expounds his ideas in the traditional dialogue form. This physician – after praising love with the help of quotes from Plato and Aristotle, seasoned with mythological and biblical references – is interrogated regarding those who 'speak a thousand ills of love'. He answers, citing the fable of Æsop regarding a lion who, while giving chase to a stag through a forest, comes upon a shepherd and asks him where his longed-for prey has hidden; the shepherd answers in a loud voice that he has not seen it, while indicating with his finger the direction taken by the stag. A comparison could be drawn, in the opinion of Barrios, between this tale and those who speak ill of love, deny it with their satires, but with their hearts, eyes and fingers point to it, revealing thus the desires that enslave them.[229] Despite this explanation, Barrios also expounds the well-known commonplaces; he explains that love enters by the eyes and inflames the blood, produces vapours (spirits) that reflect the beholded object and agitate the heart: those who love are 'at times furious, at others sad, melancholy, to the extent that they often go mad'; further on he states that those in love 'become wasted, lose their colour, have bags under their eyes and are at times out of their minds, they neither sleep nor eat', and he recommends the most varied remedies for curing lovers: from flagellations to getting them drunk, obliging them to fast or denigrating in their presence the object of their passion, or even forcing them to marry, purging them with senna and mallow or irritating their haemorrhoids with massages of fig leaves.

The chapters on melancholy and love in the *Verdadera medicina* of Juan de Barrios are a sample in miniature of the typical way of dealing with the subject in the Spanish Golden Age: a stereotyped way, inherited from the Middle Ages, in which the Renaissance and humanist spirit was opening a difficult path through the tangled undergrowth of contradictory citations and exempla. This traditional form was to culminate in that great monument – a majestic cathedral crammed full of information – which is Robert Burton's *The Anatomy of Melancholy*, the first edition of which was published in Oxford in 1621. Burton devoted a third of this immense work to 'love melancholy'; in it, a number of researchers believe have they found traces of that same sexual frustration referred to by Barrios.[230] Before Burton, the French physician Jacques Ferrand had published in 1610 his celebrated *Traité de l'essence et guérison de l'Amour ou mélancolie érotique*.[231] These and other works consecrated in the medicine of the seventeenth century a subject which was already a fundamental pillar of Renaissance culture: love melancholy was raised to the highest level and was widely disseminated, thanks to the influence of Cervantes, who created the most complex and attractive melancholy character of the Spanish Golden Age, the Knight of the Sorrowful Countenance,[232] Don Quixote.

There is a curious poem which offers another characteristic example of the complex Baroque way of approaching the subject of erotic melancholy. Hernando de Acuña (1518–80), the soldier-poet who exalted with great fervour in his verses the universal empire of Charles V, wrote some *coplas* 'To a lady suffering from a melancholy humour, who asked Don Hernando for some writings of his and fell in a rage because he did not give them to her'.[233] The *coplas* seem to be the expression of a strange battle between the soldier-poet and the melancholy lady. The poem begins with the setting-forth of a mystery: is it possible that a melancholy exists that does not originate in lovesickness? The angry lady of the *coplas* seems to be the rare example of a black humour not caused by erotic desire and the absence of the beloved, or at least not directly:

> Until this day, my lady, I
> did hold for undisputed truth,
> that from the malady of love
> alone proceedeth the sad humour
> that is known as melancholy. [1][234]
>
> . . .
>
> But since such as these be not
> cause sufficient of this strange
> distemper, what then could it be
> that doth occasion humour such
> that damage wreaks in heart so free? [3][235]

The poet assures the lady that merely looking at her can cause melancholy, and he finds it strange that she herself, who can cause sadness in others, should suffer the black humour. If the lady were to suffer her hand to be taken, in that yielding she would find alleviation: but she resists and wishes to maintain her heart free. The true cause of the lady's melancholy lies in her resistance to surrender herself:

> And for this reason alone
> you have the humour that afflicts,

> to none whereof you will surrender,
> and for which no place you find
> where it some benefit might render. [7]²³⁶

The woman does not yield to love, and thus she refuses to set off in others the passionate black humour. In a twisted sort of way she refuses to share her melancholy. The poet recommends her to be generous and share the humour that is accumulating in her heart:

> Whate'er the case, it would you profit,
> with your sadness and this ill,
> lady, to be liberal,
> since, for coming whence it came,
> none would deem it such at all.
>   Of that melancholy, I
> would fain have that part which would give
> – an'twere your will to let me choose –
> of its first dwelling and abode
> from whence it came, the amplest news. [10]²³⁷

The poet wishes to suffer from melancholy, but the lady refuses to concede him the privilege of the erotic pain. In exchange, she has requested of him something in writing, which the poet has refused to give her, with the pretext that it is better to feel and say than to write. She becomes annoyed at this, but the poet tells her – paradoxically, in the *coplas* he writes to her – that in asking for it in writing she annuls love, and with her anger she only succeeds in instilling fear. This is an elaborate Baroque and courtly interplay of comings and goings, sayings and unsayings, in which the woman suffers melancholy because she refuses to allow the poet the pleasure of enjoying the said melancholy, and the latter writes some *coplas* in order to explain his refusal to express his love in writing to a lady who has not wished, in the first instance, to give him her heart.

7. The sorrow of the Jews

It has been said that the sadness which distills from Villegas's *Ausencia y soledad de amor* reveals a feeling more radically bitter than that of the typically Renaissance melancholy which is expressed, for example, in Florentine Neoplatonism. Marcel Bataillon observes of the verses by Villegas that I quoted above that they reflect the

Platonic theory of the *Dialoghi d'amore* of Leone Ebreo, and suspects that the Spanish writer may have come from a family of Jewish *conversos*. The melancholy of Villegas is of a kind with that of such 'new Christians' as Diego de San Pedro, Fernando de Rojas and Jorge Montemayor, whose profound bitterness is characteristic of the intense melancholy that pervades the sentimental literature of the Iberian peninsula.[238] The idea that Iberian melancholy finds its explanation in the condition of the Jewish *conversos* was originally expressed by Américo Castro. Spanish Jews were living out a tragic contradiction that made them oscillate between the poles of flight and concealment, escaping and hiding themselves away: 'The contradiction experienced by these souls – of feeling at one and the same time citizens and outlaws who had to spend part of their lives lurking in the shadows – is both latent and patent in the lugubrious blossoms of the ascetic and picaresque style.'[239]

The subject of the mentality of the Jewish *conversos* is very complex and thorny. It has been said that 'Judaicizing' Spaniards and Portuguese lived on the defensive, developing endogamic mechanisms and creating habits designed to safeguard their ancient customs. But other *conversos* existed – contemptuously referred to as *mesummadim* (renegades) by the rabbis – who accepted the new mentality and even adopted a formalistic and intransigent Christianity; some championed a purified and humanistic spiritualism which brought them close to Erasmianism. Many *conversos* developed an anxious longing for integration in Christian society and endeavoured to rub out every trace of their Jewish past, even favouring anti-Jewish persecutions.[240] It has also been said that the *converso* population nurtured attitudes of expectation, was attracted by hopes of a messianic kind, and reacted in a dramatic way to any rumour of a possible redemption.[241]

It is extremely likely that the condition of the Jewish *conversos* was a cause of melancholy, and that this found its expression in literature, as Castro and Bataillon affirm. I do not wish to take sides in this discussion; on the other hand I do regard it as interesting to document the fact that in Renaissance Europe melancholy was considered an illness proper to the Jews. Johannes Reuchlin, for example, in his *De verbo mirifico* (1494), portrays the Jews as characterized by the sadness of their temperament and places them under the sign of Saturn.[242] Isaac Cardoso believed that if there was an illness that could be seen as specifically Jewish, this was melancholy, due to the sadness and fear caused by the wounds and oppressions of exile.[243] If to this we add the fact that, as I have mentioned above, many physicians were Jews or *conversos*, we may better understand the causes that led to melancholy occupying such an outstanding place in medical treatises. This leads me to suspect that Andrés Velásquez's great interest in the matter resulted from his having had Jewish *conversos* among his forebears, something very common in Andalusia. The physician of Arcos possibly knew that there had been a Jewish community in the town, with its synagogue; the remains of this had provided the foundations for the presbytery of the chapel of the Divine Compassion (*La Misericordia*), which was devoted to the burial of beggars, those subjected to execution, troublemakers and the destitute.[244] Throughout the Peninsula many physicians lived under the suspicion of being Jews, this serving in many cases as a pretext for dispossessing them of their goods and for stirring up anti-Semitic hysteria among the common people. In this regard, Menasseh ben Israel narrates in his *Vindiciae judaerum* (1656), the story of a Portuguese noble who, in order to force the Inquisition to set free his highly esteemed physician, a 'very good Catholic', who had under threat of torture confessed to being a secret practitioner of Judaism, took hold of the inquisitor himself and extracted an identical confession through similar procedures.[245]

We may find fresh support for the idea that the Jews were especially liable to melancholy in a clinical case-study of the period. The case in question also offers an opportunity for a more concrete idea of the activity of doctors during the sixteenth century. I offer the example of a Jewish-Portuguese physician who treated an Italian colleague who was also suffering the ravages of the black humour. The former was João Rodrigues de Castelo Branco, known as Amato Lusitano (1511–68), who brought together in his famous *Centuriæ* a large number of clinical case-studies. His patient was Azariah dei Rossi (1514–78), a physician and historian from Mantua, known for his studies of Hebrew, Latin and Italian literature.[246] On a certain occasion, Amato recounts, he was with Azariah in a bookshop; following a conversation regarding a text by Pietro de Galatino against the Jews, Azariah requested his help to cure an illness which was undermining his health. The patient, who was at that time thirty-five years old, had an emaciated appearance; his body was covered with dry scabs and his face had a wan hue. On examining him, Amato discovered the following symptoms: a continuous discharge or distillation from the head towards the lower parts of the body; an excessive heat in the liver; an obstruction of the spleen, which produced a murmuring in the hypochondriac region; a weak stomach unable to digest well; a 'canine' or voracious appetite; a sense of oppression in the chest; frequent insomnia; terrifying nightmares; and melancholy thoughts on awakening. Azariah suffered from melancholia, and the diagnosis is explained as follows:

> Almost all Jews are naturally subject to the black bile, which I believe arises mainly from certain diverse causes: first, because they are in captivity and consequently live submerged in fear and sadness, and thus have the black humour . . . Besides, they are all very studious and as a result of observing their religious laws with rigidity, the Hebrews are accustomed to eating foods that contain the black humour. Especially in Italy, they eat goose, duck, smoked beef, vegetables and much salted cheese . . . It is for this reason that the fact is generally accepted that all Jews are of the black humour. Azariah is no exception: he is extremely studious and he devotes himself zealously to his work as a physician.[247]

Amato Lusitano, with considerable care, describes and analyses all the effects wrought by the black bile in Azariah. He makes use of the diagnosis to refute Averroes, who had erroneously maintained that it was the humour itself, and not its colour, that produced the symptoms. Amato explains that:

> the patient awakes very perturbed, both physically and mentally, breathing heavily, and finds relief in belching and shedding tears; for in this way the humour is attenuated and transformed into a black vapour. This vapour, retained in the stomach and the heart, is liberated on yawning and eructing. In the same way, that portion of the humour which rises to the head reaches the corners of the eyelids and the nasal sinuses. Afterwards, through a violent commotion, it escapes in the tears in the same way in which that reaching the bladder is excreted in the urine. As a result of the perturbations mentioned above, we are convinced that the black bile is the cause both of the disease and of its symptoms . . .[248]

Later, he establishes that, as Maimonides explained in his *Aphorisms of Medicine*, the black bile does not derive from the black phlegm; this never produces melancholy, but other conditions of a different nature. He concludes that Azariah is affected principally by the black bile, which flows continually to his head and prevents it from becoming sufficiently heated, from assimilating what it ought to assimilate, and retaining what is necessary.

After long and complicated explanations, Amato goes on to recommend a treatment. the melancholic should avoid wet and foggy climates. To remedy his flatulence he must abstain from unleavened bread, and if during the Jewish Passover for religious reasons it cannot be avoided, then he must prepare it with sugar and eggs. He should avoid cold, salted and smoked meats, so common among the Jews. He should also desist from studying at night, since this is damaging and contrary to nature:

> For this causes serious and severe disturbance to the body; during the night the spirits retire to the internal parts, and the effort and excitation of study forces them to come out. This gives rise to a constant conflict which seriously damages the body. Study is, however, permitted during the day, though not until two hours have passed after lunch, and only light studies, since the most arduous steal away strength from the whole body. Sexual intercourse and marital relations must be of such a manner as to make the patient feel fresh and light-hearted afterwards.[249]

Since the illness was produced by an inundation of the black humour throughout the organism, the principal remedy consisted in eliminating it through several different means of evacuation. Emetics, diuretics and laxatives were often used for such purposes, and were administered in the form of enemas, infusions and purgative syrups. But the best way of eliminating the black humour, according to Galen, was bleeding; in the case of Azariah, however, it was necessary to have recourse to a special method:

> His body was so emaciated and debilitated that to prick the vein would be dangerous, and we had to use leeches applied to the veins of the anus – known as the haemorrhoids – in order to extract the black humour. Two leeches were applied, which fell off on becoming full; following which the blood continued to flow. If too much blood were to flow, as often happens, it is easy to close the openings with clay, powdered charcoal, cobweb, powdered chalk, egg-white mixed with an astringent powder, linen or lint.[250]

We know that the unfortunate Azariah dei Rossi did not merely survive this treatment, which lasted four months, but that he lived for a further thirty years after his illness, during which time he led an intense and creative intellectual activity.

Let us now consider the problem from a less practical point of view. Dr Huarte de San Juan, who was a native of a frontier region where many *conversos* took refuge,[251] also expresses the traditional idea that the Jews were a melancholic people, and expounds an interesting theory to explain this phenomenon. His starting-point consisted in seeking an explanation for the fact that the Israelites and their descendants are of an acute wit (especially apt for medicine). He finds the reason for this in the fact that, as a result of a variety of different circumstances, the ancient Jews were prone to frequent combustion of their choler. This was due not only to their dwelling in a region, like Egypt, whose inhabitants 'have their brains toasted and their choler combusted to a high degree',[252] but because during their life in the desert they ate manna, drank delicate waters and breathed pure air. His explanation goes back to Galen, who had established that rude and hot stomachs, accustomed to strong and heavy foods, on ingesting light foods converted them into adust choler: 'This very thing happened to the Hebrews with the manna, which they converted wholly into very adust choler.'[253] The same happened with the pure water of the desert, which fell into their stomachs accustomed to drinking gross, brackish and corrupted waters, and was converted into choler. The clean air, as Aristotle had already stated, enlivened wit. These conditions caused the seed of the men to become delicate and toasted and the menstrual blood of the Hebrew women to become very attenuated, and consequently the children they engendered were of an acute wit. But the later misfortunes of the Jews – hunger, subjections, persecutions, servitude and ill treatments – exacerbated the make-up of the hot, dry and burnt temperament they acquired in Egypt and in the desert:

> Because the continual sadness and vexation causes the vital spirits and arterial blood to come together in the brain, the liver and the heart; and being there one upon another, they come to be toasted and re-combusted. And so time and time again they reach high temperatures; and what ordinarily happens is that they are converted into melancholy by adustion (which all partake of down to the present day).[254]

The nature acquired by the ancient Jews was inherited by their descendants: 'the children of Israel . . . may communicate to their descendants the acuteness of wit without the latter ever having set foot in Egypt nor eaten manna.'[255] But along with their wit they also inherited the terrible illness which haunts all studious and heroic spirits, as had been posited by *Problem XXX, I*, of the Aristotelian tradition.

8. Ill-tempered instruments

On certain occasions, the close contact with strange diseases placed physicians under suspicion. This is what happened to the great Jewish doctor of Portuguese origin, Filoteo Elião de Montalto, who in the early years of the seventeenth century, spent some time at the court of Marie de Medici, where he treated Leonora Galigai, the Queen's foster-sister, for an acute nervous condition (*bulbus hystericus*) which drove her into fits of screaming and weeping.[256] Leonora and her husband Concino Concini, Marquis d'Ancre, exercised a powerful and legendary influence over Queen Marie, which generated considerable annoyance among the nobles, who ended up murdering the marquis and accusing his widow of witchcraft in 1617. When she was treated and cured by Montalto in 1606, the court physicians had already suspected that Leonora Galigai's crisis was due to her being possessed by the Devil. In 1617 she was made to stand trial as a witch and her doctor was accused of being her accomplice; she never confessed her supposed crimes and neither did she implicate Dr Montalto, despite which Leonora was found guilty, beheaded and burned on 8 July 1617. The physician remained unaffected by the accusations against him since he had died the year before, while accompanying King Louis XIII on a journey.

In 1614 Montalto published in Paris his *Archipathologia*, which contains an extensive treatise on melancholy.[257] In it we find a chapter devoted to the question of 'Whether the melancholy illness may be caused by evil spirits', in which he says:

> There are some reputed authors, among them Al-Zahravi, who believe that the probable cause of the melancholy illness is the Malign Demon, and allege that they have seen him; others base their opinion on the statements of people who, despite having knowledge of philosophy, poetry, and the mechanical arts, are not wise ... My own opinion is that these unfortunate people have always existed, both in earlier times and today, who suffer from evil spirits, which could be a punishment sent and approved by the righteous judgement of the Holy Lord God. Since the curing of such cases is beyond

the capacities of medicine, the doctor must needs have recourse to supernatural help.[258]

Montalto considers, basing his position on that of Avicenna, that it is not the physician's job to investigate whether melancholy has anything to do with the Devil. This prudent attitude could be a result of his own experience, including the case of Leonora Galigai, which had taught him the dangers of giving medical treatment to, and curing, people suspected of being possessed by the Devil. Nonetheless, Montalto refers the reader to his chapter on symptoms, which deals with the problem of how to clarify whether in the melancholy in question satanic or natural causes are to be observed. There, he expresses a more critical opinion and introduces a problem that has very ancient roots in the history of melancholy:

> There are references to miraculous events in melancholy, difficult to be believed which, they say, have been experienced by certain not very able artists, philosophers, astronomers, poets and – which is even more surprising – prophets, especially by means of dreams, while suffering from mental disturbances. Supposing that this were true, it should not be attributed to the Devil, as many do who imagine that this madness is caused by his direct and pernicious influence, but on the contrary should be explained by the peculiar nature of the melancholy humour, its quantity and quality, associated with the temperament of the subject. This was clearly Aristotle's opinion.[259]

The allusion to Aristotle brings us directly to the famous *Problem XXX, I*, which begins with the following question:

> Why is it that all men who have been exceptional in philosophy, statesmanship, poetry or the arts, have been manifestly melancholic, to the point that some of them have been affected by the evils caused by the black bile, as is told of Hercules in the relations that refer to the heroes?[260]

This problem attributed to Aristotle has exercised, as is well known, a profound and long-lasting influence on Western thought. When Andrés Velásquez confronts this problem as a doctor, he categorically opposes the Aristotelian tradition. However, he does not do so directly, but via a critique of Huarte's theses, which are in fact a recreation of the peripatetic interpretations of melancholy, according to which the black humour is capable of stimulating the capacity for prophecy, as in the case of the Sibyls and the

Bacchantes.[261] The central argument of the Aristotelian *Problem* lies in the relation which it establishes between exceptional intellectual or heroic qualities and the melancholy condition; Huarte continues along the same lines when he tries to find a link between the 'wits' (*ingenios*) and the combinations of humours and temperaments. He finds one of the proofs of the existence of such a link in the fact that a 'well-tempered' brain occasions a man, suddenly, and without having learned of the matter from anybody, to be able to speak about science with great ability.[262] Huarte gives the example of the ignorant and rustic men who, in a state of 'frenzy', suddenly began to speak Latin without ever having learned it when they were sane.[263] It is clear that he associates frenzy with melancholy, since he expressly cites in support of his contention *Problem XXX, I*, in its Latin version, in the part where he refers to the Sibyls and the black humour. This phenomenon occurs, according to Huarte, simply because the rational soul, when it reaches the sufficient degree of heat, invents the most rational words, which are those of the Latin language.[264] It may happen, therefore, that an illness causes a temperament to be produced in the brain identical with that of the man who invented Latin, so that in some way the frenetic and the maniac may once again invent a language that already exists.[265]

The origin of this idea may be traced back to the physician Antonio Guainerio, a Paduan doctor who died in 1440 and is regarded as a precursor of the ideas of Ficino on melancholy.[266] Guainerio dedicates a long chapter in his *Practica* to replying to the following question: 'Why have certain illiterate melancholics become wise and how is it that there are some among them who predict the future?'[267] Although he refers to *Problem XXX, I*, this physician gave an explanation that we recognize once more, at least in part, in Huarte and in Velásquez. According to Guainerio all souls are originally perfect and have, in equal measure, all the knowledge to which they can aspire; the differences of quality that can be observed in souls are due to the physical constitution of the bodies to which they are joined. When the soul 'incarnates' in a body it forgets almost all its innate ideas, and only study – that is to say, reason or 'discourse' – enables it to remember a part of what it has forgotten. In certain cases it comes about that the corporeal senses become paralysed and the soul – isolated for a short time – returns to direct intuition without the mediation of any discourse. This is what happens with melancholics, whose senses become blocked, leading the souls of less educated men to remember their primal knowledge to the point of becoming very wise ('*literatissimus*').

Dr Andrés Velásquez dedicated a whole chapter of his book, the last one, to refuting the idea held by certain 'very learned gentlemen, almost as if under obligation, that as a result of this *melancholia morbus*, he who did not know the Latin language may come to speak it and the rustic to philosophize'.[268] Aretæus can be cited in support of this thesis, says Velásquez, even though this is not normally done. Nonetheless, even though Aretæus says so, and is now seconded in this by Dr Huarte de San Juan, it is manifestly false. He recognizes that authorities may be cited in favour of one opinion or the other, but 'reason shows us, and confirms it to be the truth', that such sick persons cannot suddenly come to speak Latin: it is impossible that corrupted and damaged 'directive' faculties (*potencias rectrices*) may execute works that are not likewise corrupted and damaged. If the temperament is damaged, depraved and corrupted, the rational soul is incapable of working in such a way that – in a state of mania or frenzy – a person might philosophize or speak in Latin. Andrés Velásquez's conclusion does not only deny the particular case of the Latin-speaking frenetics, but emphatically opposes the Aristotelian traditions – invoked by Ficino and Guainerio – that established a relation between melancholia and genius:

> But even if it were true (which it is not) that there existed a frenetic who came to speak Latin, having acquired the temperament which is necessary for the rational soul to perform such acts, he could not do so [while suffering from] the illness to which we refer, viz. melancholy, because in this disease, apart from the serious damage which the temperament has [suffered], the spirits must of necessity have lost their natural clarity, and become obscured and shadowy. For the temperament (whence it is that the good ability emanates) being once corrupted and the instrument damaged through which it works, what work will the rational soul achieve or of what instruments will it avail itself which might come to make good consort or invention? For we must not think that as a consequence of this melancholy to which we here refer, the soul might be made more perspicacious, but that, rather, melancholy is a cause of perturbation to the soul, and not of illustration, as is clearly shown by the fear and sadness that is ever suffered by the afflicted melancholics. Thus I

hold it for very truth that no rustic manic melancholic may speak Latin nor discourse upon astrology without having first learnt of those matters.[269]

The fundamental difference between Velásquez and Huarte lies in the fact that, for the latter, the rational soul, like the Devil, is capable of operating apart from the body:

> I may not cease to understand that the rational soul set apart from the body – nay and the Devil too – enjoys the faculty of sight, smell, hearing and touch . . . For to say that the rational soul divided from the body may not reason because it has no brain is a very great folly.[270]

Velásquez meets Huarte head on:

> For the soul, inasmuch as it is in the body, may not work without instruments; and so, these being damaged and corrupted, tell me, Dr San Juan: to perform these works and acts, which of themselves have need of a sound temperament, very well accommodated and proportioned, in what way shall [the soul] work or with what instruments? For these are none other than those we have indicated.[271]

For Velásquez – and here he is indeed on the same lines as Guainerio – the rational soul in all men is of equal wisdom and capacity; the differences proceed from the instruments, to the degree that these are better or worse in each individual. His position leaves no room for doubt: 'insofar as we live, we are composed of matter, whence it is, being our form, that all our works emanate.' Melancholics suffer damage to their instruments, and so, 'the instrument being harmed, its action must also be harmed.'[272] Pedro de Mercado had already remarked in his dialogues, through the mouth of Joanicio, that the soul, 'so long as it is imprisoned in our bodies, may not work except with the aid of corporeal instruments. If these do not retain their temper and good composition the soul sickens and produces in a corrupted fashion its works.'[273] But here there is an affirmation that Velásquez does not accept: the idea that the soul itself, and not only its instruments, may become sick as a result of natural causes. For the physician of Arcos, there is not only an organic aspect that allows him to conclude that if the corporeal instruments are damaged, inevitably the resultant actions will be abnormal; he also refuses to consider that any organic modification might cause defects in the soul, since all souls 'are of an equal wisdom, perfection and capacity', and if there are differences of quality in the works of individuals, that is due to the different qualities of the organic instruments. He offers the example of two painters, equally good, one of whom is given a spoilt brush, bad colours, and a poorly finished board; one will produce works of beauty and perfection, while the other's will be defective: 'Thus the defect is not of the soul, because this is equally good, perfect, wise and capable in one case as in the other.'[274] In the same way, the defects are not to be sought in the rational soul, but in the bodily organs and instruments. In this democracy of souls, where all are equal, the differences occur in the corporeal and worldly prison, where the humours become burnt, corrupted and depraved.[275]

In contrast, Huarte took another path to defend the orthodox thesis regarding the immortality and incorruptibility of souls. He wrote a special chapter in order to avoid the accusation of maintaining that organic conditions might corrupt the soul; in his explanation he finds no remedy other than to place the Devil as a malign occupant of the soul, capable of perturbing the soul, causing it pain and sadness, but not of corrupting it.[276] He did not succeed in resolving the contradiction between the moral aspect and the natural dimension in the functioning of the mind, both in its morbid and its sane aspects. The contradiction is lodged within the Galenic tradition itself, which accepted that the humours and temperaments were the cause of serious illnesses in the soul. Juan Luis Vives in his treatise *De anima et vita* (1538) had admitted frankly that the black humour led to the obfuscation of the understanding, such that 'the soul is divested of its agility and freshness'. There is no doubt that he is referring to ills and diseases of the soul, as he calls them;[277] for Vives sadness is 'a shrinking of the soul on account of a present ill, or one that is believed to be present'; he identifies it with the *aegritūdo* (grief or distress) to which Cicero refers in his *Tusculan Disputations* (Book III). This is the interpretation of Vives:

> With grief the body dries up and the heart shrinks to the point that in some who had died of grief, it was found to be of no more substance than a membrane. The heart causes the visage, which is its image, to contract with it and, finally, gives up health itself. Inseparable companions of sadness are lamentations, moans, wailing. This passion is cold and dry, and for this reason it predominates

in cold seasons and places and generally in everything which displays a melancholic complexion, such as in autumn, in cloudy weather, at night, towards the north, regions where sadness has more victims than in Spain or Italy.[278]

Later, Vives warns that in these and other diseases of the soul, a new sorrow drives away an old one: in a soul already inured to suffering, a greater ill deadens the sensation of a lesser one.

Dr Andrés Velásquez prefers the pedestrian common-sense of a doctor accustomed to treating the most diverse forms of human suffering and illness. He completely leaves aside the problem of knowing whether the soul is contaminated in some way by organic phenomena; he prefers to remain on firm ground by simply declaring the equality of all souls, freeing himself thereby of the anxieties proper to moral theology. If all souls are identical, the doctor is free to concentrate on the instruments, the bodily mechanisms, temperaments and humours, in order to seek there the answers to his questionings. In a certain way, Velásquez, besides throwing out the Devil, has also expelled the soul from organic problems. Nor is he over-preoccupied by the intellectual consequences of the black humour in the lives of geniuses, poets and heroes. Andrés Velásquez is an ordinary doctor, profoundly concerned with the ill effects of the melancholy disease in his patients. Thus it is that, if he had ever had the chance to meet a Latin-speaking frenetic or a philosophizing maniac – something which never happened to him – he would not have paused to wonder whether perhaps the soul of the unfortunate person was trying to communicate in the perfect language thanks to a happy, though fleeting, combination of temperaments and humours. What Dr Velásquez would have done was to administer cold tranquillizing drugs and a suppository in order to make him or her evacuate the burnt bile; and in the case of the treatment failing to have effect, he would have called the confessor.

Although Velásquez never observed one of these strange cases, I believe that we may presume that the fact that they are mentioned and discussed so frequently must have been due to some empirically observed phenomena. The belief in the extraordinary capacity of some mentally ill persons to express themselves in an educated manner, although they had not received education, was very widely held. Evidence of this is that almost a century after the publication of the *Libro de la melancolía*, a text appeared that copied

Velásquez's arguments. Thomás Murillo, in his *Aprobación de ingenios y curación de hipocondríacos* (1672), devotes the first chapter to elucidating 'whether a rustic man being hypochondriac, melancholic, frenetic or maniac, may speak Latin without having studied it beforehand, and discourse of precepts of philosophy, and compose verses as if he were a poet'. His conclusion, in the third chapter, is the same as that of Velásquez: 'it is proved that no one naturally, without having studied Latin, nor other sciences, may understand them and speak of them.'[279] It has been supposed that this preoccupation with madmen talking like wise men could be due to the fact that the nonsense words with which some demented people expressed themselves were taken for an educated language.[280] This hypothesis seems to me unconvincing, among other reasons because it supposes a considerable ignorance, even stupidity, in those witnesses – whether doctors or not – of the cases of Latinizing mania.

I believe that it is in fact possible to identify the type of patients these melancholics, frenetics or maniacs with flashes of genius might have been. What syndrome unites the 'rustic' condition with that of a person who unexpectedly demonstrates knowledge of a learned language or a science? Dr J. Langdon Down, in 1887, coined the term 'idiot *savants*' to designate those persons who, suffering mental retardation or being uneducated, demonstrated possession of exceptional intellectual qualities, such as a prodigious memory or an extraordinary capacity for mental calculations.[281] Recent studies have used the term '*savant* syndrome' to describe these sick people.[282] The illness is usually detected in early infancy, which leads many to suppose that it could be a congenital biological defect, although others believe that it could be a psychogenic disequilibrium occasioned by unsatisfactory maternal care and extreme abandonment of the child to coldness and indifference. Actually, very little is known about this illness, and the different aetiologies proposed by present-day physicians often show similarities with judgments made in the sixteenth century: does the illness come from within or from without? Is it due to the wickedness of the parents or to an innate pathological condition?[283]

Those who suffer the syndrome of the idiot savant have an extraordinary memory. J. Langdon Down gave one of his patients Gibbon's *The Decline and Fall of the Roman Empire* to read: after a single reading the patient had the entire text imprinted on his memory and was able to repeat it exactly, without omission even of the errata. Other cases include one who could calculate the day of the week of any date, 40,000 years before or after, and yet did not know how to add up; another, who was blind, could reproduce on the piano any piece of music heard a single time, yet was unable to hold a fork in his hand. We may well imagine that the cases discussed by Huarte and Velásquez involved people who had memorized entire sermons in Latin, conversations on astrology or theological discussions. Nowadays it is known that most of these cases of hypertrophied memory are patients suffering from autism, and it is estimated that one in every ten autistic persons displays the idiot savant syndrome; with some degree of frequency they also suffer from mental retardation. Despite their dramatic incapacities and their disconnection from the world, some autistic people acquire an extraordinary development of the olfactory, tactile, visual or auditory senses, and show a prodigious ability for feats of memory and calculation 'without having ever learnt how to do these things', as Huarte might have said. One physician has compared these studies of autism with the experience of an anthropologist on Mars: this is such a strange field that it seems to him that the skills of an ethnologist are necessary in order to try to study a completely unknown group of human beings. The deviation found in autistic human beings is so radical that, according to Oliver Sacks, we find ourselves face to face with a subject that touches the deepest problems of ontology.[284]

9. Decadence and *Angst*

The publication in 1585 of Andrés Velásquez's book on melancholy could be taken as an ill omen or as a manifestation of heightened sensibility regarding the black humours which were beginning to threaten Spain. Scarcely two years after the appearance of the book, Arcos sent a force of 100 lancers and 400 harquebusiers, all of them residents of the town, to go rapidly to the port of Cadiz, which was being sacked by Sir Francis Drake.[285] The much-feared English privateer sank, burned or captured there a score of vessels at the end of April, 1587, which was a very heavy blow to the Spanish Armada and a premonition of the fate that awaited it the following year, when it was destroyed as a result of its ill-fated campaign against the English. The Duke of Arcos in person – the son of the man who had usurped the property of the residents of the town – participated in the defence of Cadiz and was sent afterwards to defend the coasts of Granada, which were being constantly invaded and sacked by Algerian or other Barbary corsairs.[286] It was to this Duke, Don Rodrigo Ponce de León, that Dr Velásquez dedicated his *Libro de la melancolía*; one is tempted to wonder whether, in the midst of such turmoil, the Duke of Arcos would have had time to read Velásquez's treatise and to reflect on its 'importance for the health and well-being of the public', as the author said in his introduction to the book.

Of course, the idea that Spanish society was sick and suffering from a process of decadence is not new; it was voiced by the Spaniards of the Golden Age themselves. In an acute essay, J. H. Elliot has shown just how widespread was a fatalistic vision among politicians and thinkers regarding what has been called Spain's 'decline', expressed for example in the well-known *Memorial de la política necesaria* by Martín González de Cellorigo, published in 1600. Jerónimo de Ceballos even used medical metaphors to explain Spanish decline, which was similar to that of a body that, as a result of excess or from natural causes, enters into decay. An interesting document presented to the Cortes in 1623 declared that monarchies are mortal and compares the condition of Castile with that of one of the human bodies described by Galen, undergoing a process of gradual corruption caused by the bad humours that, nonetheless, maintain it painfully alive and which the doctors dare not purge, for fear of inducing a sudden death.[287] The corruption of the body politic could lead to melancholy in men, as we have already seen. But it was also suggested for the first time that knowledge of the natural processes of the illness, such as they affected individuals, could contribute to the understanding of social life and the improvement of political life. It is not by chance that it was precisely a physician, Miguel Sabuco de Nantes, who developed the idea that the new philosophy must be of interest to kings, since through the knowledge and understanding of the nature and properties of men they would be able better to rule them and govern their world. Thus, his *Nueva filosofía de la naturaleza del hombre* (1587) includes a significant 'Coloquio sobre las cosas que mejoran este mundo y sus repúblicas' (*A dialogue regarding things that improve this world and its republics*).[288] Sabuco begins his recommendations with a curious reflection on those 'affects' which do damage, in contrast with those which give health. He bases his ideas, naturally, on the theory of humours. He mentions more than a dozen negative affects, among them sadness, fear and love. Solitude may be positive but it also produces damage: it is healthy for good Christians and bad for melancholics and sad people, for the solitary person 'is either like God or like a beast'.[289]

In 1588 the Duke of Medina Sidonia, Alonso Pérez de Guzmán – one of the richest and most powerful grandees of Spain – was designated by Philip II to command the Armada and lead it in what was to turn out to be a disastrous attack against the English fleet. Perhaps a reading of the books of Drs Sabuco and Velásquez – which had recently left the presses – would have led him to a better understanding of the misfortune. Many years later, as we shall see, the Duke hired the services of Dr Velásquez. But in the year of the failure of the 'Invincible Armada' our doctor of melancholics was living in Arcos, where he was to continue to exercise his profession a further twenty years. During that time his little town lived under continual tensions: the permanent threat from the English kept them ready for war, prepared to go to the rescue of the port of Cadiz. Paradoxically, the warlike Arcenses – always prepared to defend the honour of king and country against foreigners – did not hesitate to file a number of suits against Philip II and against neighbouring towns in defence of their own properties and interests. That same year of 1588 they filed a complaint against Philip II for having appropriated lands forming part of the communal property of the city (in 1590 they came to an understanding with the king and paid him the sum of 20,000 ducats, in exchange for keeping the disputed estates in favour of the commonalty). In the following year they once again entered into litigation with the king on refusing to pay him the *moneda forera* (a kind of feudal tribute which was payable to the king every seven years), a tax from which they considered themselves to be exemp. And again, in 1591, they resisted payment of the *almojarifazgo*, a duty on internal or external imports and exports, and initiated a costly lawsuit in defence of their traditional privileges. At the same time, they entered into litigation with Jerez and Seville over problems of boundaries and properties; but the worst disputes were with the neighbouring town of Villamartín, which even led to bloody clashes in 1590 and 1594, when the Arcos guards killed some foresters who were cutting down trees on their common lands. The fear of the English mobilized the residents of Arcos in 1589, when they lent twenty carts for the transport of stone for the fortifications of Cadiz and Santa María, as well as a further six to carry gunpowder. In April, 1591, an English squadron was sighted off Cadiz, and so Arcos rapidly sent a hundred cavalrymen to the port; they returned shortly afterwards when the English withdrew. The turmoil intensified, due to the unexplained homicide of a priest at the hermitage of San Miguel; despite the intervention of the Inquisition and the arrest and interrogation of many people, the strange crime was never solved. Five years later another humiliation was suffered: the Cadiz garrison, with the support of horsemen from Arcos, Chiclana and Jerez was unable to prevent the seizure, by an English expedition led by the Duke of Essex, of the port, which they held for the period of two weeks, ample time to effect the pillaging of the entire city; the English on retiring carried off a number of hostages for whom they demanded payment of a ransom; among these was a citizen of Arcos who, on account of his knowledge of English, was chosen as one of those commissioned to negotiate the liberty of the captured Spaniards.[290]

Inspired by this episode, Cervantes wrote what is, according to Otis Green, a revealing sonnet regarding the melancholy that was increasingly taking hold of the Spanish, who believed themselves to be God's chosen people but felt that the realization of their destiny was receding into the remote future. The last lines of the sonnet are as follows:

> Bellowing, the Calf put order in the field;
> the earth did tremble, and the sky grew dark
> threatening utter ruin on every side;
> and finally into Cadiz, with full measure
> of gravity and pomp – the Earl having gone
> undaunted – great Medina's Duke did ride.[291]

Cervantes refers to the recovery of the port by the Duke of Medina Sidonia, who arrived when the English had already departed, supported by Sevillian soldiers hurriedly organized and with the aid of the Calf of God, without whose apocalyptic bellowing the Spaniards could not have 'triumphed'.[292] After this bitter experience, the town council of Arcos, realizing that its citizens lacked good armaments, purchased in Seville 400 harquebuses; the same year it was agreed also to repair the town clock, which was situated in the tower of St. Mary's church.[293] Did they perhaps feel that Spain's time was no longer in step with that of the epoch?

But time followed its course and in 1607 Rodrigo Ponce de León, Duke of Arcos and protector of Andrés Velásquez, who had dedicated his *Libro de la melancolía* to him, died. Velásquez had envisaged his book as a ship that 'blew with the favour and tide of such an excellent prince; I am confident that it will find a good port, and rest assured that no squall, such as those that are stirred up by murmurers, shall be a nuisance to it.' Dr Andrés Velásquez, his protector having grown old and died, ceased to be the physician of Arcos, and the winds blew him to Sanlúcar de Barrameda, to assist the Duke of Medina Sidonia, who was still Commander of the Ocean and at the head of the now vanquished Armada. The town council of Arcos, on 4 May 1608, appointed as its doctor a certain Montoya in replacement of Dr Velásquez,

> who has been unable to excuse himself from attending upon the commands of the Duke of Medina Sidonia, whom he is assisting in his home in order to cure his person as a result of the fame of his much learning and his medicine which is enjoyed by the said doctor.

The Duke had been feeling very ill, and his personal physician, Dr Maldonado, had declared himself unable to cure him. Two messengers were sent, one to Cadiz and the other to Arcos, to bring urgently Drs Toquero and Velásquez; it was the latter who succeeded in curing the Duke. The Duchess of Medina Sidonia commented on the matter in a letter: 'Dr Velásquez is already installed at home. And I am most happy with the good report you make of his person, with which I shall remain all the more contented to have him with us.'[294] Consequently, the Duchess signed orders to pay the former physician of Arcos 51,000 *maravedís* for his journey to Sanlúcar and to assign him an annual salary of 500 ducats, 500 *fanegas* of wheat and another 50 of barley, 'and I command that [the said salary] be liberated and paid to him in four-monthly portions as is the case with our other physicians' starting in January 1608.[295]

It is very likely that, in Sanlúcar, Dr Velásquez would have been able to treat the members of the Medina Sidonia family for the effects of melancholy and had time to explore in his own soul the damage caused by the black humour. Despite the luxury in which he lived and his ownership of one of the largest fortunes in the whole of Europe, the Duke must surely have been sorely burdened by the memory of his enormous failures at the head of the Armada. Dr Velásquez also lived surrounded by comforts, and he even permitted himself the luxury of acquiring a silver jug and some crimson velvet cushions, in 1609 and 1610; they cost him less than 400 copper *reales* at the auctions in which some goods belonging to the recently deceased Duchess were sold off. The fact that the immensely rich Duke of Medina Sidonia, in order to deal with some pressing cash-flow problem, should have been obliged to liquidate certain superfluous belongings is in itself somewhat melancholic. This timely purchase is the last news we have of Dr Velásquez.[296] According to the ledgers of the ducal house, our physician received his salary, in cash and in kind, every four months until August 1615; his name no longer appears on the list of doctors who received that year a sheep, by way of a Christmas box. According to a plan of burials dating from the seventeenth century his tomb was in the first row of the presbytery of St Mary's church in Arcos.[297] Thus, in the same way that we have found no firm evidence as to his origin or that of his ancestors, we are likewise unaware of the circumstances in which, undoubtedly in 1615, Dr Andrés Velásquez crossed the last frontier.

NOTES

[1] Juan Huarte de San Juan, *Examen de ingenios para las ciencias*, critical edn by Guillermo Serés (Madrid: Cátedra, 1989), ch. V, p. 325.

[2] Andrés Velásquez, *Libro de la melancholia, en el qual se trata de la naturaleza desta enfermedad, assi llamada Melancholia, y de sus causas y simptomas. Y si el rustico puede hablar Latin, ò philosophar, estando phrenetico ò maniaco, sin primero lo aver aprendido* (Sevilla: Hernando Díaz, printer, and Alonso de Mata, bookseller, 1585), p. 294. All references are to the edition of this text published in Roger Bartra, *El Siglo de Oro de la melancolía. Textos españoles y novohispanos sobre las enfermedades del alma* (Mexico City: Universidad Iberoamericana, Departamento de Historia, 1998).

[3] Ibid., p. 286.

[4] Huarte, *Examen de ingenios*, ch. V, p. 326.

[5] Nemesius, *De natura hominis*, IV, cited by Jackie Pigeaud, 'De la mélancolie et de quelques autres maladies dans les *Etymologies* IV d'Isidore de Seville', in *Textes médicaux latins antiques*, ed. G. Sabbah (Saint-Étienne: Publications de l'Université de Saint-Étienne, 1984), p. 93. The subject of *phantasia* is enormously complex and highly significant; it has been addressed brilliantly, from a number of different points of view, in the third part of the book by Giorgio Agamben, *Stanze, La parola e il fantasma nella cultura occidentale* (Turin: Einaudi, 1977), and in the first

part of Ioan P. Couliano, *Eros and Magic in the Renaissance* trans. Margaret Cook (Chicago: University of Chicago Press, 1987).

6   Velásquez, *Libro de la melancolía*, p. 275.
7   Ibid., p. 297. Francisco Vallés compared morbid cerebral activity to a dung-heap: 'since as there is no dung-heap that always exhales corruption, but only on being moved around and turned over, with greater reason – since the causes of the illness become moved at certain times, with a certain order or erratically – it is necessary that melancholics become sad when the seat of their soul becomes invaded by black vapours, and that from time to time, on ceasing the copious smoking and being mitigated the movement of the black juice, they become free from sorrow. [. . . pues así como no hay estercolero que siempre exhale fetidez, sino sólo al ser agitado y removido, con mayor razón – puesto que las causas de la enfermedad se agitan en ciertas épocas, con un cierto orden o de un modo errático – es necesario que los melancólicos se entristezcan al ser invadida la sede del alma por vapores negros, y que de vez en cuando, al cesar la copiosa ahumadura y mitigarse el movimiento del jugo negro, queden libres de la tristeza].' Quoted by Vicente Peset Llorca, 'La psiquiatría de un médico humanista (Francisco Vallés, 1524–1592)', *Archivos de neurobiología*, third part, p. 63.
8   Velásquez, *Libro de la melancolía*, pp. 289 and 291.
9   Ibid., pp. 289–91. Velásquez not only insists that the nerves are 'somewhat hard and solid', but demonstrates by means of an empirical proof that the spirits do not flow like liquids along them: when the functioning of the brain is obstructed, feeling and movement are *immediately* lost, which would not happen if it were fluids that were being transmitted, since these would animate the body for a time, before being consumed.
10 See Stanley W. Jackson, *Melancholia and Depression. From Hippocratic Times to Modern Times* (New Haven: Yale University Press, 1986), pp. 123, 129, 283. Isaac Newton had published in his *Principia* (1713) his ideas on the subject, developed originally in 1675: 'animal bodies move at the command of the will, namely, by the vibrations of this spirit, mutually propagated along the solid filaments of the nerves'; quoted by Jackson, ibid., p. 122.
11 Huarte, *Examen de ingenios*, ch. 7, pp. 367 ff.
12 Ibid., VII, p. 372.
13 Velásquez, *Libro de la melancolía*, p. 318.
14 Ibid., pp. 319–20.
15 Huarte, *Examen de ingenios*, ch. 7, pp. 368–9.
16 An account of the problem within the perspective of the present day may be found in Simone Clapier-Valladon, 'L'homme et le rire', p. 250: 'Laughter – and this is perhaps the major problem – is at the same time emotion and thought. It thus presents, from both the philosophical and psychological point of view the problem of the interactions between affectivity and intelligence and, from the physiological point of view, the problem of the relations between the palaeoencephalon – the phylogenetically most ancient parts of the

brain, which rule the emotions – and the neoencephalon – the brain of intellectual manifestations –.'
17. At p. 98 et seq 'The Golden Age of Melancholy'.
18. Velásquez, *Libro de la melancolía*, p. 318.
19. Huarte was not the only one who expressed this idea, which was apparently widely held. For example, Alfonso de Santa Cruz, physician to Philip II and a professor at Valladolid, was convinced that melancholics could speak Latin without having previously learn it, maintaining this in a book which he wrote in the same period in which Velásquez's left the press (*Dignotio et cura afectuum melancholicorum*, dialogue I, published in 1622 by his son, also a physician).
20. [Cuántos leemos que se han dado desastradas muertes. Unos colgándose, otros despeñándose, y otros abrasándose en fuegos, y así han acabado miserablemente sus vidas; ¿qué cosa hay de tanto espanto, ni tan digna de llorar, como es ver las potencias todas en un hombre afligido de esta enfermedad tan estragadas, arruinadas y perdidas? Que más se puede decir bestia brava que hombre racional, tanta es la fuerza de esta estupenda enfermedad.] Velásquez, *Libro de la melancolía*, p. 354.
21. According to the Galenic tradition the temperaments were four: hot, cold, moist and dry, but here Velásquez refers only to the first two.
22. Dr Francisco Vallés distinguished between lesions in the internal senses and the symptoms of dementia; *fatuitas, amentia* and *oblivio* are classified as 'sensum internorum laesiones qui non sunt insaniæ'; in another section, in the category of 'dementia, aut insania, vel delirium' he places the following illnesses: *phrenitis, lethargus, melancholia, mania* and *paraphrenitis*. See Peset Llorca, 'La psiquiatría de un médico humanista', third part, p. 63.
23. Jackie Pigeaud, 'De la mélancolie et de quelques autres maladies dans les *Etymologies* IV d'Isidore de Seville', in *Textes médicaux latins antiques*, ed. G. Sabbah (Saint-Étienne: Publications de l'Université de Saint-Étienne, 1984), pp. 94–5.
24. *Etimologías*, IV, 7, 9, cited by J. Pigeaud, ibid., pp. 92, 95–8.
25. Velásquez, *Libro de la melancolía*, p. 349.
26. Ibid., p. 345.
27. Ibid., p. 329.
28. [Algunos filósofos naturales quisieron sentir que la incorruptibilidad de los cielos, y aquello diáfano y transparente que tienen, y el gran resplandor de las estrellas, nacía de la suma sequedad que había en su composición. Los viejos, por esta mesma razón, discurren tan bien y duermen tan mal: por la mucha sequedad de su celebro todo lo tienen diáfano y transparente, y los fantasmas y figuras relumbrando como estrellas; y, porque la sequedad endurece la sustancia del celebro, toman tan mal de memoria.] Ibid., p. 307.
29. Huarte, *Examen de ingenios*, VI, p. 358, ch. IX of the 1594 edn.
30. See José Antonio Maravall, *Estado moderno y mentalidad social*, 2 vols (Madrid: Alianza Editorial, 1986).
31. A 'strange loop' is what Douglas R. Hofstadter would call it; see *Gödel, Escher, Bach. An Eternal Golden Braid* (New York: Basic Books, 1979).

32 G. Jahoda, *Psychology and Anthropology. A Psychological Perspective* (London: Academic Press, 1982), p. 182; cited by G. E. R. Lloyd, *Demystifying Mentalities* (Cambridge: Cambridge University Press, 1990), p. 5.
33 Alfonso de Santa Cruz, *Dignotio et cura afectuum melancholicorum* (Madrid: Tomás de Junta, 1622). On the tensions surrounding the Galenic system see Francisco Barrenechea, 'Modelos para romper: Velásquez y la crítica de la autoridad en la medicina del Siglo de Oro'.
34 The text on chronic diseases was published for the first time in 1529 at Basle (printed by Heinrich Petri). The book on acute diseases was printed in Paris in 1533 by Simon de Colines.
35 Cælius Aurelianus, *Tardarum passionum*, I, ch. 6, pp. 180–2, of the Latin text and tr. into English by I. E. Drabkin, *On Acute Diseases and On Chronic Diseases* (Chicago: University of Chicago Press, 1950).
36 Sor Juana Inés de la Cruz, *El sueño*. See a commentary in this respect by Héctor Pérez-Rincón, 'Del leteo al beleño. Un hipnótico mitológico y uno natural en dos fragmentos poéticos del Siglo de Oro'.
37 'un cadáver con alma, / muerto a la vida y a la muerte vivo . . .'
38 'templado hoguera del calor humano, . . .'
39 'de los atemporados cuatro humores, . . .'
40 'y el que hervor resultaba bullicioso / de la unión entre el húmedo y ardiente . . .'
41 'Y del cerebro, ya desocupado, / las fantasmas huyeron, / y – como de vapor leve formadas – / en fácil humo, en viento convertidas, / su forma resolvieron.'
42 Octavio Paz, *Sor Juana Inés de la Cruz o las trampas de la fe* (Mexico City: Fondo de Cultura Económica, 1982), pp. 505–6.
43 Frances A. Yates, *The Occult Philosophy in the Elizabethan Age* (London: Routledge & Kegan Paul, 1979), ch. 6.
44 Jorge Alcázar, 'La figura emblemática de la melancolía en *El sueño* de Sor Juana', *Poligrafías*, 1 (1996). Although there are images of melancholy blackness, Sor Juana also refers to the sanguine humour, when she speaks of 'boiling' in the fusion of the 'moist' and the 'ardent'.
45 Elías Trabulse, 'El hermetismo y Sor Juana Inés de la Cruz', in *El círculo roto* (Mexico City: Lecturas mexicanas, 1984).
46 *Libro de la melancolía, en el qual se trata de la naturaleza desta enfermedad, assi llamada Melancholia, y de sus causas y simptomas. Y si el rustico puede hablar Latin, ò philosophar, estando phrenetico ò maniaco, sin primero lo aver aprendido* ('Book of melancholy, which treats of the nature of this illness called Melancholy, and of its causes and symptoms; and of whether a simple rustic can speak Latin, or philosophize, being frenetic or maniac, without having first learned to do so'). All the references are to the critical edition of the work published in my book *El Siglo de Oro de la melancolía*. The text of this chapter is itself an expanded version of that which appeared in the above-mentioned book.
47 Translated from the Italian version by Richard Carew, this highly successful book went through four English editions between 1594 and 1616 under the title *Examen de Ingenios. The Examination of Mens Wits*. In

1698, Edward Bellamy published a new translation – using Carew's and collating it with the Spanish original – this new or revised translation was entitled *Examen de Ingenios, or the Tryal of Wits*.

48 *Examen de ingenios para las ciencias*, critical edn by Guillermo Serés (Madrid: Cátedra, 1989). See also the well-documented study by Gabriel A. Pérouse, *L'Examen de Esprits du Docteur Juan Huarte de San Juan. Sa diffusion et son influence en France aux XVIe et XVIIe siècles* (Paris: Les Belles Lettres, 1970), and the already outdated essay by Arturo Farinelli, *Dos excéntricos: Cristóbal de Villalón – El Dr. Juan Huarte* (Madrid: Revista de Filología Española, Anejo 24, 1936). The latter study denigrates Dr Velásquez for censuring Huarte's 'elevated concepts' without advising remedies for melancholy, and qualifies him as a 'very partial judge of the *Examen*' (p. 70 and bibliographical notes).

49 A Committee of Preservation from Contagion kept watch over the application of the quarantine to visitors, who had to remain in the unhealthy '*cotarro*', easy victims to the attacks of thieves and in danger of infection from those fleeing from the plague in other nearby towns and villages. See Manuel Pérez Regordán, 'El doctor don Andrés Velázquez y su libro de la melancolía', unpub. typescript (Arcos de la Frontera, 1972), p. 2.

50 The term *converso* referred not only to those recently converted from Islam or Judaism to Christianity, but also to the descendants of original converts, often down through many generations (*translator's note*).

51 [Galeno é Hipocrás / gentiles fueron por cierto, / y con ellos hemos muerto / un millón de hombres y más. / Abiçena moro es, / Isac y Rabí Moisés / judíos son de natura, / mas por ende su scriptura / no es quemada después.] Verses sent by the physician Francisco López de Villalobos to the Admiral of Castile; in *Algunas obras del Doctor Francisco López de Villalobos*, p. 91. The name Isaac refers to the famous philosopher and physician known as Isaac Judaeus (Isḥāq ibn Sulaymān al-Isra'īli, c.855–955). Rabbi Moisés is Moisés ben Maimón or Maimonides. These verses are also quoted, in a different version, by Otis H. Green, *Spain and the Western Tradition*, III, p. 246. López de Villalobos, a Jewish *converso*, was born in 1469; he was physician to King Ferdinand the Catholic, the Emperor Charles V and Philip II. Guillermo Serés thinks it is possible that Villalobos was the doctor sent by Charles V to the king of France when the latter requested of him a Jewish surgeon (see Serés's edition of Huarte's *Examen de ingenios*, p. 505, n. 28). In a letter of 1525 the Admiral of Castile had warned Villalobos, on learning that he was in the vicinity of Cordoba, to beware of the terrible inquisitor Lucero, who had launched a persecution of those believed to be practising Jews in secret; the doctor replied: 'And were Lucero, in Judea, / to sit in judgement on the twelve tribes, / may Lusitania afford us protection / being a province of Galilee' (Y si el Lucero en Judea / las doce tribus juzgare, / Lusitania nos ampare, / provincia de Galilea; in *Cartas castellanas, Algunas obras del Doctor Francisco López de Villalobos*, XXI, p. 75). Dr Villalobos was held prisoner for eighty days accused of being a 'sorcerer expert in philtres and maleficiations' (*mago conocedor de filtros y*

maleficios), 'a charlatan and witch' (*charlatán y hechicero*), who by means of pacts with the demons deceives and takes command of the wills of others; he is accused of being a soothsayer and of being 'master of [the art of] binding and unbinding and making women attend by night against their will' (dueño de ligar y desligar y de hacer que las mujeres acudiesen de noche contra su voluntad) at his summons (letter written in Latin to Don Cosme de Toledo, Bishop of Plasencia, 1510, *Cartas latinas*, ibid., pp. 241–8).

52 Yosef Hayim Yerushalmi, *From Spanish Court to Italian Ghetto. Isaac Cardoso: A Study in Seventeenth-Century Marranism and Jewish Apologetics* (New York: Columbia University Press, 1971), p. 70.

53 Marcel Bataillon, '¿Melancolía renacentista o melancolía judía?', in *Estudios hispánicos. Homenaje a Archer M. Huntington* (Wellesley, MA: Spanish department, Wellesley College, 1952).

54 See Donald W. Bleznick, 'La teoría clásica de los humores en los tratados políticos del Siglo de Oro', *Hispanofila*, 2, 2 (1959). An especially interesting example is the application of the humoural conception to New Spain made by Juan de Cárdenas in his *Problemas y secretos maravillosos de las Indias* (Mexico City: Pedro Ocharte, 1591). It is also worth consulting the treatise by the Catalan physician Hieronymo Merola, *República original sacada del cuerpo humano* (Barcelona: Pedro Malo, 1587), which sets forth the correspondence between the human body and the political republic. An interesting commentary on this work can be found in Augustin Redondo, 'La métaphore du corps de la république à travers le traité du médecin Jerónimo Merola (1587)', *Le corps comme métaphore dans l'Espagne des XVIᵉ et XVIIᵉ siècles*, ed. A. Redondo (Paris: Publications de la Sorbonne Nouvelle, 1992).

55 Andrés Velásquez himself refers to these explanatory notes (*escolios*) to the ninth book of Rhazes. I imagine they must have been written in Latin and were perhaps published in some edition of the famous book of Rhazes (known in Arabic as Abu Bakr Muhammad ibn Zakariya ar-Razi), who was born *c.*865 and died between 923 and 932.

56 See Esteban Torre, *Averroes y la ciencia médica. La doctrina anatomofuncional del «Colliget»* (Madrid: Ediciones del Centro, 1974); Nancy G. Siraisi, *Avicenna in Renaissance Italy. The Canon and Medical Teaching in Italian Universities after 1500* (Princeton: Princeton University Press, 1987); Giuliano Tamani, *Il 'Canon medicinae' di Avicenna nella tradizione ebraica. Le miniature del manoscritto 2197 della Biblioteca Universitaria di Bologna* (Padua: Editoriale Programma, 1988); Elinor Lieber, 'Galen in Hebrew: the transmission of Galen's works in the medieval Islamic world', in Vivian Nutton (ed.), *Galen: Problems and Prospects* (London: Wellcome Institute for the History of Medicine, 1981); Gotthard Strohmaier, 'Galen in Arabic: problems and prospects', in Vivian Nutton (ed.), *Galen: Problems and Prospects* (London: Wellcome Institute for the History of Medicine, 1981).

57 In this chapter an ethnological perspective has been adopted in order to study melancholy as a myth. The so-called 'glass men', who suffered a peculiar form of melancholy, is one of the clearest examples of the

evolution of the myth, as has been brilliantly demonstrated by Gill Speak in her essay 'An odd kind of melancholy: reflections on the glass delusion in Europe (1440–1680)'; the same author has examined a celebrated character from Cervantes's *Examplary Novels* who suffered this peculiar form of melancholia, in '*El licenciado Vidriera* and the glass men of early modern Europe', *Modern Language Review*, 85, 4 (1990). See also Otis H. Green, '*El Licenciado Vidriera*: its relation to the *Viaje del Parnaso* and the *Examen de Ingenios* of Huarte', in *The Literary Mind of Medieval & Renaissance Spain* (Lexington: University Press of Kentucky, 1970).

58 José Antonio Maravall, *Estado moderno y mentalidad social*, I, pp. 123–9.
59 *Moriscos*: the Muslim population remaining in territories won by the Christian kingdoms.
60 Miguel Mancheño y Olivares, *Apuntes para una historia de Arcos de la Frontera* (Arcos: Tipografía El Arcobricense, 1893), pp. 261–2.
61 Ibid., pp. 288–90.
62 Ibid., p. 297.
63 Fernand Braudel, *El Mediterráneo y el mundo mediterráneo en la época de Felipe II*, 2 vols (Mexico City: Fondo de Cultura Económica, 1976), II, part 3, ch. 3, para. 2, p. 559.
64 Baptismal Register of the St Mary's Parish Archive (Archivo Parroquial de Santa María, Libro de Bautismos), 5th (1562–78), fo. 56v. See also José Antonio Delgado y Orellana, 'Tres insólitos arcenses', *Hidalguía*, 31, 178–9 (1983), p. 403; this is one of the few texts that refer to Velásquez. Another mention is found in B. Piga Sánchez-Morate, 'Sobre algunas ideas interesantes acerca de la melancolía morbus en la medicina española del siglo XVI', *Medicina*, 11, 5 (1943), a brief and not particularly interesting article.
65 Delgado y Orellana, 'Tres insólitos arcenses', p. 403.
66 Baptismal Register of the St Mary's Parish Archive (Archivo Parroquial de Santa María, Libro de Bautismos), 5th (1562–78), fo. 54v. These data were obtained by Manuel Pérez Regordán, who kindly provided me with copies of them.
67 Baptismal Register of the St Mary's Parish Archive (Archivo Parroquial de Santa María, Libro de Bautismos), 6th (1578–91), fos 327v, 389v, 436; book 7 (1591–1603), fos 66, 111, 152v, 235, 306, 368.
68 Archives of the Notarial Register: Cadiz Provincial Historical Archive (Archivo de Protocolos Notariales: Archivo Histórico Provincial de Cádiz). Document located and copied by Manuel Pérez Regordán. The reference to 'whiteness of the eyes' (*ojos claros*) indicates that she has healthy sight, being free of cataracts or other defects in the eyes. The autograph signature of the doctor uses the *s* in his surname, while the clerk spells it with a *z*.
69 See Hugh Thomas, *La trata de esclavos. Historia del tráfico de seres humanos de 1440 a 1870* (Barcelona: Planeta, 1998), p. 800. Originally published in English as *The Slave Trade: The History of the Atlantic Slave Trade, 1440–1870* (London: Phoenix, 2006).
70 Ibid., p. 118.
71 '... sus buenas letras e ingenios', *Libro de la melancolía*, p. 267.

72 Ibid., p. 313.
73 Ibid., p. 352. Francisco Vallés, in *De sacra philosophia*, had categorically established: 'Melancholia non fit sine melancholico succo, genito aut in ipso cerebro, si est affectus proprius; aut alibi si est per consensum' (melancholy does not occur without the melancholy juice, whether engendered in the brain itself, if the affection is local, or elsewhere, if it is of the whole body); quoted by J. B. Ullersperger, *La historia de la psicología y de la psiquiatría en España*, p. 85. Vallés's book was expurgated by the Inquisition and republished with corrections in 1613. But in 1618 the Inquisition demanded new corrections, which apparently were never incorporated. In 1900 this book still appeared in the index of forbidden books. Vallés's work displeased the Church on account of its sceptical approach (Otis H. Green, *Spain and the Western Tradition. The Castilian Mind in Literature from El Cid to Calderón*, 4 vols (Madison: University of Wisconsin Press, 1963–8), III, p. 305). See also the informative, though now out-of-date, study by Eusebio Ortega and Benjamín Marcos, *Francisco Vallés (El Divino)* (Madrid: Biblioteca Filosófica, 1914).
74 See Luis García Ballester, *Los moriscos y la medicina. Un capítulo de la medicina y la ciencia marginadas en la España del siglo XVI* (Barcelona: Labor, 1984), pp. 21–2; and Ullersperger, *La historia de la psicología y de la psiquiatría en España*, pp. 63–4.
75 Velásquez, *Libro de la melancolía*, p. 327.
76 An interesting panorama of the historic background to the religious tensions in Spain can be found in Norman Roth, *Jews, Visigoths, and Muslims in Medieval Spain. Cooperation and Conflict* (Leiden: E. J. Brill, 1994).
77 Even today there is a street in Arcos named after the Gomeles, as a vestige of the existence of the district of that name. See Manuel Pérez Regordán, *Historias y leyendas de Arcos*, 3 vols (Arcos de la Frontera: published by the Arcos town council, 1988 and 1994), vol. I, p. 46.
78 Archive of the Inquisition of Cuenca, leg. 245, no. 3270A, cited by Louis Cardaillac, *Moriscos y cristianos. Un enfrentamiento polémico (1542–1640)* (Mexico City: Fondo de Cultura Económica, 1979), pp. 26 and 31.
79 It is interesting, for example, that Jean Bodin (*Les Six livres de la république* (Paris: 1583)), in order to illustrate his theory that the influence of geography and climate had a decisive influence on the character of men, stated that the Mediterranean peoples had a greater tendency towards madness than others; according to Bodin this explained the fact that the city of Granada had so many hospitals devoted exclusively to the care of the mentally ill. Cited by H. C. Erik Midelfort, *A History of Madness in Sixteenth-Century Germany* (Stanford: Stanford University Press, 1999), p. 41, who stresses that the fact was actually related more to the great Arab-Islamic medieval tradition of caring for the mentally ill in special hospitals.
80 See the important book by Teresa Scott Soufas, *Melancholy and the Secular Mind in Spanish Golden Age Literature*. On melancholy in Spain – although in connection with later periods – see: Folke Nordström,

Goya, Saturn, and Melancholy (Estocolmo: Alquist & Wiksell, 1962); and María Bolaños, *Pasajes de la melancolía. Arte y bilis negra a comienzos del siglo XX* (Madrid: Junta de Castilla y León, 1996). A general panorama, although somewhat clumsy, may be found in Guillermo Díaz-Plaja, *Tratado de las melancolías españolas* (Madrid: Sala, 1975).

81 Tirso de Molina, *El melancólico* [1611], in *Obras dramáticas completas*, vol. I (Madrid: Aguilar, 1946).

82 This was the opinion of, for example, Juan Eugenio Hartzenbusch, well-known dramatist and editor of the works of Tirso de Molina in the nineteenth century. Walter Benjamin observed, in his study on the *Trauerspiel*, that 'The prince is the paradigm of the melancholy man' (*The Origin of German Tragic Drama* (London: Verso, 1977), p. 142). A good example of this paradigm may be seen in Segismundo in Calderón de la Barca's *La vida es sueño*.

83 On the medieval precedents of melancholy, especially erotic or love melancholy, as an illness linked to nobility, see Mary F. Wack, 'The *Liber de heros morbo* of Johannes Afflacius and its implications for medieval love conventions', *Speculum*, 62 (1987) and, by the same author, *Lovesickness in the Middle Ages. The Viaticum and Its Commentaries* (Philadelphia: University of Pennsylvania Press, 1990), pp. 60–2.

84 *Leal conselheiro*, ch. 18, 'Da tristeza'; cited by Kimberley S. Roberts and Norman P. Sacks, 'Dom Duarte and Robert Burton: two men of Melancholy', *Journal of the History of Medicine*, 9 (1954), p. 22. See also Yvonne David-Peyre, 'D, Duarte Roi du Portugal: une névrose exemplaire', *Littérature, medecine, societé*, 1 (1979).

85 Moses Maimónides, *On the Causes of Symptoms (Maqālah fībayān ba'ḍ? al-'arāḍ? wa-al-jawāb 'anhā – Ma'amar ha-hakra'ah – De causis accidentium)*, Hebrew text with English trans. ed. J. O. Leibowitz and S. Marcus (Berkeley: University of California Press, 1974), ch. 3, 136r, ll. 5–6.

86 Ibid., ch. 2, 134v, ll. 9–14.

87 Ibid., ch. 3, 147r, ll. 3–7.

88 [Mi vida no ha sido vida sino una muerte prolija; mi vivir no ha sido vivir sino largo morir; mis días no han sido días sino sombras muy pesadas; mis años no han sido años sino unos sueños enojosos; mis placeres no fueron placeres sino unos alegrones que me amargaron y no me tocaron; mi juventud no fue juventud sino un sueño que soñé y un no sé qué que me vi; finalmente, digo que mi prosperidad no fue prosperidad, sino un señuelo de pluma y un tesoro de alquimia.] Antonio de Guevara, *Menosprecio de corte y alabanza de aldea*, edición de Asunción Rallo (Madrid: Cátedra, 1984), XVIII, pp. 262–3. Such melancholic complaints at the injustices of the world may also be seen in one of the books that influenced the configuration of the mental cosmos of Menocchio, the exemplary case studied by Carlo Ginzburg. This is a satirical (*bufonesco*) poem, whose title-page to the Venice edition of 1541 contains the illustration of one of the characters, the jeweller Caravia, sunk in melancholy, in the manner of the angel engraved by Dürer; his sadness is due to his contemplating a world full of injustice; the buffoon of the poem, Zanpolo, tells him: 'You look just

like Melancholy / painted by a great master' (*Il sogno dil Caravia*, cited by Carlo Ginzburg in *El queso y los gusanos* (Mexico City: Oceano/ Muchnik, 1997), p. 63.

89   Miguel Mancheño y Olivares, *Apuntes para una historia de Arcos de la Frontera*, p. 263.
90   Antonio de Guevara, *Menosprecio de corte y alabanza de aldea*, XVIII, p. 263.
91   Manuel Pérez Regordán discovered in the archives of the Monastery of the Incarnation (Convento de la Encarnación) a document referring to the doctor's house, which was situated at what is now number 8 in the street known as Pesas del Reloj; the existing façade is not the original one, but some cellars of the adjoining house – which until a few years ago still conserved the manacles with which the slaves were chained up at night – almost certainly formed part of the doctor's house (personal communication, April 1999).
92   José and Jesús de las Cuevas, *Arcos de la Frontera* (Cádiz: Departamento de Publicaciones de la Diputación Provincial, 1967), p. 70.
93   See the transcription of the claims in Miguel Mancheño y Olivares, *Apuntes para una historia de Arcos de la Frontera*, pp. 264–71.
94   See the entry for 'Dobla' in Sebastián de Covarrubias's *Tesoro de la lengua castellana o española* [1611], ed. F. C. R. Maldonado (Madrid: Castalia, 1995).
95   See the transcription of the document testifying to the agreement (*escritura de concordia*) in Miguel Mancheño y Olivares, *Apuntes para una historia de Arcos de la Frontera*, pp. 272–87.
96   Ibid., pp. 289–90.
97   The University of Osuna was founded in 1549 by the father of the first Duke of Osuna. See Richard L. Kagan, *Students and Society in Early Modern Spain* (Baltimore: Johns Hopkins University Press, 1974), p. 66. The lay nobility also supported the creation of the small College of Santa Catalina at Alcalá and the University of Gandía.
98   He graduated on 7 October 1555, according to the degree book of the University of Osuna. This was found to have gone astray when José Antonio Delgado y Orellana tried to locate it ('Tres insólitos arcenses', p. 403), but it had been consulted on a previous occasion by Francisco Rodríguez Marín, who transcribed the information (with mistakes) in his *Estudios cervantinos* of 1947; the book of records was at some time put up for public sale and the buyer agreed to return it to Osuna. This was the 'First Register of lower and higher degrees that have been conferred at this illustrious University of the Immaculate Conception at Osuna' [Registro primero de grados menores y mayores que se han conferido en esta insigne Universidad de la Puríssima Concepción de Ossuna] (fos 10r and 23v); there it can be seen that the degree of bachelor was obtained by Velásquez on 24 February 1554 (and not in 1553, as Rodríguez Marín says). He was examined by Dr Miguel Ferrer, and by Masters Diego de la Magdalena and Diego de Avellaneda. The degree of *bachiller en artes* was conferred on him, and he is cited as 'Andrés Velázquez, native of Arcos, in the diocese of Seville' (the surname here being written with a z). My having obtained a copy of

this register is due to the kindness of Manuel Pérez Regordán. At the same university, Pedro de Peramato gained his degree in medicine in 1557, it being recorded that he was a native of Ledesma, in the diocese of Salamanca, although the seventeenth-century Spanish literary historian Nicolás Antonio believed him to have been Portuguese. Dr Peramato was personal physician (*médico de cámara*) to the Duke of Medina Sidonia between 1568 and 1583. In the *Libro de la melancolía* (p. 332) Velásquez cites his *De humoribus*, included in the *Opera medicinalia* of Peramato published in Sanlúcar de Barrameda by Fernando Díaz in 1576. The two doctors were almost certainly friends since the period when Peramato held the 'Chair in Aphorisms' (*translator's note:* the word *aforismos* – literally brief summaries of medical science for didactic purposes – seems to have been virtually a synonym for medical knowledge during this period) at the University of Osuna, where he graduated in medicine in 1557. See Francisco Rodríguez Marín, *Estudios cervantinos* (Madrid: Patronato del IV centenario de Cervantes, Ediciones Atlas, 1947), p. 37.

[99] The child was Leonor Núñez de Prado. One of Dr Velásquez's daughters got married in 1613 to a member of this family, Luis Núñez de Prado; likewise, in 1606, another daughter, Elvira, married Francisco Manuel Núñez de Prado y Ponce de León (a descendant of the dukes of Arcos). As may be seen, Dr Velásquez had established excellent relations with the noble families of Arcos. José Antonio Delgado y Orellana, 'Tres insólitos arcenses', p. 403.

[100] This is the opinion of Mauricio de Iriarte, who found among the names enrolled in the matriculation books (*matrículas*) of the University of Alcalá those of Andrés Velásquez, native of Arcos, and Juan de San Juan, de Baeza; we cannot be completely sure that the latter is identical with Juan Huarte de San Juan, author of the *Examen de ingenios*. See Iriarte, *El doctor Huarte de San Juan y su 'Examen de ingenios'. Contribución a la historia de la psicología experimental* (Madrid: Consejo Superior de Investigaciones Científicas, 1948), p. 20.

[101] [hecho aljufaina de viejo a pura saliva] Francisco de Quevedo, *Historia de la vida del Buscón llamdo Don Pablos*, in *Obras completas*, vol. I (Madrid: Aguilar, 1958), V, p. 299.

[102] See Peter Burke, *The Fortunes of the Courtier* (University Park, PA: Pennsylvania State University Press, 1995), p. 29. On the relations between the myth of the wild man and melancholy, see my books *Wild Men in the Looking Glass: The Mythic Origins of European Otherness* (Anne Arbor: Michigan University Press, 1994) and *The Artificial Savage: Modern Myths of the Wild Man* (Anne Arbor: Michigan University Press, 1997).

[103] Wolf Lepenies, *Melancholy and Society* (Cambridge: Harvard University Press, 1992), pp. 35–44. Regarding the Spanish context see J. H. Elliott, 'The Court of the Spanish Habsburgs: a peculiar institution?', in *Spain and Its World, 1500–1700* (New Haven: Yale University Press, 1989).

[104] [La soledad poníame tristeza y la mucha compañía, importunidad. El mucho ejercicio cansábame y la ociosidad dañábame. Si estaba sano

atormentábanme los cuidados, y si estaba enfermo justiciábanme los médicos. Finalmente digo y afirmo que muchas veces me vi en la corte tan aborrido y yo mismo de mí mismo tan desabrido que ni osaba pedir la muerte, ni tomaba gusto en la vida.] Antonio de Guevara, *Menosprecio de corte y alabanza de aldea*, XVIII, p. 267.

[105] [. . . el rey no me daba lo que yo quería y el privado me negaba la puerta], ibid., p. 266.

[106] A. Redondo, 'Du beatus ille horacien au *Mépris de la cour et éloge de la vie rustique* d'Antonio de Guevara' (*L'humanisme dans les lettres espagnoles*, Paris, 1979), cited by Asunción Rallo in her critical edition of *Menosprecio de corte y alabanza de aldea* (Madrid: Cátedra, 1984), p. 81.

[107] *Aviso de privados o despertador de cortesanos*, 1539.

[108] [. . . vimos estar sentada en un rincón una muy rota y desarrapada muger. Ésta era el lloro y tristeza miserable, estaba sentada en el suelo puesto el cobdo sobre sus rodillas, la mano debajo de la barba y mexilla. Vímosla muy pensativa y miserable por gran pieza sin se menear, y como al meneo de nuestros pies miró, alcançé a la ver un rostro amarillo, flaco y desgraçiado: los ojos hundidos y mexillas que hazían más larga la nariz, y de rato en rato daba un sospiro de lo hondo del coraçón, con tanta fuerza y afliçión que parecía ser hecho artificial para sólo atormentar almas con las entristeçer. Es este gemido de tanta efficacia que traspasa y hiere el alma entrando allí, y con tanta fuerça que le trae cada momento a punto de desesperación; y ésta es la primera miseria que atormenta y hiere las almas de los condenados y es tan gran mal que sin otro alguno bastaba vengar la justiçia de Dios.] Cristóbal de Villalón, *El Crótalon de Cristóforo Gnofoso*, p. 342. An interpretation of Dürer's famous engraving can be found in Klibansky, Panofsky and Saxl, *Saturne et la Mélancolie* (Paris: Gallimard, 1989); an alternative interpretation, of Jungian approach, which emphasizes the alchemical symbolism of the engraving, can be found in Maurizio Calvesi, *La Melanconia di Albrecht Dürer* (Turin: Einaudi, 1993). Another curious interpretation suggests that the engraving is in fact a representation of the horoscope of the Emperor Maximilian, and that the winged figure would not be the ascendant, but the *medium caelum*, Virgo, presented as Lucina, goddess of birth-giving; T. D. Barlow, *The Medieval World Picture and Albert Dürer's Melancholia* (Cambridge: The Roxburghe Club, 1950).

[109] Velásquez, *Libro de la melancolía*, p. 369.

[110] Huarte de San Juan, *Examen de ingenios para las ciencias*, IV, p. 310.

[111] Ibid., IV, pp. 306–7. A text by Belleforest, from his *Histoires tragiques*, which has been recognized as one of the sources of Shakespeare's *Hamlet*, mentions the relation between melancholy and diabolic divinatory power: 'Amleth . . . avoit esté endoctriné en celle science, avec laquelle le malin abuse les hommes, et advertissoit ce Prince (comme il peut) des choses ja passes . . . et si ce Prince, pour la vehemence de la melancholie, avoit receu ces impressions, devinant ce qu'autre ne luy avoit jamais declairé . . .' (quoted by Harold Jenkins in his 'Introduction', Arden edn of *Hamlet* (London: Routledge, 1989), p. 95, n. 1). In Shakespeare the same idea appears thus: 'The spirit that

I have seen / May be the devil: and the devil hath power / To assume a pleasing shape; yea, and perhaps / Out of my weakness and my melancholy. / As he is very potent with such spirits— /Abuses me to damn me— (*Hamlet*, II, ii, 635–40). A translation to English of Belleforest's text was published in 1608 as *The Hystorie of Hamblet*.

112 Huarte de San Juan, *Examen de ingenios para las ciencias*, IV, pp. 317–18. This is an explanation similar to those given by other physicians, who accepted the existence of a 'natural magic'.

113 Mauricio de Iriarte strays far from the truth when (in *El doctor Huarte de San Juan y su 'Examen de ingenios'*, p. 278) he exalts Huarte's 'scientific spirit' in trying to explain by biological causes the 'absurd' fact of prophesy of the future, while, on the other hand, despising Velásquez for doubting the fact itself; Velásquez only accepts as a last resort the supernatural intervention of the Devil. I shall return to this subject below, when I examine the linguistic problem of the rustics who spoke Latin. On these subjects, see also Vicente Peset, 'Las maravillosas facultades de los melancólicos (Un tema de psiquiatría renacentista)', *Archivos de neurobiología*, 18, 4 (1955).

114 I use the French version of 1579, reprinted in 1885, cited in the previous note.

115 See Christopher Baxter, 'Jean Bodin's *De la démonomanie des sorciers*: the Logic of Persecution', in Sydney Anglo (ed.), *The Damned Art. Essays in the Literature of Witchcraft* (London: Routledge & Kegan Paul, 1977); Sydney Anglo, 'Melancholia and witchcraft: the debate between Wier, Bodin, and Scot', in *Folie et déraison à la Renaissance*, Colloque International, November 1973 (Bruselas: Éditions de l'Université de Bruxelles, 1976). It is possible that the sudden expansion of demonology responds to the same causes that caused a boom of interest in madness among doctors. Between 1550 and 1650 in Germany 56 per cent (136 of a total of 241) of the academic dissertations in medicine dealt with mental diseases; of these, 64 per cent were devoted to subjects linked to disorders caused by the black humour, whether melancholy or hypochondria (H. C. Erik Midelfort, *A History of Madness in Sixteenth-Century Germany*, p. 158, which tabulates data provided by Oskar Diethelm, *Medical Dissertations of Psychiatric Interest Printed Before 1750* (Basilea, 1971‡).

116 Jean Bodin, *De la démonologie des sorciers* (Paris, 1580), fo. 226, cited (in the original French) by Anglo, 'Melancholia and witchcraft', p. 215. On this point Bodin showed his ignorance of the classical medical canons and even contradicts the *Malleus maleficarum*, which warns: 'It should also be noted that women are not always molested by an incubus, [often] they merely believe they are. If this type of case is more common among women than among men, this is due to the fact that women are more fragile and feel more inclined to imagine extraordinary things. This is the reason why the so often cited William [of Paris] says: many fantastical apparitions arise from the melancholy illness in many people, and especially among women, as may be seen in their dreams and visions' (tr. from the Spanish version: *El martillo de las brujas [Malleus maleficarum]*, II, bk. 1, p. 356). In the controversy

regarding the satanic possession of the Ursuline nuns of Loudon, in 1635 Hippolite Pilet de la Ménardière repeated Bodin's thesis in his *Traité de la mélancholie. Savoir si elle est la cause des Effets que l'on remarque dans les Possédées de Loudun* (La Flèche, no pub. 1635), maintaining that the nuns really were possessed by the Devil and that women have no predisposition towards melancholy.

117 Anglo, 'Melancholia and witchcraft', p. 215.
118 Jean Wier, *Histoires, disputes et discours des illusions et impostures des diables, des magiciens infâmes, sorcières et empoisonneurs: des ensorcelez et demoniaques et de la guérison d'iceux: item de la punition que méritent les magiciens, les empoisonneurs et les sorcières*, 2 vols (Paris: A. Delahaye et Lecrosnier, 1885), I, bk. 3, ch. 17, pp. 377–81.
119 Christopher Baxter, 'Johann Weyer's *De praestigiis daemonum*: unsystematic psychopathology', in Sydney Anglo (ed.), *The Damned Art. Essays in the Literature of Witchcraft* (London: Routledge & Kegan Paul, 1977), p. 61. The debate on the relation between demonology and melancholy also permeated the famous case of the Ursuline nuns of Loudun, in 1635. A Huguenot doctor (the Scotsman Marc Duncan, who was living in Saumur) wrote that the Ursulines were victims of melancholia, and therefore, were liable to simulation (*Discours de la possession des religieuses ursulines de Lodun*, 1634); an orthodox priest, H.-J. Pilet de la Ménardière, of the Faculty of Medicine at Nantes, refuted this immediately (*Traité de la mélancholie. Savoir si elle est la cause des Effets que l'on remarque dans les Possédées de Loudun*). Ménardière also stated that melancholy stimulated prediction through visions of the future. Duncan in turn replied in another book, entitled *Apologie pour Monsieur Duncan*. See Mario Galzigna, 'L'enigma della malinconia. Materiali per una storia', *Aut aut*, 195–6 (1983), p. 91. Michel Foucault, in his *Histoire de la folie à l'âge classique* (Paris: Gallimard, 1972), p. 282, refers to this polemic, but without mentioning its relation with satanic possession. As a curious piece of information, we might add that Father Jean-Joseph Surin – the severe exorcist of the Mother Superior, known as Sister Jeanne 'of the Angels' (Soeur Jeanne dite Des Anges), and the Ursuline nuns possessed by the Devil – was driven by his own mystical excesses to a kind of melancholic desperation which he himself, in an autobiographical text, compared with the dark night of the soul of St John of the Cross (*Lettres spirituelles* (Toulouse: Cavallera, 1928), pp. 10 f.). Surin refers directly to the polemic in his *Guide Spirituel por la perfection* (VII, ch. 7, pp. 307 ff.), where he devotes a chapter to 'the Hell of the Soul'. He mentions Sister Jeanne 'of the Angels', who attempted, prompted by her anxiety, to cut open her body with knife (she imagined she was pregnant); but the knife was torn from her hand by an invisible force and deposited in the hand of an image of the crucified Christ, which stood before her. He also mentions the case of a Dominican monk, and goes on to mention those who have tried to explain the mystical condition in terms of melancholy, and states that this was all that could be expected of those who take doctors as judges of the extraordinary things that take place in the soul. Immediately afterwards, Surin wonders whether

the sufferings he describes are due to melancholy; he states that there are three types of sufferings (*penas*): (1) those caused by the corporal temperament, melancholy or accidents that perturb the spirit; {2) those produced by Grace in order to test souls (this is when Divine Providence hands over the reins to the Devil, as is recounted in the Book of Job; {3) those of a mixed origin, both natural and providential. Surin's anxieties are reflected dramatically above all in his correspondence of the first years; see *Correspondance*, letters 1–17 (1626–30). See also Michel de Certeau, *La Possession de Loudun* (Paris: Julliard, 1970).

[120] Anglo, 'Melancholia and witchcraft'. A different interpretation of Wier has been proposed by H. C. Erik Midelfort, for whom the author of *De praestigiis daemonum* established that witches hallucinated or dreamed their pacts with the Devil due to the fact that, paradoxically, the malign spirit was much more powerful than what was commonly believed (*A History of Madness in Sixteenth-Century Germany*, pp. 196 ff.). In any case, the severest and most orthodox theologians saw Wier as an advocate of witches ('*sagarum patronus*'), according to the expression of the Jesuit Martín del Río, a descendant of Spanish *conversos*, native of Antwerp, who published in Louvain in 1599 his *Disquisitionum magicarum*. The disdainful reference to Wier occurs in ch. 4 of bk. II, translated into Spanish as *La magia demoníaca* by Jesús Moya; Martín del Río does not even mention Wier by name and refers to his *argumentillos* ('insignificant little arguments'), saying that he prefers to 'despise them and ignore them than to refute them, above all on account of the fact that others have already done so with more care than difficulty' [despreciarlos y pasarlos por alto, mejor que rebatirlos, sobre todo teniendo en cuenta que ya otros lo han hecho con más cuidado que dificultad] (p. 187).

[121] *Histoires, disputes et discours des illusions et impostures des diables, des magiciens infâmes, sorcières et empoisonneurs*, I, bk 3, ch. 6, p. 300.

[122] Ibid., I, bk 4, ch. 25, p. 603.

[123] Ibid., I, bk 4, ch. 26, pp. 603–4. He clarifies that this was, rather, a case of mania; he cites as melancholic an old woman who, after rubbing her body with ointments, dreamed she was travelling over the sea and the mountains, without actually leaving her room (I, bk 3, ch. 17, p. 378). Buderic is almost certainly a locality on the banks of the Rhine; there are two places called Büderich, one near Düsseldorf and another further north.

[124] 'It is beyond doubt that the demons, being subtle and elusive spirits, insinuate themselves into human bodies and, hidden in the bowels, ruin the health secretly, causing diseases, producing terrifying dreams, agitating souls and shaking minds with furies, so that we may wonder whether it is such fury that agitates the insane or that they are being moved in that way by a spirit.' Jason Pratz, *De cerebri morbis* (Basilea, 1549), ch. 17, pp. 213–14, adapted from versions given by Jean Céard ('The Devil and lovesickness: views of 16th century physicians and demonologists', p. 39) and by H. C. Erik Midelfort (*A History of Madness in Sixteenth-Century Germany*, p. 153).

125 The Devil 'is not born secretly in the body itself; he penetrates it from without in order to bring it sickness; and in this way he brings sicknesses that depend on materials in a way that is no different to that in which procathartic causes do, for example by exciting within us the melancholy illness, increasing the melancholy fluid, corrupting that which is already there, transporting black vapours to the brain and to the sites of the internal senses. He may increase the natural melancholy by preventing it from being evacuated or by exciting diverse causes of adustion ... and by accumulating heavy fluids in the ventricles of the brain and at the very roots of the nerves' [no nace secretamente en el cuerpo mismo, lo penetra desde afuera para traerle enfermedad; por lo tanto trae enfermedades que dependen de materias en una forma que no es diferente a como lo hacen causas procatárticas, por ejemplo excitando dentro de nosotros la enfermedad melancólica, al aumentar el fluido melancólico, al corromper el que ya estaba allí, al transportar vapores negros al cerebro y a los lugares de los sentidos internos. Puede aumentar la melancolía natural al evitar que sea evacuada o al excitar diversas causas de la adustión ... y al acumular fluidos espesos en los ventrículos del cerebro y en la raíz misma de los nervios]. De iis quae scripta sunt physice in libris sacris, sive sacra philosophia (Lyon: F. Le Fevre, 1587), pp. 226–7, cited by Jean Céard, 'The Devil and lovesickness: views of 16th century physicians and demonologists', in Donald A. Beecher and Massimo Civolella (eds), *Eros and Anteros: The Medical Traditions of Love in the Renaissance* (Toronto: University of Toronto Italian Studies 9, Dovehouse Editions, 1992), p. 39. François Azouvi describes the connections that link the plague, melancholy and the Devil: blackness, adustion and putrefaction ('The Plague, Melancholy and the Devil', *Diogenes*, 108 (1979)).

126 *Diálogos de filosoofía natural y moral* (Granada: Hugo de Mena and René Rabilio, 1558). Pedro de Mercado published another book on fevers, in which, mainly, he sets forth the Greek and Arab doctrines on the subject: *De febrium differentiis carumque causis, signis, medela tam in universali quam in particulari ex antiquorum et iuniorum tum graecorum tum arabum authoritate* (Granada, in quarto, lacking name of printer or year of publication [licence date: 1581]). See Luis S. Granjel, 'Los «Diálogos» de Pedro Mercado', in *Médicos españoles* (Salamanca: Universidad de Salamanca, 1967).

127 [una mudanza de la imaginación de su curso natural a temor y tristeza, hecha por la tiniebla y obscuridad de los espíritus claros del cerebro] *Diálogos de filosofía natural y moral*, p. 375. All references are to the edition of the sixth dialogue which appears in Roger Bartra, *El Siglo de Oro de la melancolía*.

128 *Duende*: a supernatural being something like a pixie or a poltergeist; here clearly in the sense of an invisible and intangible agent (*translator's note*).

129 [... el 'aprovechamiento del tiempo (teniéndolos suspensos, en vanas imaginaciones y tristes), como en persuadirles el aborrecimiento de sí

mismos, amonestándoles mil géneros de desesperaciones, proponiéndoles medios para ejecutarlas, sin dejarlos un solo momento'] Ibid., pp. 376–7.

[130] [muchas malas cosas pueden imaginar los hombres de sí mismos, sin que a ellas concurra el demonio] Ibid., p. 384.

[131] Ibid., pp. 389–90.

[132] [tomara yo ahora más aína un cuartal de pan o una hogaza y dos cabezas de sardinas arenques, que cuantas yerbas describe Dioscórides, aunque fuera el ilustrado por el doctor Laguna] Miguel de Cervantes, *Don Quijote de la Mancha*, ed. Francisco Rico (Barcelona: Instituto Cervantes/Crítica, 1998), I, ch. 18, p. 197. The English version is from the 1612 translation by Thomas Shelton (*www.bartleby.com*). Regarding this fascinating doctor, see Marcel Bataillon, 'Andrés Laguna, Autor del *Viaje a Turquía* a la luz de las recientes investigaciones', *Estudios segovianos*, 15 (1963). See also the book by Joaquín Olmedilla y Puig, *Estudio histórico de la vida y escritos del sabio español Andrés Laguna, médico de Carlos I y Felipe II y célebre escritor y botánico del siglo XVI* (Madrid: El Correo, 1887).

[133] Andrés Laguna, *Pedacio Dioscórides Anazarbeo acerca de la materia medicinal y los venenos mortíferos, traducido de la lengua Griega en la vulgar castellana, & ilustrado con claras y sustantiales Annotaciones y con las figuras de innúmeras plantas, exquisitas y raras* (Antwerp: Iuan Latio, 1555). Volume in folio of 616 pages with woodcuts intercalated in the text.

[134] Ibid., p. 421. The *hierba mora*, or black nightshade (*Solanum nigra*), was used as a tranquillizer; taken in excess, it produces convulsions and death.

[135] [hice untar de pies a cabeza a la mujer del verdugo, que de celos de su marido había totalmente perdido el sueño y vuéltose cuasi medio frenética, y esto así por ser el tal sujeto muy apto, en quien se podían hacer semejantes pruebas, como por haber probado otros infinitos remedios en balde y parecerme que aquel era mucho a propósito y no podía dejar de aprovechar, según de su olor y color se colegía. La cual, súbito en siendo untada, con los ojos abiertos como conejo, pareciendo también ella una liebre cocida, se adurmió de un tan profundo sueño, que jamás pensé despertarla. Por donde, con fuertes ligaduras y fricciones de las extremidades, con perfusiones de aceite costino y de euforbio, con sahumerios y humo a narices y, finalmente, con ventosas, la di tal prisa que al cabo de treinta y seis horas la restituí a su juicio y acuerdo, aunque la primera palabra que habló fue: '¿Por qué en mal punto me despertastes, que estaba rodeada de todos los placeres y deleites del mundo?' Y vueltos a su marido los ojos, díjole sonriéndose: 'Tacaño, hágote saber que te he puesto el cuerno, y con un galán más mozo y más estirado que tú.' Y diciendo otras cosas muchas y muy extrañas, se deshacía porque de allí nos fuésemos y la dejásemos volver a su dulce sueño, del cual poco a poco la divertimos, aunque siempre le quedaron ciertas opiniones vanas en la cabeza.] Ibid., fo. 422.

[136] Christine Orobitg offers a broad description of the explanations given by Spanish doctors of the sixteenth and seventeenth centuries of cases

of possession by malign and diabolic spirits ('Between evil and malady: cures of melancholy in Spanish Golden Age').

[137] See an excellent description of this subject in Stuart Clark, 'The scientific status of demonology', in Charlotte F. Otten, *A Lycanthropy Reader. Werewolves in Western Culture* (Syracuse, NY: Syracuse University Press, 1986).

[138] As Harry Friedenwald has observed in 'Andres a Laguna, a pioneer in his views on witchcraft', in *The Jews and Medicine, Essays*, 2 vols (Baltimore: Johns Hopkins Press, 1944).

[139] [. . . podemos conjeturar que todo cuanto dicen las desventuradas brujas es sueño, causado de brebajes y unciones frías, las cuales de tal suerte las corrompen la memoria y la fantasía, que se imaginan las cuitadas y aun firmísimamente creen haber hecho despiertas todo cuanto soñaron durmiendo.

Allégase a todo lo suso dicho un no liviano argumento, y es que ansí aquella, como todas las que en tan infames ejercicios fueron hasta aquí convencidas, a una voz confesaron (según consta por sus procesos) que habían conocido muchas veces carnalmente al Demonio; y preguntadas en particular si habían sentido notable deleite en su acceso, respondieron constantemente que no, y esto a causa de la incorportable [*sic*] frialdad que sentían en las partes diabólicas: de las cuales también, a su parecer, se les revertía un humor frío como el hielo, y a manera de granizo, por las entrañas. Los cuales accidentes no pueden proceder d'otra causa sino de la excesiva frialdad del ungüento, que las traspasa todas, y se les mete en los tuétanos. Ansí que las tales, dado caso que sean escandalosas y merezcan un castigo ejemplar por hacer pactos con el demonio, todavía la mayor parte de cuanto dicen es devaneo; pues ni con el espíritu, ni con el cuerpo, jamás se apartan del lugar donde caen agravadas del sueño, y esta es la opinión de la mayor parte de los Teólogos, aprobada también por decretos de algunos Santos Concilios, conviene a saber: que el demonio no puede obrar sino por medio de naturales causas, aplicando activa passivis; y que así, por su demasiado saber y agudeza, conociendo la virtud de semejantes ungüentos, se los enseña a las vanas brujas, para hacerlas soñar y creer infinitas burlas y vanidades.] Andrés Laguna, *Pedacio Dioscórides Anazarbeo acerca de la materia medicinal y los venenos mortíferos, traducido de la lengua Griega en la vulgar castellana, & ilustrado con claras y sustantiales Annotaciones y con las figuras de innúmeras plantas, exquisitas y raras* (Amberes: Iuan Latio, 1555), fo. 422.

[140] . . . algunos Varones Píos tienen por resoluto que el Demonio las puede transformar en cien mil fantasmas y llevarlas en cuerpo y en ánima por el aire . . .

[141] [algunos autores dicen que el Demonio se alegra con el humor melancólico (pero que) aunque el Demonio pueda causar enfermedades innumerables, puede el Médico, como instrumento de la Divina Justicia, o cualquier otro varón de vida inculpable, pie & devotè, ahuyentar al Demonio.] Thomás Murillo, *Aprobación de ingenios y curación de hipocondríacos, con observaciones y remedios muy particulares*, fos 31r and 33v.

142 *Si los melancólicos pueden saber lo que está por venir, o adivinar el suceso bueno o malo de lo futuro, con la fuerza de su ingenio, o soñando.* This is a text with its own page numbering, but appended to Freylas's book *Conocimiento, curación, y preservación de la peste* (Jaén: Fernando Díaz de Montoya, 1606). Alonso de Freylas was a native of Jaén and was physician to Cardinal Bernardo de Rojas y Sandoval, Archbishop of Toledo.

143 ['melancolía negra causada por adustión y encendimiento de cólera' [which] 'causa grandísimas enfermedades, como son locuras, melancolías extrañas, depravadas imaginaciones, y varios furores y pensamientos maníacos.'] Ibid., fo. 1v.

144 Ibid., fo. 2.

145 [... sin culpa suya, ni pacto hecho con el demonio, son engañados, y aprovechándose el demonio del humor melancólico moviéndose en el cuerpo, y representando con él en la imaginación algunas cosas debajo de especie de bien, con resplandores que parecen celestiales: para dar a entender que es revelación del Cielo.] Ibid., fos 3 and 4r.

146 [pienso que con la fuerza del humor melancólico, ayudado de conjeturas o de causa interior natural que nos mueva ... se podría en alguna manera decir algo de lo que está por venir ... Y el humor melancólico, aunque dispone, no es causa sino porque los que tienen abundancia de él tienen profunda imaginación y el cerebro caliente; y con este calor suelen discurrir mucho y hablar mucho, y de aquí les viene acertar en algo.] Ibid., fos 5v and 6r.

147 Ibid., fo. 5v.

148 This is the idea developed by Leland L. Estes in 'The medical origins of the European witch craze: a hypothesis.' It is symptomatic that such a critical and heterodox thinker as Tomasso Campanella, author of the famous utopia *The City of the Sun* (*Città del sole*), written while he was a prisoner of the Spanish Inquisition, should have accepted the relation between melancholy and the Devil. Campanella wrote a treatise on magic and the meaning of things (*De sensu rerum ac magia*), which contains a chapter devoted to explaining the causes of the wisdom and the ability to predict the future that melancholics were supposed to possess. There is a melancholy that invites the Devil, says Campanella; the black humour, which is mixed with the blood, is a fuliginous humour which causes lycanthropy and irrational fears, bedevils men who 'delight in fetid and filthy places, with tombs and corpses'; the Devil avails himself of dark vapours, Campanella believes. He rejects the 'impious opinions' that hold 'that it is not the demons but merely the melancholy humour which produces these disorders in the infected spirit'. When the doctor purges the melancholic, 'the humour going, the Devil who availed himself of it departs too' (Tomasso Campanella, *Del senso delle cose e della magia*, bk III, ch. 10, 'Della sagacità de' malinconici puri e impuri e demonoplassia e consentimento dell'aria', pp. 193–4.

149 [más no perdieron sus habilidades de buenos ingenios, ni las ciencias que ellos alcanzan por su natural ingenio ... Y ansí tienen ciencia de toda la orden del mundo Corporal, y de todo el curso de la natura ... Saben la astrología, filosofía y medicina mejor y más perfectamente

que todos los filósofos y sabios del mundo que son y fueron en los hombres.] I use the Barcelona edition published in 1628: Pedro Ciruelo, *Tratado en el qual se repruevan todas las supersticiones y hechizerías*, II, ch. 8, p. 66. What gave impulse to demonology was not 'wild', archaic and shamanic thinking, as Christine Orobitg maintains ('Between evil and malady: cures of melancholy in Spanish Golden Age', p. 200); paradoxically, it was scientific thought with its explanations based on humoral theory which guided the Inquisition in support of witch-hunting.

150 Reginald Scot, 'A discourse upon divels and spirits', appendix to *The Discoverie of Witchcraft* ([London: William Brome, 1584] facs. edn Da Capo Press, Amsterdam, 1971), ch. 32, p. 540.

151 As Stuart Clark explains in 'The scientific status of demonology', on the basis of his interpretation of the appendix that Scot added to his *Discoverie of Witchcraft.*

152 Anglo, 'Melancholia and witchcraft'.

153 Miguel Mancheño y Olivares, *Apuntes para una historia de Arcos de la Frontera*, p. 317.

154 Ibid., p. 317.

155 Ibid., p. 305. That year (1587), in Arcos, a pound of pork cost 32 *maravedís*, and beef or mutton 24 *maravedís*.

156 Ibid., p. 319.

157 Giorgio Agamben, *Stanze, La parola e il fantasma nella cultura occidentale* (Turin: Einaudi, 1977), first part, ch. IV. On acedia see also the following: Siegfried Wenzel, *The Sin of Sloth: Acedia in Medieval Thought and Literature* (Chapel Hill: University of North Carolina Press, 1967), and Reinhard Kuhn, *The Demon of Noontide. Ennui in Western Literature* (Princeton: Princeton University Press, 1976).

158 Bert Kaplan states that the indifference proper to acedia is the most acute crisis in people's lives ('Acedia: the decline of desire as the ultimate life crisis').

159 [ser melencolía no lleva camino nenguno; porque la melencolía no hace y fabrica sus antojos sino en la imaginación; estotro procede de lo interior del alma]. *Moradas del castillo interior* VI, bk 2, ch. 7, p. 530. All references to texts by St Teresa are to the Spanish edition of the Complete Works (*Obras completas*)

160 [*puede ser antojo, en especial en personas de flaca imaginación u melancólicos, digo de melancolía notable*] Ibid., VI, bk 3, ch. 1, p. 531.

161 Ibid., VI, bk 6, ch. 12, p. 547.

162 *Libro de la vida*, 4 and 5.

163 Ibid., bk 8, ch. 12, p. 63.

164 *Moradas del castillo interior* IV, bk 1, ch. 8, p. 497.

165 Ibid., IV, bk 1, ch. 9, p. 497.

166 Ibid., IV, bk 1, ch. 10, p. 498.

167 Regarding Teresa of Avila's afflictions, see Francisco Marco Merenciano's 'Psicoanálisis y melancolía en Santa Teresa', which presents the great mystic as a psychoanalyst *avant-la-lettre*. Octavio Paz described another nun of the Baroque period, Sor Juana Inés de la Cruz, as a 'genuine melancholic' and found in her poem *Primero sueño*

an unsettling reminiscence of Dürer's engraving *Melencolia I* (*Sor Juana Inés de la Cruz o las trampas de la fe*, pp. 286 and 505).
168 *Libro de las fundaciones*, 7, ch. 4, p. 701.
169 Ibid., 7, ch. 7, p. 702. See Juan José López Ibor's theologizing psychiatry in 'Ideas de Santa Teresa sobre la melancolía'; this writer sets out to explain the contradiction in Teresa, who – despite having herself suffered melancholy (like her brother too) – shows such severity towards the distempered nuns. Her own melancholy is portrayed as a tragic but praiseworthy acceptance of the human condition, sunk in terrible corruption since the Fall, while the black humour of the nuns is seen as a free fruiting of the consequences of sin and as a complacent enjoyment of illicit and repugnant passions and imaginings.
170 Quoted by Melquiades Andrés, *Historia de la mística de la Edad de Oro en España y América* (Madrid: Biblioteca de Autores Cristianos, 1994), p. 108. Others who concerned themselves with melancholy were Jerónimo de Segorbe (*Navegación segura para el cielo*, Valencia, 1611), María de San José, disciple of St Teresa, and Alonso de Ledesma, who wrote: 'With her falling sickness dire / there stands Lady melancholy / dealing ceaseless blows against the soul, / for even the soul falls victim to this ill [*Con su mal de corazón / está la melancolía, / dando mil golpes al alma, / que es mal que hasta el alma tira*]' (*Conceptos espirituales y morales*, Madrid, 1600); these references are from the above-mentioned book by Melquiades Andrés, p. 108, n. 41.
171 *Moradas del castillo interior* III, bk 1, ch. 5, p. 489. Long before Teresa de Jesús, another great mystic, Hildegard von Bingen (1098–1179), known as the 'Sibyl of the Rhine', had been concerned with the way in which the humours influenced women. With considerable originality, and concerned mainly with sexual behaviour, she describes melancholy women as follows: 'Their thoughts are inconstant and wander freely, and they are painfully consumed by distress; they have little resistance and at times melancholy wears them out. They suffer much loss of blood in their menstruation, and are sterile due to their having a weak and fragile womb; they are thus unable to lodge or retain the seed of the man, and for this reason are healthier, stronger and happier without a husband than married, above all, since when they lie with their husbands, they tend afterwards to feel weak. But men stay apart from them and shun them, because they do not talk affectionately to men and love them little. If for the space of an hour they experience sexual pleasure, this fades very quickly. Nevertheless, some of these women, if they marry robust and sanguine husbands, may occasionally, arriving at a suitable age, such as around fifty years, bear at least one child . . . If they do not receive help in their illness, freeing themselves of it with God's help or thanks to medicine, they die rapidly.' It is possible that, as a result of fleeing from men, many female melancholics ended up in convents and were recognized there for their afflictions. Hildegard's text comes from *Causae et curae*, quoted by Peter Dronke in *Women Writers of the Middle Ages. A Critical Study of Texts from Perpetua (†203) to Marguerite Porete (†1310)* (Cambridge: Cambridge University Press, 1984), pp. 180–1. A Spanish version of

Causae et curae is available in *El arte de sanar de santa Hildegarda* ed. Manfred Pawlik (Gerona: Tikal, n.d. *c*.1997)) (the text cited on p. 112).

172 [un 'camino de oscura contemplación y sequedad' en que el alma se cree perdida ante tantos trabajos, aprietos y tentaciones, sobre todo cuando le dicen 'que es melencolía, o desconsuelo, o condición, o que podrá ser alguna malicia oculta suya'.] *Subida al Monte Carmelo*, Prologue, ch. 4, p. 90. All references to texts by St John of the Cross are to the Complete Works in Spanish (*Obras completas*).

173 [por 'conocer si es melencolía o otra imperfección acerca del sentido o del espíritu'] Ibid., ch. 6, p. 90.

174 [¡Oh noche que guiaste, / oh noche amable más que la alborada; / oh noche que juntaste / Amado con amada, / amada en el Amado transformada!] Ibid., *Canción*, p. 5.

175 Ibid. II, bk 13, ch. 6, pp. 161–2. Modern psychiatric and psychological studies generally reject the distinction St John makes between melancholy and the contemplative or illuminated state. See: M. Laignel-Lavastine, 'Concomitance des états pathologiques et les «trois signes»', *Illuminations et sécheresses*, ed. Bruno de Jésus-Marie (Paris: Desclée de Brouwer, 1937); Denis Turner, 'St John of the Cross and depression', *The Downside Review*, 106 (1988); Mary Meadow, 'The dark side of mysticism: depression and the "dark night"', *Psychology and Christianity*, 5 (1991).

176 *Noche oscura del alma*, ch. 1, pp. 8–9.

177 Javier Álvarez, *Mística y depresión: san Juan de la Cruz*. He compares the poet's metaphors with the modern clinical description of depression, especially that formulated by Hubertus Tellenbach, and not with that of Renaissance medicine (i.e. as regards melancholy). For this reason he fails to notice that John of the Cross is also inspired by the processes of healing (in his evident and constant references to purgations).

178 *Noche oscura del alma*, bk 2, ch. 10, p. 2.

179 In another text (*Llama de amor viva*, 2, pp. 2–14) St John also clearly uses medical metaphors; he compares the Holy Spirit to the cauterization that produces a scar: it is a cauterization by love, such that, the more it hurts, the more it cures; the more it burns, the more it delights.

180 [Si yo tuviera poder sobre esa persona (i.e. Lucrecia de León) la exorcizara como a energúmeno sin que ella entendiera lo que era, y pudiera ser que con eso pasara los sueños en que ella, a lo que parece, anda inocente] Letter from Fray Luis de León to Don Alonso de Mendoza, 12 February 1588, published by Juan Blázquez Miguel in *Sueños y procesos de Lucrecia de León* (Madrid: Tecnos, 1987), pp. 132–3. Apparently there is an error in Blázquez's transcription, where Fray Luis would seem to affirm that the case was one of melancholy or illusion. I prefer the transcription by Richard L. Kagan in *Lucrecia's Dreams. Politics and Prophecy in Sixteenth-Century Spain* (Berkeley: University of California Press, 1990), p. 121 (Archivo Histórico Nacional de Madrid, Sección de Inquisición, 3712/2/6, no. 50).

181 On rejecting the medicines given him by the doctor, he poured scorn

upon him, saying to his face that 'if he thinks that he [in reference to Alonso de Mendoza] is a melancholic on account of the time that he has been a prisoner, he is wrong, baring to [the doctor] his legs entirely as far as the waist to show him how thick-set he is' [que si piensa que está melancólico por el tiempo que ha que está preso, que se engaña, descubriéndole todas las piernas hasta la cintura para mostrar cuán grueso está] (Report of the Inquisition on the madness of Don Alonso de Mendoza, A.H.N. Inq. leg. 3079/55 del 12 de septiembre de 1593, quoted by Juan Blázques Miguel, *Sueños y procesos de Lucrecia de León*, p. 186).

[182] [cuando las tinieblas espesas y la soledad que nace del silencio de todo, causan horror en el ánimo, y cuando todo lo que se ve o se imagina ver, como no se devisa, hace asombramiento que espeluzna el cabello; y cuando el humor melancólico, que escalentado con el sueño y esforzado con el alejamiento del sol, se mueve en el cuerpo, y con los humos que envía, apretando el corazón y ennegreciendo la imaginación y sentido, cría sueños pesados y horribles.] *Exposición del Libro de Job*, in *Obras completas castellanas* (Madrid: Biblioteca de Autores cristianos, 1944), 4: 13.

[183] [porque las enfermedades de humor melancólico, cual éste era, toman fuerza con las tinieblas, que son la hora propia cuando la melancolía hierve y humea; de manera que, si se vela, arde en negras llamas el lecho, y, si se duerme ... el humor negro, movido con el sueño, turba en la imaginación las especies y tíñelas de su mala color, de que resultan espantables figuras que atemorizan y espantan el ánimo del que duerme.] Ibid., 7: 13–14.

[184] Américo Castro, 'La mística y humana feminidad de Teresa la Santa', p. 35.

[185] Ibid., 6: 4.

[186] Ibid., 6: 4. The references come from Galen, *De anima mor.*, p. 3, and from Aëtius, *Tetrabiblos*, I, ch. 6, p. 9.

[187] [por una parte, ennegrece la luz, y ansí borra todo lo que es alegría, y por la misma razón representa la vida como cosa escura y tristísima; y, por otra parte, los temores de las visiones que el mismo humor acarrea, hácenla odiosa y aborrecible. Y ansí por natural consecuencia los tocados de esta calamidad apetecen el salir de la vida luego, y por cualquier manera que sea; y es señal del deseo lo que acontece en el hecho en muchos de estos que lo ponen por obra, y se despeñan o ahogan.] Ibid., 7: 15. See a modern medical diagnosis of Job's depression in Jack Kahn, *Job's Illness: Loss, Grief and Integration. A Psychological Interpretation* (Oxford: Pergamon Press, 1975).

[188] [una caja de unos polvos que ella solía hacer y enviarme para mis melancolías y pasiones del corazón que ella sola los sabe hacer y nunca tuve de ellos más necesidad que ahora] Letter of 13 March 1572 to the Inquisitorial Tribunal, cited by Luciano Rubio, 'El temperamento «melancólico» de fray Luis de León y sus actuaciones prácticas', in S. Álvarez Turienzo (ed.), *Fray Luis de León. El frayle, el humanista, el teólogo* (Real Monasterio de El Escorial: Ediciones Escurialenses, 1992), p. 636.

[189] Jacob Böhme, *Aurora (Morgenröthe im Aufgang)*, in *Sämtliche Schriften*, vol. I, ed. W. E. Peuckert (Stuttgart: F. Romann, 1955–61), I, ch. 19, pp. 5–9; the second of the two quotations is from the translation by John Sparrow, *The Aurora* (London: John M. Watkins, 1914). On the German mystic's melancholy, see the curious book by Isidoro Reguera, *Objetos de melancolía (Jacob Böhme)* (Madrid: Ediciones Libertarias, 1985); and Bernard Gorceix, 'La mélancolie aux XVIe et XVIIe siècles. Paracelse et Jacob Böhme', *Recherches germaniques*, 9 (1979). Melancholy was an important subject for Paracelsus, despite his critical outlook on Galenism.

[190] In a letter to Caspar Lindner of 1621, Böhme enumerates his works and mentions in the seventh place a text called *For the Melancholy*. This book is better known under the misleading title *Von den vier Complexionen (De quattuor complexionibus)*. Written in 1621, this work contains a chapter devoted to each of the four complexions (choleric, sanguine, phlegmatic and melancholic); but the long chapter 5, which is devoted wholly to the black humour, takes up three-quarters of the book, barely two or three pages remaining for each of the other humours.

[191] I have used the seventeenth-century English translation: Jacob Behmen, *A Consolatory Treatise of the Four Complexions, that is, an Instruction in the Time of Temptation for a Sad and Assaulted Heart . . .* (London: H. Blunden, 1654).

[192] Alexandre Koyré, *La Philosophie de Jacob Boehme* (Paris: J. Vrin, 1979), p. 30.

[193] *Libro de la melancolía*, pp. 349–50. In this, Dr Velásquez adopted the point of view expressed by Vallés, who in his *Controversiae medicae et philosophicae*, published in Alcalá in 1556, dedicated a chapter to discussing 'the cause by which fear and sadness are produced by melancholy [la causa por la que el miedo y la tristeza son producidos por la melancolía]' (ch. 14). Vallés in this text refutes Averroes, for whom it is a temperamental imbalance, and not the dark colour of the humour, that originates the fear and sadness proper to melancholy. Averroes maintains that, since the brain does not have sensations directly, it cannot perceive the black colour of the bile. 'It is true (Vallés recognizes) that a blind man is no happier in the light than in the darkness' (p. 331). Nevertheless, Vallés insists that the cause is to be found in the black colour and not in the disequilibrium of temperaments, but that this does not take place through the senses, since effectively the brain does not see. It happens that the animal spirits, which are the instrument by means of which the soul acts, need their own natural light, but 'the black colour of the humour obscures the brilliance of the spirits, and thus the mind moves in an altered manner by the defect of its own instrument [el color negro del humor oscurece el resplandor de los espíritus, y por ello la mente se mueve en forma alterada por defecto de su propio intrumento]' (p. 332). See José María López Piñero and Francisco Calero, *Los temas polémicos de la medicina renacentista: 'las Controversias' (1556), de Francisco Vallés* (Madrid: Consejo Superior de Investigaciones Científicas, 1988), from

which I take the translations quoted. A long time before, Arnau de Vilanova had established that sadness 'throws a shadow over the spirits, they grow dense [*entenebra los espiritz, els engroseex*]' (*Regiment de sanitat*, in *Obres catalanes*, ed. Miquel Batllori (Barcelona: Barcino, 1947), II, pp. 132–3).

194 [hay muchos de estos melancólicos que vienen a perder de tal manera el sentido y la razón, y quedar tan espantados y faltos, que de todas las cosas quedan ignorantes y, desacordados de sí mismos, guían y pasan su vida a manera de bestias] Ibid., p. 354.

195 [. . . a la gente recogida, melancólica, de profunda imaginación y muchas vigilias y ayunos, no dar crédito con facilidad a sus melancólicas visiones, revelaciones, raptos, sino que al punto se humillen conociendo su miseria y bajeza, y consulten confesor sabio, prudente y devoto, ejercitado en semejantes casos] Alonso de Freylas, *Si los melancólicos pueden saber lo que está por venir*, fo. 4r.

196 [No hay hombre grande, prudente y sabio que no tenga algo de esta melancolía. Los que fueron coléricos en su juventud en la vejez tienen esta melancolía. Los que tienen este humor son buenos para gobernar, grandes consejeros, profundos letrados; y si dan en ser espirituales, son buenos para maestros de espíritu, por ser de ordinario prudentes y discretos] Miguel Godínez (Michael Wadding), *Practica de la Theologia Mystica* (Sevilla: Juan Vejarano a costa de Lucas Martín de Hermosilla, 1682), pp. 341–2. The book was originally published in Puebla, Mexico, in 1681, but I quote from the Sevillian edition of 1682 (with modernized spelling and punctuation). Godínez was Professor of Philosophy at Puebla, Rector of the College of San Ildefonso in Mexico City and missionary to the Indians of Sonora and Sinaloa. For Godínez as the confessor of a nun with mystical inclinations, see Doris Bieñko, *Azucena mística. Isabel de la Encarnación, una monja poblana del siglo XVII* (Mexico: Escuela Nacional de Antropología e Historia, 2001).

197 Melchor Cano, *Tratado de la victoria de sí mismo* (Madrid: Biblioteca de Autores Españoles, 1873), vol. 65, p. 310. This text, published in 1550 at Valladolid, is in fact a translation and adaptation of a work by Fray Battista da Crema, which is curious, since this Dominican theologian was regarded as an 'illuminist'. Chapters 8 and 9 of this treatise refer to acedia (which is distinguished from sloth). In Cano's version da Crema's *iluminismo* is transformed into a dry asceticism. See Marcel Bataillon, *Erasmo y España. Estudios sobre la historia espiritual del siglo XVI* (Mexico City: Fondo de Cultura Económica, 1966), p. 703. See also Noel L. Brann, 'Is acedia melancholy? A re-examination of this question in the light of Fra Battista da Crema's *Della cognitione et vittoria de se stesso* (1531)', *Journal of the History of Medicine*, 34 (1979).

198 Where there is neither consent nor deliberation, Cano notes, sin can only be venial. *Tratado de la victoria de sí mismo*, pp. 311–12.

199 See the extensive comments on love sickness in Mary F. Wack, *Lovesickness in the Middle Ages. The Viaticum and Its Commentaries*, and in the critical introduction to Jacques Ferrand's, *A Treatise on Lovesickness*, prepared by Donald A. Beecher and Massimo Ciavollela. On the

ancient tradition of erotic or love melancholy see: Samuel Henry Butcher, 'The melancholy of the Greeks'; Marie-Paule Duminil, 'La mélancolie amoureuse dans l'Antiquité'; John Livingston Lowes, 'The Loveres Maladye of Hereos'; Jackie Pigeaud, *La maladie de l'âme*.

200 2 Samuel 13:1–22.

201 [También es enfermedad / el amor, y aunque es afeto / del alma, cuyo sugeto / es señor, la voluntad; / como obra por instrumentos / corporales, y es pasión / que asiste en el corazón, / suelen los medicamentos / hallar cura en la experiencia; / que el alma espiritual / presa en el campo mortal, / obra siempre en su presencia. / El pulso tenéis amante.] *El amor médico*, act II, scene xv. See a commentary on this in Rafael Sancho de San Román, *La medicina y los médicos en la obra de Tirso de Molina*, p. 33. In a curious play by Gaspar de Aguilar (1561–1623), doctors easily diagnose the illness afflicting the gypsy, Irene, who is suffering because of her love for the soldier Numa: 'For considering the cold sweat, / The slight temperature, the pallid visage, / and the blackened colour of the eyes, / It is the melancholy humour [Porque, considerando el sudor frío, / La poca calentura, el rostro pálido, / Y el color denegrido de los ojos, / Es humor melancólico]'; the remedy eludes the pharmacopoeia: she must go to parties and games for recreation, 'For things of pleasure and joy / Are of more benefit than herbs / For this disease [Que las cosas de gusto y alegría / Son de mayor provecho que las yerbas / Para esta enfermedad]' (*La gitana melancólica*, pp. 145–6). Gaspar de Aguilar, a Valencian, apparently died of grief on being despised by his employers, the duke and duchess of Gandía.

202 953b, p. 35. I use the translation by Jackie Pigeaud, in *L'homme de génie et la mélancolie. Problème XXX, 1*. The association between melancholy and love crystallized in Renaissance thought; see, for example, Marsilio Ficino's *De amore* (English translation by Jayne Sears, *Commentary on Plato's Symposium on Love*, Woodstock, CT: Spring Publications, 1985), in which he establishes that vulgar love is born of the corruption of the blood, especially of melancholic blood (Speech VII, ch. 7, p. 164)

203 The chapter 'De spiritibus' in the *Isagoge* of Johannitius (Hunayn ibn Ishaq) sets forth: 'Thus there are three spirits: first the natural which takes its origin from liver; second the vital from the heart; and third the psychic from the brain. Of these the first is diffused from the liver over the whole body through the veins which have no pulse. The second is directed from the heart to the whole body by the arteries. And the third is directed from the brain into the whole body by the nerves.' Quoted by Owsei Temkin, 'On Galen's pneumatology', pp. 160–1. Andrés Velásquez did not agree that the nerves conducted the animal pneuma, since they were not hollow; he believed they conducted the sensations 'by illustration' (see the second chapter of the *Libro de la melancolía*).

204 [tengo por muy mala manera de granjería, para ganar honra, querer

morder los graves autores ... aunque es un poco lasciva, será bien tratemos en suma y con la mayor brevedad posible] *Libro de la melancolía*, p. 311.

205 [si fuera verdad lo que Galeno dice, parece que la imaginación y la contemplación de los actos venéreos no aprovecharan para la dilatación y erección de los miembros genitales: y vemos que estas contemplaciones más que otra cosa los levantan] Ibid., p. 312.

206 [De donde se sigue muy bien que por ir ellos a aquel miembro fistuloso y correr a él se levanta, y no como dijo Galeno: que por se alterar él y se levantar ex naturae instincto, sucedían los espíritus, sino que esto se hace por acudir allí los espíritus al movimiento de la imaginación, y así se levantan las partes genitales] Ibid., p. 313. Dr Velásquez's arguments may throw light on the discussion of the meaning of the religious nude in Renaissance art. Caroline W. Bynum ('The body of Christ in the later Middle Ages: a reply to Leo Steinberg') has cast doubt on the idea that the *ostentatio genitalium* had sexual or erotic repercussions. Nevertheless, the attitude of the censors of the Inquisition allow us to suppose otherwise; these 'overseers (*veedores*)' were suspicious of nudes in painting and some were scandalized on seeing the frescos of the Sistine Chapel. The fear that the contemplation of naked bodies and sexual organs in works of art illustrating religious or mythological themes might be a cause of erotic excitation caused writers on painting to criticize the exhibition of naked figures. Francisco Pacheco, teacher of Diego Velázquez, in his *Arte de la pintura* of 1649 even went so far as to prohibit the nakedness of the Christ Child (see Julián Gállego, *Visión y símbolos en la pintura española del Siglo de Oro*, p. 69). As Leo Steinberg has shown, portraying the genitals of Jesus, apart from being a manifestation of his human masculinity, might bring to the imagination those 'venereal acts' to which Dr Velásquez refers (*The Sexuality of Christ in Renaissance Art and in Modern Oblivion*).

207 Augustine supposes that, in the absence of sin, Adam would have been able to reproduce himself, achieving at will an erection without libido or passion, since 'the organ created for this purpose would sow the field of generation as the hand of man sows the earth' (*The City of God*, bk 14, ch. 23, p. 3; see also bk 14, ch. 20).

208 *Malleus maleficarum* (*The Witches' Hammer*), I, bk 8, ch. 124: 'Quando virga nullatenus movetur, et nunquam potuit cognoscere, hoc est signus frigiditatis; sed quando movetur et erigitur, perficere autem non potest, est signum maleficii.' See a commentary on this subject in Winfried Schleiner, *Melancholy, Genius, and Utopia in the Renaissance*, p. 174.

209 The story of the elimination of the gargoyle's genitals was told to Manuel Pérez Regordán, as he himself explained to me, by people who had witnessed the act. See the *Historias y leyendas de Arcos*, vol. I, pp. 206–7, by this historian of Arcos.

210 Mary F. Wack, *Lovesickness in the Middle Ages. The Viaticum and Its Commentaries*, p. 41. See also Danielle Jacquart, 'La maladie et le remède d'amour dans quelques écrits medicaux du Moyen Age'.

Marsilio Ficino (Speech VII, ch. 12, p. 168) prescribes coitus in the curing of love; as well as relying on the recommendations of the doctors, he cites Lucretius in legitimation of this remedy (*De rerum natura*, IV, pp. 1059–73).

[211] Klibansky, Panofsky and Saxl, *Saturne et la Mélancolie*, p. 148.

[212] Wack, *Lovesickness in the Middle Ages*, p. 235.

[213] Petri Hispani, *Thesaurus pauperum* 37 and 38, in *Obras médicas de Pedro Hispano*, pp. 234–42. A curious adaptation of the traditional cures to the conditions of New Spain (colonial Mexico) can be found in Agustín Farfán's *Tratado breve de medicina y de todas las enfermedades*, pub. in Mexico in 1592.

[214] Wack, *Lovesickness in the Middle Ages. The Viaticum and Its Commentaries* (Philadelphia: University of Pennsylvania Press, 1990), p. 41. Since the fifteenth century there had been a street in Arcos – that which is now known as the Calle Callejas – given over to public prostitution, and every year the city council designated a doctor to make a daily visit to the brothel (Miguel Mancheño y Olivares, *Apuntes para una historia de Arcos de la Frontera*, p. 253).

[215] Manuel Pérez Regordán, *Historias y leyendas de Arcos*, vol. I, p. 145; and, by the same author, 'El doctor don Andrés Velázquez y su libro de la melancolía', p. 3.

[216] 'How many enemies has miserable man? The world, the Devil and woman. [¿Quantos enemigos tiene el mezquino ombre? El mundo, el diablo e la muger].' Alfonso Martínez de Toledo, *Arcipreste de Talavera o Corbacho*, ed. Michael Gerli (Madrid: Cátedra, 1992), bk 3, ch. 10, p. 250.

[217] [Son sañudos, e luego las puñadas en la mano, porfiados, mentirosos, engañosos ... son podridos, gargajosos, ceñudos e crueles] Ibid., bk 3, ch. 5, pp. 209–10.

[218] Ibid., bk 3, ch. 10, p. 229. It is possible that the extreme misogyny of Martínez de Toledo may have been related to some personal misfortune in love; not only was he accused of having contracted marriage while a priest, but data have come to light that allow us to suspect that he had a lover: a woman named Mari Gómez who appears as 'cousin' and 'niece', and whose lodging he paid for (Carmen Torroja Menéndez and María Rivas Palá, 'Teatro en Toledo en el siglo XV. Auto de la pasión de Alonso del Campo', *Boletín de la Real Academia Española*, Anejo 35 (1977)).

[219] Alan Deyermond, 'The text-book mishandled: Andreas Capellanus and the opening scene of La Celestina.' See an analysis of Capellanus's book in Irving Singer, *The Nature of Love. 2: Courtly and Romantic* (Chicago: University of Chicago Press, 1984), ch. 3. A useful study of Capellanus's *De amore*, as well as of anatomical descriptions, the eroticism of the troubadours and venereal diseases, can be found in Danielle Jacquart and Claude Thomasset, *Sexualité et savoir médical au Moyen Age* (Paris: Presses Universitaires de France, 1985).

[220] [Tragicomedia de Calisto y Melibea, compuesta en reprehensión de los locos enamorados que, vencidos en su desordenado apetito, a sus

amigas llaman y dicen ser su Dios] Fernando de Rojas, *La Celestina*, ed. Bruno Mario Daminani (Madrid: Cátedra, 1985), Prologue, p. 52.

221 Ibid., I, p. 59.

222 As has been analysed by F. A. de Armas, '*La Celestina*: an example of love melancholy', *Romanic Review*, 66, 4 (1975). As this author has pointed out, Robert Burton in his *The Anatomy of Melancholy*, ed. Floyd Dell and Paul Jordan Smith (New York: Tudor, 1955) recognized in Calisto's passion the effects of melancholy. The examination of Burton's references to the Celestina has been taken further by Ricardo Castells in *Fernando de Rojas and the Renaissance Vision: Phantasm, Melancholy, and Didacticism in 'Celestina'* (ch. 4). Castells also analyses in detail a possible direct reference, in the first act of the *Celestina*, to love melancholy. In the first edition of 1499 Calisto exclaims: 'O, if you were to come now, Eras and Crato, physicians, you would feel my sickness! O pity of silence, inspire in the pleberic heart [of Melibea] (*translator's note:* the adjective *pléberico* seems to be a humorous invention by Rojas, based on the Latin word *plebs*, meaning 'plebeian': see the edition of *La Celestina* published by Peter Russell in Clásicos Castalia, p. 215), lest without hope of health it may send the lost spirit away with star-crossed Pyramus and star-crossed Thisbe.' In later editions, however, there is a change in this passage: the physicians are now 'Crato and Galieno', and instead of 'pity of silence,' we read 'celestial pity' (I, p. 29). This change has been imputed to a possible error of transcription or a correction of the original by Rojas himself, and it has been proposed that the text of the anonymous first author used by Rojas was actually making a reference to the physician Erasistratus and the 'pity of Seleucus', the king of Babylon who summoned the famous doctor to cure his son Antiochus, who was in love with his stepmother; Seleucus's mercy was praised because he handed over his wife to the melancholic son. This interpretation has been supported by, among others, Ramón Menéndez Pidal and Martín de Riquer, but is rejected by Castells, who maintains that, since it has been demonstrated – against what was once believed – that the physicians Heras and Cratos (associated with the treatment of problems of sight and hearing), did exist, albeit very little known, the original reference must be to them; he points out that erotic or love melancholy is caused by *looking* at the loved one and, moreover, that it leads to various morbid effects in the eyes and ears (sunken and dry eyes, humming in the ears); the association of these doctors with lovesickness would therefore not be out of place. Ricardo Castells devotes the third chapter of his book to a detailed exposition of this problem of interpretation. In any case there is no doubt at all that the aetiology of the sickness, both in Calisto's and Melibea's case, is love melancholy.

223 [la entrada, causa de la ver y hablar; la habla engendró amor; el amor parió tu pena; la pena causará perder tu cuerpo y el alma y la hacienda] de Rojas, *La Celestina*, II, p. 96.

224 Ibid., IV, p. 123.

225 [es un huego escondido, una agradable llaga, un sabroso veneno, una dulce amargura, una delectable dolencia, un alegre tormento, una

dulce y fiera herida, una blanda muerte] Ibid., X, p. 203. (*huego* = *fuego*). On the subject of love melancholy in the theatre, see Donald A. Beecher, 'Lovesickness, diagnosis, and destiny in the Renaissance theaters of England and Spain: the parallel development of a medico-literary motif'. See also: James F. Burke, 'The *Estrella de Sevilla* and the tradition of saturnine melancholy', *Bulletin of Hispanic Studies*, 51, (1974); Florencio L. Pérez Bautista, 'La medicina y los médicos en el teatro de Calderón de la Barca', *Cuadernos de Historia de la Medicina Española*, 7 (1968); and Teresa Scott Soufas, 'Calderón's melancholy wife-murderers', *Hispanic Review*, 52, 2 (1984). Yvonne David-Peyre has prepared a detailed and erudite study of physicians in Golden Age literature in her book *Le Personage du médecin et la relation médecin-malade dans la littérature ibérique XVIe et XVIIe siècle* (thesis for *doctorat ès lettres*) (Paris: Ediciones Hispano-Americanas, 1971).

[226] *Taqiyya* (which means 'precaution') refers to the act of dissimulation by Muslims who abstained from practising their religion, feigning the adoption of Christianity. José Ramón Enríquez, in his magnificent essay 'Gerión el mestizo y el teatro del Siglo de Oro', in *Pánico escénico* (Mexico City: Dirección de Literatura, UNAM, 1997), points out correctly that this idea applies not only to the Moors of Spain, but to much of the literature of the Golden Age. On the *taqiyya* see Louis Cardaillac, *Moriscos y cristianos. Un enfrentamiento polémico (1542–1640)*, pp. 85 ff. Rojas himself explains this invitation to the enjoyment of love as the 'sweetmeat' which attracts the reader to swallow the 'bitter pill' of the condemnation of the erotic madness. It is paradoxical to teach the delights of erotic pleasure for the purpose of giving a lesson on the dangers of love. Rojas, in his prologue, is perfectly aware of the fact that some readers will choose to ignore the bitter lesson and take note only of the 'wayfarer's tale' and the 'amusing expressions and commonplaces'.

[227] The balsams, ointments, distillations, lustres, oils, lyes and waters prepared by the old Celestina were used 'to remedy love and to make the patient loved [para remediar amores y para se querer bien]', and she used surgery to mend hymens: 'some she made out of a bladder and others she cured by sewing [unos hacía de vejiga y otros curaba de punto]', with such skill that she managed to sell the same housemaid as a virgin to the French ambassador three times over. De Rojas, *La Celestina*, I, pp. 75–7. See in this respect J. Martínez Ruiz and J. Albarracín Navarro, 'Farmacopea en La Celestina y en un manuscrito árabe de Ocaña', in *La Celestina y su contorno social*, ed. Manuel Criado del Val, Actas del I Congreso Internacional sobre La Celestina (Barcelona: Borrás, 1977); and G. Folch Jou, P. García Domínguez and S. Muñoz Calvo, 'La Celestina: ¿hechicera o boticaria?', in *La Celestina y su contorno social*, ed. Manuel Criado del Val, Actas del I Congreso Internacional sobre La Celestina (Barcelona: Borrás, 1977).

[228] [El amor nasce en el cielo / de aquella divina Idea; / allí se engendra y recrea / y de allí llueve en el suelo. / Las criaturas le reciben; / unas a otras se quieren; / sin el amor luego mueren / y mediante el amor viven.] [El amor y sus passiones, / aquel rabioso cuydado / es cáncer

dissimulado / que come los coraçones. / Los que en sus libros escriven / por vasallos de solar, / tristes se pueden llamar, / quando más gozo reciben.] In Francisco López Estrada, 'Estudio y texto de la narración pastoril «Ausencia y soledad de amor», del «Inventario» de Villegas', *Boletín de la Real Academia Española* 29, 126 (1949), lines 304–11, p. 109. Certainly we should add Garcilaso de la Vega's work to the large reservoir of melancholy in Golden Age Spanish poetry. See Christine Orobitg's extensive study, *Garcilaso et la mélancolie* (Toulouse: Presses Universitaires du Mirail, 1997).

[229] Juan de Barrios, *Verdadera medicina, cirugía, y astrología* (Mexico City: Fernando Balli, 1607), p. 440. The reference is to the edition of chs 9 and 10 reproduced in Roger Bartra, *El Siglo de Oro de la melancolía*. Regarding the scientific context in New Spain, see the excellent study by Elías Trabulse, *Ciencia y religión en el siglo XVII* (Mexico City: El Colegio de México, 1974). Several cases of melancholy in colonial Mexico are analysed by María Cristina Sacristán in *Locura e Inquisición en Nueva España, 1571–1760* (Mexico City: Fondo de Cultura Económica, 1992) (cases 1, 10, 15, 16, 18 and 25).

[230] Bergen Evans, *The Psychiatry of Robert Burton* (New York: Columbia University Press, 1944), p. 19; J. R. Simon, *Robert Burton (1577–1640) et l'Anatomie de la Mélancholie* (Paris: Didier, 1964), p. 166, n. 115; Jackie Pigeaud, 'Reflections on love-melancholy in Robert Burton', in *Eros and Anteros: The Medical Traditions of Love in the Renaissance*, Donald A. Beecher and Massimo Ciavolella (eds) (Toronto: University of Toronto Italian Studies Dovehouse Editions, 1992), p. 220. A useful overview of the subject can be found in Lawrence Babb, *The Elizabethan Malady. A Study in English Literature from 1580 to 1642* (East Lansing: Michigan State College Press, 1951). See also Carol Falvo Herffernan, *The Melancholy Muse. Chaucer, Shakespeare and Early Medicine* (Pittsburgh: Duquesne University Press, 1995).

[231] Published in Toulouse. The second and enlarged edition is of 1623, published in Paris under a different title: *De la maladie d'Amour, ou mélancolie érotique, discours curieux qui enseigne à cognoistre l'essence, les causes, les signes, et les remèdes de ce mal fantastique* (Paris: Denis Moreau, 1623).

[232] The sobriquet assigned to Don Quixote by Sancho Panza in Book I, ch. 19, in the original Spanish is *el Caballero de la Triste Figura*, translated 'Knight of the Mournful Countenance' by Samuel Putnam (1948), and – more prosaically – 'Knight of the Ill-favoured Face' by the *Quijote*'s first English translator, Thomas Shelton (published 1612).

[233] [A una dama doliente de humor melancólico, que pidió a Don Hernando escritos suyos, y se enojó porque no se los daba] Published by his widow in the posthumous edition *Varias poesías* of 1591. See Hernando de Acuña, *Poesías*, pp. 137–40. Luis de Góngora, in three poems in a satiric vein, also established a link between love and melancholy; he refers, more precisely, to 'melarquía', the word of Arabic origin which denotes the most dangerous form of the illness, caused by the black humour when it affects the belly. In the romance 'A vosotras digo' those courting disdainful girls are admonished: 'You

new Maciases / resist the ice, / lose color, / *melarchias*. [Resistan al hielo / los nuevos Macías, / pierdan el color, / sufran melarchías].' In the romance 'Hanme dicho, hermanas' Góngora joyfully 'pays a thousand pensions / to *melarchia* [paga mil pensiones / a la melarchía]' (romances 744 and 756). In a *letrilla* (no. 16) the flirtations described are so false that they reduce melancholy to the condition of a knave (*truhán*). See in this respect the essay by Germán Franco Toriz, 'Una singular aportación indiana al tema de la melancolía: la cura de la «merarquía» por cauterios', in Roger Bartra, *El Siglo de Oro de la melancolía. Textos españoles y novohispanos sobre las enfermedades del alma* (Mexico City: Universidad Iberoamericana, Departamento de Historia, 1998), pp. 222–6.

[234] 'Hasta ahora yo tenía / por cierto, señora mía, / que sólo del mal de amor / procediese el triste humor / que llaman melancolía.'

[235] 'Pero ya que éstas no son / causas de ese mal extraño, / ¿cuál podrá ser la ocasión / de un humor que hace daño / en tan libre corazón?'

[236] 'y que por eso tenéis / el humor que padecéis; / y que a ninguno le dais, / porque lugar no halláis / adonde bien le empleéis.'

[237] 'De cualquier suerte conviene, / señora, ser liberal / de la tristeza y el mal / que por venir de do viene / nadie lo tendrá por tal. / Mas de esa melancolía / aquella parte querría, / si yo escogerla pudiese, / que más nuevas me dijese / del lugar donde vivía.'

[238] Marcel Bataillon, '¿Melancolía renacentista o melancolía judía?', in *Estudios hispánicos. Homenaje a Archer M. Huntington* (Wellesley, MA: Spanish Department, Wellesley College, 1952), pp. 42 and 48.

[239] Américo Castro, *España en su historia. Cristianos, moros y judíos* (Buenos Aires: Losada, 1948), p. 578. The book *Aspectos del vivir hispánico. Espiritualismo, mesianismo, actitud personal en los siglos XIV al XVI* (Santiago de Chile: Cruz del Sur, 1949), by the same author, is also interesting. A historical enemy of Castro, Claudio Sánchez-Albornoz, wrote in his book, *España, un enigma histórico*, a furious rejoinder, in which he accused Castro of being pessimistic, 'Judaicizing' and 'Arabicizing'. This angry, stubborn reaction, inflamed with Catholic fervour and adoration for a particular vision of Spain, is typical of those who would like to bury the work of Américo Castro and 'seal it with seven locks' in order to put an end to what they view as its pernicious influence.

[240] Moisés Orfalí, 'El judeoconverso hispano: historia de una mentalidad', in Carlos Barros, (ed.), *Xudeus e conversos na historia*, Actas do Congreso Internacional, Ribadavia, 14–17 October 1991 (Santiago de Copostela: Editorial de la Historia, 1994), pp. 117–18. See also the monograph by Luis Coronas Tejada, *Conversos and Inquisition in Jaén* (Jerusalem: Magnes Press/Hebrew University, 1988).

[241] Moshe Idel, 'Religion, thought and attitudes: the impact of the expulsion on the Jews', in Elie Kedourie (ed.), *Spain and the Jews. The Sepharadi Experience. 1442 and After* (London: Thames and Hudson, 1992), p. 136. See also Haim Beinart, 'The conversos and their fate', in Elie Kedourie (ed.), *Spain and the Jews, The Sephardi Experience. 1442 and After* (London: Thames and Hudson, 1992), pp. 115–18.

242 Cited by Frances A. Yates, *The Occult Philosophy in the Elizabethan Age*, p. 23. A medical treatise of the eighteenth century still describes melancholy, together with hypochondria and haemorrhoids, as a Jewish disease, and refers to an environment of misery, excessive irritability, squalor and bad food that is a breeding ground for sadness (Elcan Isaac Wolf, *Von den Krankheiten der Juden* (Mannheim, 1777); cited by Harry Friedenwald, 'Concerning the diseases of the Jews', in *The Jews and Medicine, Essays*, 2 vols (Baltimore: Johns Hopkins Press, 1944), p. 524).

243 Isaac Cardoso, *Las excelencias de los hebreros* (Amsterdam: David de Castro Tartas, 1679, p. 347), cited by Yosef Hayim Yerushalmi, *From Spanish Court to Italian Ghetto. Isaac Cardoso: A Study in Seventeenth-Century Marranism and Jewish Apologetics* (New York: Columbia University Press, 1971), p. 437.

244 The old Jewish quarter was situated in what is now the Calle Cuna; the synagogue consisted of a double nave, separated by six stone pillars (today there are only four), which supported ten circular vaults (Manuel Pérez Regordán, *La Real Justicia y el Santo Oficio de la Inquisición en Arcos de la Frontera* (Arcos de la Frontera: author's own publication, 1992), pp. 18–23). See Haim Beinart, *Andalucía y sus judíos* (Córdoba: Monte de Piedad-Caja de Ahorros, 1986) and María Antonia Bel Bravo, *El auto de fe de 1593. Los conversos granadinos de origen judío* (Granada: Universidad de Granada, 1988). It is very likely that Huarte de San Juan also would have had Jewish ancestors, as likewise would Melchor Cano (Antonio Domínguez Ortiz, *Los judeoconversos en España y América*, pp. 183–5). See the same author's excellent study, *La clase social de los conversos en Castilla en la Edad Moderna* (Granada: Universidad de Granada, 1991).

245 Mentioned by Cecil Roth in his stupendous book *A History of Marranos* (New York: Sepher-Herman Press, 1974), ch. 5, n. 6.

246 The case-study is taken from Amatus Lusitanus, *Curationum medicinalium centuriae quatuor*, Venecia: Balthesarem Constantinum, 1557 (fourth century, case 42). I use the Portuguese translation by Firmino Crespo (Amato Lusitano, *Centúrias de curas medicinais*) and that into English by Harry Friedenwald, 'Two Jewish physicians of the sixteenth century', in *The Jews and Medicine, Essays*, 2 vols (Baltimore: Johns Hopkins Press, 1944), pp. 392–403.

247 *Centúrias de curas medicinais*, III, p. 75, and Friedenwald, 'Two Jewish physicians of the sixteenth century', p. 395.

248 *Centúrias*, III, p. 77 and Friedenwald, 'Two Jewish physicians of the sixteenth century', p. 397.

249 *Centúrias*, III, p. 82 and Friedenwald, 'Two Jewish physicians of the sixteenth century', p. 400.

250 *Centúrias*, III, p. 83 and Friedenwald, 'Two Jewish physicians of the sixteenth century', p. 401. Bleeding was a treatment much used by physicians; there is a sonnet by Góngora devoted to the subject, in which melancholy is also mentioned, and which begins thus: 'Wounded the white foot by the brief iron / Healthy, if sharp, my friend, / My face you tinge with melancholy, / While you stain the

snow with pink. [Herido el blanco pie del hierro breve, / Saludable si agudo, amiga mía, / Mi rostro tiñes de melancolía, / Mientras de rosicler tiñes la nieve]' ('A una sangría de un pie [On the bleeding of a foot]').

251 He was born at St Jean Pied-de-Port in the French Basque country, not far from the cities of Biarritz and Bayonne, which provided a haven for groups of *conversos* (Haim Beinart, 'The conversos and their fate', p. 119).

252 [... *tienen el cerebro tostado y la cólera requemada*] Huarte de San Juan, *Examen de ingenios*, ch. 12, p. 510.

253 [Eso mesmo les aconteció a los hebreos con el maná, que todo se les convertía en cólera retostada] Ibid., ch. 12, p. 514.

254 [Porque la continua tristeza y vejación hace juntar los espíritus vitales y sangre arterial en el cerebro, en el hígado y corazón; y estando allí unos sobre otros, se vienen a tostar y requemar. Y así muchas veces levantan calenturas; y lo ordinario es hacer melancolía por adustión (de la cual casi todos participan hasta el día de hoy).] Ibid., ch. 12, pp. 516–17.

255 [el pueblo de Israel ... puede comunicar a sus descendientes el agudeza de ingenio sin estar en Egipto ni comer maná] Ibid., ch. 12, p. 523.

256 Harry Friedenwald, 'Montalto, A Jewish physician at the court of Marie de Médicis and Louis XIII', in *The Jews and Medicine, Essays*, 2 vols (Baltimore: Johns Hopkins Press, 1944), pp. 481–2.

257 Filoteo Elião de Montalto, *Archipathologia, in qua internarum capitis affectionum essentia, causae, signa, praesagia et curatio accuratissima indagine edisseruntur* (Paris: F. Jacquin, 1614). The book consists of eighteen treatises, the fourth – which consists of 148 pages and is divided into thirty-six chapters (almost a fifth of the whole) – being devoted to melancholy.

258 *Archipathologia*, pp. 247–8. Cited by Friedenwald, 'Montalto. A Jewish physician at the court of Marie de Médicis and Louis XIII', p. 481. The Arab doctor cited as al-Zahravi was the Cordoban surgeon also known as Albucasis (Abū al-Qasim al-Zaharaui Khalaf ibn Abbas, *c.*936–1013).

259 *Archipathologia*, pp. 297–8, quoted by Friedenwald, 'Montalto', p. 482.

260 See the bilingal edition prepared by Jackie Pigeaud: *L'homme de génie et la mélancolie. Problème XXX, 1.*

261 *Problème XXX, 1*, 954^a, p. 36.

262 Huarte, *Examen de ingenios*, IV, pp. 293–300.

263 Ibid., ch. 4, pp. 309, 314–15.

264 Further on he says: '...there is no reason to wonder at the fact that things said and written in Latin sound so good, and in other languages so bad, since the first inventors of these were barbarians.' Ibid., ch. 8, p. 421.

265 Ibid., ch. 4, pp. 314–15.

266 Klibansky, Panofsky and Saxl, *Saturne et la Mélancolie*, pp. 160 ff.

267 Fourth chapter of *Practica* (Venecia, 1517). I use the summary that appears in Klibansky, Panofsky and Saxl, *Saturne et la Mélancolie*,

pp. 160 ff. Long afterwards, in 1620, Tomasso Campanella still supported the ideas affirming the prophetic ability and wisdom of melancholics. In his *De sensu rerum ac magia* he defends the idea that, besides the malign and impure form of melancholy, another, pure, form existed, giving rise to intellectual clarity, insight or 'wit' (*agudeza*) and ability to predict the future: this pure kind of melancholy 'occurs because the blood is well cooked and the fuliginous elements transpire to the exterior [of the body] through the fibres, and the melancholy is in a state of much repose in the gall-bladder, and this is a sign of great heat because the blood blackens and burns; thence are born subtle and very peaceful spirits, like firewood burning, which at first makes a heavy and dark smoke, afterwards a thinner [*mediocre*] and purer smoke, and at the last a very subtle and invisible fume, as a result of the great action of heat; the coals, however, remain black: in the same way the melancholy remains very hot, and this is a sign of wise spirits, but it is not their cause; the cause is the subtlety and peacefulness of the spirits.' The spiritual mechanics is interesting: Campanella says that 'the subtle spirit is more capable of receiving the almost imperceptible movements of the air, in the same way that the air is more [able to] receive movements than the water and that languid movements are received more easily by tenuous things. And thus, when [melancholics] see a man, they divine his thought, on receiving the tiny movements that the thinking spirit communicates to the air' (Tomasso Campanella, *Del sensu delle cose e della magia*, bk III, ch. 10, 'Della sagacità de' malinconici puri e impuri e demonoplassia e consentimento dell'aria', pp. 194–5).

[268] Velásquez, *Libro de la melancolía*, p. 355.

[269] [Mas aunque fuese verdad (que no lo es) que viniese un frenético a hablar latín llegando a tener el temperamento necesario que se requería para que el alma racional hiciese estos actos, no los podía hacer en la enfermedad de que tratamos, que es en la melancolía, porque en esta enfermedad, demás del grave daño que tiene el temperamento, necesariamente los espíritus tienen perdido su natural resplandor y están obscurecidos y tenebrosos. Pues corrompido el temperamento (que es de donde emana la buena habilidad) y el instrumento con que obra dañado, ¿qué obra hará el alma racional o de qué instrumentos se aprovechará que venga a hacer buena consonancia o invención? Porque no se ha de pensar que por razón de esta melancolía de que tratamos se hace el alma más perspicaz, sino antes es causa la melancolía de perturbar el alma, que no de ilustrarla, como se muestra claro del miedo y tristeza que siempre padecen los afligidos melancólicos. Así que tengo por verdad averiguada que ningún melancólico maníaco rústico hablará latín ni tratará de astrología sin las haber primero sabido.] Ibid., p. 360. It is interesting to note that in 1634 the physician Marc Duncan of Saumur doubted that the Mother Superior of the Ursuline nuns could have spoken Latin without having learned it previously, simply because of being possessed by the Devil (M. Duncan, *Discours de la possession des religieuses ursulines de Lodun*,

The Golden Age of Melancholy 161

    1634 (printed pamphlet of 64 pp., no publisher's or printer's imprint, in the Bibliotèque nationale de France, 16-LB36-3961), pp. 18–19).

270 [yo no puedo dejar de entender que el ánima racional apartada del cuerpo, y también el demonio, tenga potencia visiva, olfativa, auditiva y tactiva ... Pues decir que el ánima racional apartada del cuerpo no puede raciocinar por no tener cerebro es desatino muy grande] Huarte, *Examen de ingenios*, ch. 8, pp. 388–9.

271 Velásquez, *Libro de la melancolía*, p. 359.

272 [dañándose el instrumento ha de ser de necesidad su acción dañada] Ibid., pp. 358–9.

273 [mientras está encarcelada en nuestros cuerpos no obra sin instrumentos corporales. Y si estos no guardan su templanza y buena composición el ánima enferma y corrompidamente produce sus obras] de Mercado, *Diálogos de Philosophia natural y moral* (Granada: Hugo de Mena and René Rabilio, 1558), p. 389.

274 [Así que el defecto no es del alma, porque igualmente es buena, perfecta, sabia y capaz en el uno como en el otro] Velásquez, *Libro de la melancolía*, p. 365.

275 Huarte, like Guainerio, also believed that 'all rational souls and their understandings, set apart from their bodies, are of equal perfection and knowing [todas las almas racionales y sus entendimientos, apartadas del cuerpo, son de igual perfección y saber]' (*Examen de ingenios*, ch. 6, p. 356). This phrase formed part of a paragraph that was expurgated and replaced in the 1594 edition by another: '. . . the power that is in the soul . . . is in all men of equal perfection [. . . la potencia que está en él ánima . . . en todos los hombres es de igual perfección]', ch. 9 of the revised edition). In *Los trabajos de Persiles y Sigismunda* Cervantes puts a similar idea into the mouth of Mauricio: 'because all souls are equal and of a similar mass in their beginnings, created and formed by their Maker, and in accordance with the receptacle of the body in which they are enclosed, and its temperament, do they thus appear more or less discreet, and take note of, and have interest in knowing, the sciences, arts or skills that the stars most incline them towards [porque las ánimas todas son iguales y de una misma masa en sus principios, criadas y formadas por su Hacedor, y según la caja y temperamento del cuerpo, donde las encierra, así parecen ellas más o menos discretas, y atienden y se aficionan a saber las ciencias, artes o habilidades a que las estrellas más las inclinan]' (I, p. 18). It has been noted that Cervantes possibly took this idea from Huarte.

276 Huarte, *Examen de ingenios*, ch. 7, p. 390. This chapter was expurgated in its entirety from the second edition.

277 *De anima et vita*, III, ch. 18, p. 1302 and III, ch. 19, p. 1304; I use Lorenzo Riber's Spanish translation in *Tratado del alma*.

278 [Con la pesadumbre se reseca el cuerpo y el corazón se contrae hasta el punto en que algunos que de pesadumbre murieron se halló no más abultado que una membrana. El corazón contrae consigo el rostro, que es su imagen, y, por último, entrega la salud misma. Compañeros inseparables de la tristeza son lamentaciones, gemidos, llantos. Esta

pasión es fría y seca; por esto prepondera en épocas y sitios fríos y, generalmente, en todo cuanto ostenta complexión melancólica, como en otoño y en el invierno, en tiempo de nublado, de noche, hacia el Norte, regiones en las cuales la tristeza hace más víctimas que en España o en Italia.] Ibid., III, ch. 19, p. 1303. (*Trnaslator's note:*The text quoted here is a translation by Lorenzo Riber of Vives's original Latin, which it has not been possible to consult; it will be noted that the words *pesadumbre* (grief) and *tristeza* (sadness) are used here apparently as synonyms).

[279] Thomás Murillo, *Aprobación de ingenios y curación de hipocondríacos, con observaciones y remedios muy particulares* (Zaragoza: Diego de Ormer, 1672). This is a highly involved and confused book, overloaded with learned references to everyone from Hippocrates and Galen to Ficino and Mathiolo de la Tarántula, without ignoring Avicenna and St Thomas Aquinas, and yet it never mentions Andrés Velásquez, whom he is obviously plagiarizing. The second chapter is devoted to 'the temperaments, and which of them is the most appropriate for wit (*ingenio*)', but on this occasion it is Juan Huarte de San Juan that he fails to cite.

[280] This is the supposition of Alberto Escudero Ortuño, *Concepto de la melancolía en el siglo XVII (un comentario a las obras de Robert Burton y Alfonso de Santa Cruz)* (Huesca: Imprenta provincial, 1950), p. 49, n. 3. This is a doctoral thesis by the director of the Provincial Asylum of Huesca, which was published in 1950.

[281] J. Langdon Down, *Mental Affections of Childhood* [1887]; (Oxford: MacKeith Press, Blackwell Scientific Publications, 1990).

[282] See Darold A. Treffert, *Extraordinary People. Understanding 'Idiot Savants'* (New York: Harper and Row, 1989).

[283] See Bruno Bettelheim, *The Empty Fortress: Infantile Autism and the Birth of the Self* (New York: Free Press, 1967), who emphasizes exogenous factors in autism.

[284] Oliver Sacks, 'An anthropologist on Mars', in *An Anthropologist on Mars* (New York: Knopf, 1995), p. 246. The same author has dealt with this subject in other medical case-studies: 'Prodigies', 'The Autist Artist', 'The Twins' and 'A Walking Grove'.

[285] Miguel Mancheño y Olivares, *Apuntes para una historia de Arcos de la Frontera*, p. 303. Sixty infantrymen of Arcos had already embarked in 1585 at Cadiz in pursuit of Drake, who had attacked the Spaniards at Vigo, at Santo Domingo and at Cartagena de Indias. The Arcos infantry reinforced a squadron of the Marquis of Santa Cruz.

[286] Ibid., p. 313. His father was Luis Cristóbal Ponce de León, who died in 1573.

[287] Jerónimo de Ceballos, *Arte real para el buen gobierno de los Reyes, y Príncipes, y de sus vassallos* (Toledo, 1623), fo. 4. *Actas de las Cortes de Castilla*, ch. 38, pp. 141, 146. Cited by J. H. Elliot, 'Self-perception and decline in early seventeenth-century Spain', in *Spain and Its World, 1500–1700* (New Haven: Yale University Press, 1989), pp. 248–50.

[288] *Nueva filosofía de la naturaleza del hombre [y otros escritos]* (Madrid: Editora Nacional, 1981). Dr Sabuco decided to attribute the text that

he himself had written to his daughter Oliva, and for a long time she was believed to have been the author.

289 Ibid., p. 137. Other negative affects are: anger, pleasure, mistrust, enmity, shame, grief or distress (*congoja*), pity, servitude, lust, sloth, jealousy and vengeance (chs 3–21). The positive affects are: joy, hope, good temper, love for one's neighbours, friendship and, at times, solitude (chs 23–9). Different from the 'affects' are the 'contraries', which also cause damage, such as the plague, poisons, overweight, excess of noise or overwork, bad smells, gluttony, lack of sleep or food, annoyance, heat, imagination, etc. It is a curious fact that, even in the eighteenth century, a physician, in a trial for heresy and blasphemy of a person who had been attacked by melancholic delirium while in the secret dungeons of the Inquisition in Mexico, should have cited the authority of Sabuco de Nantes to describe the damage caused by sadness, which is a discord of soul and body (Archivo General de la Nación, Inquisición, vol. 1086, fo. 105v. Advisory opinion of Dr Juan Joseph de la Peña y Brizuela in the action against Joseph de Silva, native of San Martín Texmelucan, Puebla, 1770).

290 Miguel Mancheño y Olivares, *Apuntes para una historia de Arcos de la Frontera*, pp. 306–9, 311–12.

291 'Bramó el Becerro, y púsoles en sarta: / tronó la tierra, oscurecióse el cielo, / amenazando una total ruina; / y al cabo, en Cádiz, con mesura harta, / ido ya el conde sin ningún recelo, / triunfando entró el duque de Medina.'

292 The 'Calf' (*el Becerro*) is a play on words which refers both to the name of a captain who participated in the entry into Cadiz and to the animal. Cervantes's sonnet has the following title: 'On the entry of the Duke of Medina Sidonia into Cadiz in July 1596, with the aid of troops trained in Seville by Capt. Becerra, after the city was evacuated by the English troops and sacked during the period of twenty-four days under the command of the Earl of Essex [A la entrada del Duque de Medina Sidonia en Cádiz en julio de 1596, con socorro de tropas enseñadas en Sevilla por el Capitán Becerra, después de haber evacuado la ciudad las tropas inglesas y saqueándola por espacio de veinticuatro días al mando del Conde de Essex].' Cited by Otis H. Green, *Spain and the Western Tradition, The Castilian Mind in Literature from El Cid to Calderón*, 4 vols (Madison: University of Wisconsin Press, 1963–8), III, p. 364, n. 70.

293 Miguel Mancheño y Olivares, *Apuntes para una historia de Arcos de la Frontera*, p. 313.

294 Quoted by Luisa Isabel Álvarez de Toledo, *Alonso Pérez de Guzmán: General de la Invencible* (Cádiz: Servicio de Publicaciones de la Universidad, Consejería de Educación y Ciencia de la Junta de Andalucía, 1994), p. 135.

295 Archivo Ducal de Medina Sidonia (Medina Sidonia Ducal Archive): *Libramientos y provisiones*, vol. 57, file 2854, fos 1 and 27v, of 1608. Also cited by José Antonio Delgado y Orellana, 'Tres insólitos arcenses', *Hidalguía*, 31, 178–9 (1983), pp. 403 and 405. The payment of each four-monthly portion to Dr Velásquez amounted to 52,500 *maravedís*;

for purposes of comparison, another bedside physician, Dr Diego Maldonado, received only 6,666 *maravedís*, little more than the barber Alberto Lumel, who received 5,000 *maravedís* (Archivo Ducal de Medina Sidonia: *Libramientos y provisiones*, vol. 57, file 2870, fo. 231v, and vol. 58, file 2879, fos 142, 269, 6v. These data were obtained by Manuel Pérez Regordán, who kindly made them available to me.

296 Delgado y Orellana, 'Tres insólitos arcenses', pp. 407–8.

297 Ibid., pp. 406–7. The plan is framed and exhibited in the church of Santa María. It is not known whether his body was actually buried in the space reserved for him there or was, rather, entombed at Sanlúcar, which is almost certainly where he died.

Chapter 3

Melancholy and Christianity: On Don Quixote's Sadness

For my children—
Arí, Belisa, Bruno and Iliana—
who have brought me so much joy

If we were able to give a vigorous shaking to Christianity's family tree, the oddest of branches bearing the strangest of fruits would come tumbling around our ears. This experience would be enough to convince us that the notion of the unity of the West – a result of the monodic chant of Christian culture – is an unsustainable vision of European history. I do not wish to spend much time considering this widely accepted fact; what interests me now is to ponder on the function of these strange fruits and boughs that, despite their exotic nature, form part of the genealogy of Christianity. For although these are exogenous elements of ancient, barbarous and pagan origin, they have become embodied in the corpus of Christian belief, thus forming a consubstantial part of European culture. I propose to examine this problem, taking as my example the ancient canon of melancholy – such as it was defined by the Hippocratic and peripatetic traditions – and the way in which it was absorbed by the culture of the Spanish Golden Age, to become one of its most important axes.

This way of looking at the problem brings us to the classic theme of what are sometimes referred to as 'survivals', the 'continuity' of ancient myths embedded in cultural forms which, in principle, reject them as alien to the dominating faith or reason. Jean Seznec devoted a memorable book to this subject, *La Survivance des dieux antiques*,[1] in which he performed an erudite dissection of the evolution of pagan myths during the Middle Ages as vehicles of ancient ideas that were in the process of taking on new forms. Another important book that addresses, even more directly, the subject I have broached was written by Raymond Klibansky, Erwin Panofsky and Fritz Saxl: this is *Saturn and Melancholy*.[2] I have cited these two extraordinary works not only in order to exemplify the importance of the subject which I wish to consider, but also in order to offer a very different approach to the problem. Most of the works which deal with the subject of 'survivals' of pagan antiquity, such as those I have just mentioned, fall into the category that Braudel called *histoire événementielle* (history of events): a history of ideas which leads us along a path strewn with 'key ideas' and myths as events, leaving aside the study of the cultural networks that surround them. In opposition to this approach we have the structuralist interpretations that have given pride of place to the study of cultural textures and the functions of their components.

How are we to interpret the long history and the permanence over many centuries of a cultural and mythic canon such as that of melancholy? How are we to explain that this peculiar conglomeration of ideas and myths has survived such a long passage through such different cultural, social and historical contexts? And, more specifically, how did it survive Christianity? Of course, melancholy is not the only pagan ingredient that we can find in Christian culture; there are many others, and some may even be found inscribed in biblical texts. Two aspects of melancholy – that exotic fruit of the family tree of Christianity – are of particular interest to me. First, the fact that its integration is relatively recent and well documented; secondly, that its adoption – or so it appears to me – has been one of the most important factors facilitating what we might call the 'modernization' of Christianity; for the canon of melancholy has ensconced itself in the heart of the West, in a line of evolution that connects Hildegard von Bingen and Jacob Böhme with Kierkegaard, and to which we could add other milestones represented by St John Cassian, Ficino and Robert Burton. In the Spanish cultural tradition the great landmarks of melancholy include the physician Arnau de Vilanova, Miguel de Cervantes and Calderón de la Barca, and extend right down to Antonio Machado.

I propose, with the aid of the Knight of the Sad Countenance, to examine melancholy as a myth that has found itself a niche within Christianity. The study of myths tends to draw us towards the exploration of their origins and thus toward primeval eras of human history in which, it is supposed, we might rediscover not only the foundations of religions but the roots of language and thought themselves. This idea is something we have inherited from the Renaissance: Pico de la Mirandola believed that myths concealed primordial truths whose knowledge had been lost, but could be recovered by cabbalistic means capable of deciphering the hidden meaning of ancient fables.[3] The study of myths, five centuries later, is not so distant as some would like to think from the ideas of Pico, although the emphasis has shifted more and more towards a conception of mythology as a peculiar manner of approaching reality, rather than as a kind of chest containing a hidden treasure. Studies of myths, down to the present day, have given pride of place to the search for primeval and immutable elements whose origin would be found in an original human condition; attempts have been made to discover the logic inscribed in myth, a primitive symbolic language or an archetype deeply embedded in the collective psyche. The study of myth tends to be an invitation to look back into the past – to reconstruct genealogies – and to think in terms of the essential immutability of certain canons that would contain within themselves the keys to their meaning and their permanence.

If we continue along this path we might arrive at the conclusion that the Christian religion simply found in the canon of melancholy a valuable treasure, a primordial truth inscribed in the Hippocratic-Galenic codex of illnesses afflicting the soul. Or perhaps it would be better to express it the other way round: an ancient and powerful structure, having found its classic expression in Greek culture, took on a new form first in medieval Arabic culture and then in the Christian culture of the Renaissance. The explanation of the presence of this strange fruit could also be expressed in a modern, psychoanalytical or structuralist form: the canon of melancholy would respond to a Jungian archetype, to a message inscribed in the human spirit or a mental structure, such as those postulated by Chomskyan generative grammar.

I believe that such explanations cloud over the extraordinary complexity and richness of the process that lies concealed behind the phenomenon of 'survivals'. At base, what is at stake is not the survival of certain outstanding intellectual achievements, nor, for that matter, the reinterpretation of a codex inscribed indelibly in the minds of all human beings. Confronted by these alternatives, while engaged in other research (on the myth of the wild man in

Europe) I chose what I like to call an evolutionist perspective. It is from this point of view that I intend to offer certain reflections on the way in which the myth of melancholy adapted itself in Renaissance Spain to the requirements and contradictions of Christian culture. I believe it is necessary to focus our attention on certain moments of transition, during which symptomatic mutations take place regarding both the composition of the myth and its function within the surrounding cultural texture. I shall refer to several facets of this process: the gestation of new patterns of suffering and renewed models of alterity. In each one of these facets the canon of melancholy underwent mutations that allowed it to adapt itself to the new cultural conditions and to fulfill innovatory functions; these mutations are what enable us to understand the long evolution of the canon of melancholy.

The incorporation of melancholy into the Christian corpus helped to solve an old problem: how, Christians asked themselves, once the persecutions to which they had been subjected had come to an end and their faith had become the dominant religion, could they continue to offer to God their suffering and their pain? The ancient Hippocratic-Galenic model of melancholy was adapted, via a curious mutation, to the new needs.

Melancholy offered models for rejecting demonic otherness and for channelling suffering towards new socially accepted forms. But demonology and mysticism were not the only ways in which Christian culture assimilated the melancholic canon; there were others, among which it is worth stressing its use in the reprobation and condemnation of courtly love and, in general, the manifestations of passional eroticism that from the twelfth century onward expanded across Europe. Humoural theory added arguments for condemning the new expressions of eroticism, exemplified by the poetry of the Provençal troubadours, since it allowed worldly love to be defined as a dangerous illness: the so-called erotic or love melancholy. In Spain we find important manifestations of this condemnation of mad love in works such as the *Celestina*, written by the *converso* Fernando de Rojas, an extraordinary text, at whose base we can hardly fail to discern melancholy as the cause of the morbid eroticism of the lovers. In the *Celestina* – as occurred also in the Florentine Neoplatonic tradition – fleshly and worldly love is condemned with a kind of good-humoured passion that leads us to suspect that the apparent condemnation merely serves to veil a surreptitious admiration for the lovers who sacrifice their lives for the sake of love.[4]

Not all the models offered to explain melancholy had a negative character, nor were they all associated with a condemnation of the body and worldly and fleshly pleasures. The process of individualization – from ancient times impelled by religious impulses towards a personal salvation – was enormously accelerated by the positive evaluations of the melancholic sentiments, both in cultivated poetry and popular *romances* or ballads, and by the rebirth of the ancient Aristotelian idea of the black humour, understood in the famous *Problemata* as a source of inspiration, intellectual vigour and heroic valour. Such models have received ample attention from scholars.[5]

In contrast, there have been few studies directed at observing these processes in the history of Spain. Based largely on the concepts established by Florentine Neoplatonism in the fifteenth century, Spain was the great soundboard of melancholy in Europe, resonating and raising the theme to a higher level. Without examining the Spanish process it is difficult to understand the sudden blooming of the myth of melancholy throughout Europe as a whole in the seventeenth century, its most outstanding exponents, aside from Cervantes, being Shakespeare and Montaigne. For this reason it is worth stressing the importance of the interpretations of Teresa Scott Soufas, since they shed light on a fundamental problem.[6] She adopts Edgar Wind's idea of the 'transvaluation' of traditional values and concepts in order to refer to a process of readaptation of ancient expressions to new needs, without eliminating or invalidating them. According to Wind, Renaissance melancholy was a transmutation of the ancient vice of sloth and indolence, known to theologians as *acedia*.[7] This horrendous sin had undergone a mutation and – transformed into the noble melancholy – was henceforth a privilege of inspired men.[8] Similar mutations could be observed in the mortal sins represented by *ira* and *luxuria*, which were transformed into the worthy and honourable irascibility and the noble *voluptas*.

Teresa Soufas refers to a similar process of 'dialectical transvaluation of traditional values'. Her prime example is Don Quixote, a character whose melancholy was to be the cause of both his madness and his health: through a process similar to the transformation of acedia as described by Wind, Cervantes had been able to acknowledge, in his melancholy hero, the power and autonomy of the secular mind, without thereby throwing doubt on the traditional negative evaluation of melancholy.[9] Not only did he accept the traditional model, but – as Soufas observes – the description of the sufferings occasioned by melancholy was a way of pointing to the failure of the new independent secular mentality from a conservative viewpoint, as Lope de Vega and Calderón also did.[10]

From another point of view, it could be said that the survival of melancholy in the context of the Spanish Renaissance and Baroque might be explained by the fact that – without modifying the ancient canon – a transvaluation of its negative sense had occurred; in other words, an adaptation that merely altered the direction of the flux of value without modifying the structure itself. Thus, the survival of the myth would suppose an adaptation to new functions, without the necessary existence of significant precedents or previous mutations of the canon of melancholy. Giorgio Agamben has directed an important critique against this interpretation; he points out that even such a careful researcher as Edgar Wind committed a serious error in supposing that acedia during the Middle Ages had only a negative value. Agamben thinks that, on the contrary, during the Middle Ages from the ancient Patristic period onward, the double polarity of *tristitia–acedia* was well known, thus paving the way for the Renaissance revaluation of the black humour.[11]

The existence of a moral complex grouping both acedia and sadness has been well documented.[12] The Levantine ascetic St John Cassian (360–435), on the basis of the experiences of the anchorite monks of the Egyptian desert, described acedia in detail as one of the eight mortal sins or vices, similar, but not identical, to the vice of sadness (*tristitia*), and associated it with the strange 'demon of noontide' (*daemonio meridiano*) mentioned in Psalm 90, v. 6 (Vulgate):[13]

> Our sixth combat is against what the Greeks call '*akedia*': it is a torpor, a laziness of the heart; in consequence, it is very close to sadness (*tristitia*); it attacks especially those monks who wander from place to place or who live in isolation. It is the most dangerous and persistent enemy of those who live in solitude.[14]

But in the list of the seven deadly sins that was later drawn up by Gregory, acedia was assimilated to sorrow (*tristitia*);[15] and the latter was always, since the teachings of St Paul, a concept with two different facets: 'For godly sorrow worketh repentance to salvation not to be repented of: but the sorrow of the world worketh death', explained Paul to the Christians of Corinth, in order to justify a furious letter of protest at the offences suffered by one of the Apostle's envoys.[16] This exaltation of a sadness that led to salvation can be compared with the positive evaluation of the melancholy that affects exceptional men according to the Aristotelian tradition (*Problem XXX, I*). However, both in Christian theology and in Hippocratic-Galenic medicine, the positive aspects of sorrow and the black humour were relatively marginal when set against the serious damage that was accorded to acedia, *tristitia saeculi* or the melancholy illness. The important thing here, however, is to underline the fact that two nuances – which I like to think of as mutations – present both in the Christian tradition and the pagan, served Renaissance culture as a foundation for re-evaluating melancholy. These two ancient mutations – *tristitia secundum Deum* and the appreciation of the *melancholikoi* – made possible the survival of a pagan canon at the very centre of Christian culture.

Renaissance melancholy, therefore, is not simply a revaluation of medieval acedia, since we have evidence that such a revaluation had already taken place within theology itself and within ancient Greek thought. Wenzel, however, sets forth another problem: he maintains that the survival of medieval acedia subsumed in Renaissance melancholy is a purely hypothetical development, and that it is impossible to demonstrate that it occurred, in the way that one can show that a plant grows or a chemical reaction takes place. Wenzel states that he has not come across any document that draws an explicit equivalence between acedia and melancholy. The only written reference he mentions is very late: the abbot Claude Fleury (1640–1723), a friend of Fénelon and disciple of Bossuet, in a treatise published in 1686, mentions melancholy as one of the most ancient sources of sin (and in the margin makes a reference to acedia).[17] This is an indication that men of letters of that period recognized acedia as an antecedent of melancholy.

Acedia and melancholy share many similar features, and this presented complex problems to medieval theologians: if the melancholic complexion in the body of a person could predispose that person to melancholy, this could serve as a moral exoneration. St Bonaventure, the great thirteenth-century Italian theologian, a Franciscan and the son of a physician, vigorously rejected this idea; acedia did not assail people in the same way as sensual passions did, but, rather, one arrived at this sinful state by one's own free will. Nevertheless – as Rainer Jehl observes – for Bonaventure spiritual liberty is dominion over the body, and free will is mastery both of the lower – vegetative and sensitive – faculties, and of the rational will itself.[18] Consequently, even corporeal influences called, in the final instance, for moral repression; otherwise, freedom would remain restricted and thus the very basis of sin would be annulled: for without freedom, there would be no call for moral exoneration. This idea could lead us to think that the demand for a complete mastery of the will over the body is the condition that makes freedom possible, and is thus also the ground of existence for sin and vice. But since this total dominion or mastery is rarely attained, acedia as a sin must be of very scarce occurrence, and we would be faced rather by melancholy, a pathological condition irrelevant from the moral point of view. This interpretation of Bonaventure's thought led to certain confusions later on. The way out of this vicious circle is the idea of grace, since this divine gift offered to humanity gives human beings the necessary will to attain virtue, but also the liberty to indulge in vice. Acedious man, distancing himself – like other sinners – from transcendental goodness and straying towards temporal goods, produces a curvature of the soul with cosmic consequences, since this confounds and implies not only man but physical nature as a whole. Unlike other mortal sins, however, in the case of acedia the definition of the worldly good that attracted the curved soul was not very clear. Bonaventure mentions *quies* (which can be translated as tranquillity or repose, also as peace, neutrality or truce) as the aim of acedia, understood simply as inactivity and as a caricature of the *apátheia* of the stoics; but he also saw it as the inverted mirror-image of the blessedness towards which men aim by means of a will – aided by divine Grace – capable of dominating the body and the lower faculties of the soul. The emphasis on tranquillity and repose, more bodily than spiritual, led to an assimilation of acedia and sloth.

A stimulating study by Noel Brann has shown how the theologians of the Renaissance, who were concerned to establish a relation between acedia and humoral theory, divided into two major tendencies. In the first place, those who accepted the Gregorian dissolution of acedia in sorrow emphasized the links between this sin and melancholy. In the second place, those who preferred the original Cassinian version of the eight sins related acedia primarily to the phlegmatic humour.[19] In the first line of interpretation we find the poet Francesco Petrarch, who assimilated the *accidia* that he himself suffered with the *tristitia* of Seneca and the *ægritudo* of Cicero.[20] Another very different interpretation

Melancholy and Christianity

was that of Battista da Crema, who in his *Della cognitione et vittoria de se stesso* (1531) separates *tristitia* from *accidia*. Sadness or sorrow has its origin in the melancholic complexion and, according to the Pauline doctrine, may have a negative, secular expression or alternatively a divine form; in this, Battista da Crema reflects the Florentine Neoplatonists, such as Ficino, who had stressed the dual character of melancholy: 'a person of Saturnine nature is either an angel or a devil.'[21] In contrast, *accidia* does not harbour any positive alternative: on being associated with the phlegmatic humour it loses any intrinsic possibility of becoming inflamed and thus stimulating a vivacity of soul or even a spark that would light up the spirit to genius or mysticism. Acedia is a vice that keeps man submerged in a state of vexation, boredom, apathy and negligence. The Spanish version of Battista da Crema's book prepared by Melchor Cano in 1550 points out that the acedia provoked by the melancholic humour may drive the soul to desperation and, in certain cases, become a mortal sin beyond the reach of the physicians of the body.[22] In Battista da Crema acedia is connected more with the phlegm, a humour that, according to the Galenic tradition, cannot engender the dangerous 'adust' or combusted black bile; only the three remaining humours – blood, choler and natural black bile or *atrabilis* – may become inflamed to produce adust melancholy. By the sixteenth century Avicenna's thesis according to which the phlegm can also produce melancholy by adustion was beginning to be rejected.

It is the other line of interpretation which is of most interest to us here, since, thanks to the Gregorian fusion of acedia and sorrow, a connection could be made between the deadly sin and melancholy.[23] Petrarch, in his *Secretum*, defines acedia as a great sadness occasioned by discouragement in the face of the misfortunes of life, the frustrating remembrance of efforts made and fear of an uncertain future; this produces a hatred and contempt for the human condition, and reveals a great dissatisfaction with fortune. Petrarch does not limit himself to describing the capital sin: in the suffering of acedia he discovers a secret pleasure, a voluptuousness that grows alongside the pain; the delights produced by this sadness are a symptom of acedia, not a cure or a way out. Wenzel stresses that this conception of acedia makes no reference to the ills of the religious life, but describes it as a 'humanist sin' caused by intellectual reflection on the ups and downs of fortune.[24] This transformation of the traditional Christian meaning of acedia is a secularization that brings it close to the idea of melancholy.

Before Petrarch, we can point to an important example that provides evidence of a link between acedia and melancholy. I refer to the humoral images, images of blackness, with which Dante associates certain miserable characters, replete with 'acedious smoke (or fumes)' who, in the same circle of Hell (the fifth) in which the wrathful are made to suffer, are submerged in the mire, causing the black waters to bubble with their sighs: 'Sullen were we / in the sweet air, that's gladdened by the Sun, / bearing acedious smoke within our hearts; / now lie we sullen here in the black mire.'[25] Giorgio Agamben believes he has found another, even older, example of convergence between *tristitia-acedia* and melancholy: a letter from St Jerome establishes a connection between the black humour described by Hippocrates and the typical malaise affecting monks undergoing excessive solitude, fasting and study.[26] On the other hand, Wenzel himself recognizes the existence of iconographic evidence for this relation: the medieval representation of acedia was used in the Renaissance to symbolize melancholy, as has been shown by Klibansky, Panofsky and Saxl.[27]

In spite of the terrifying visions that accompanied acedia and melancholy, a texture survived that made it possible to understand that sorrow and the black humour could accompany – and even help – men in their path toward salvation and wisdom. There is no doubt, as Max Weber has noted, that Calvinism knew how to manipulate the affliction and distress brought on by the practice of asceticism, manifested in the form of terrible feelings of interior loneliness in individuals.[28] Weber also perceived that disillusioned and pessimistic individualism – as manifested for example in the melancholy of Robert Burton – is an expression of the national character of peoples with a Puritan past; nonetheless, the importance of the suffering of religious melancholy passed Weber by.[29] On the other hand, we should remember that Marsilio Ficino had already laid the foundations of a Renaissance tradition that turned its gaze toward Aristotelian ideas about the relation between genius and the black bile, and while perfectly aware of the baneful nature of the Saturnine humour which he strove to explain (having personally suffered its effects throughout his life), he originated an influential polyvalent canon that established the extraordinary though dangerous virtues of the black humour.[30] The legendary drama of Torquato Tasso – who in 1579, as a result of his melancholic madness, was imprisoned at Ferrara, where he remained for six years – is paradigmatic: the great poetic genius suffered an excess of melancholy, as he himself confessed.[31] The fact should also be mentioned that Galenic medicine, with the extensive application of the symptoms of melancholy, contributed to secularizing the notion of sorrow (*tristitia*), but gave pride of place to its malignant dimension. An important departure was Juan Huarte de San Juan, who, in his *Examen de ingenios para las ciencias* (1575), vindicated the positive aspects of the black bile.[32]

Thus we arrive at an extraordinary point of inflection, which has not been sufficiently studied: the conceptual axis that connects the *Examen de ingenios* with the *Ingenioso hidalgo don Quijote de la Mancha* is symptomatic and revealing of the many-faceted process by means of which Renaissance and Baroque Christian culture absorbed melancholy. It is worth pausing to consider the fact, since despite the wide dissemination in Europe both of *Don Quixote* and the *Examen*, and the latter's decisive influence on the expansion of the renewed interest in melancholy, this book has not received the attention it deserves.[33] The influence of the *Examen* on *Don Quixote* has indeed been noticed by researchers since 1905, when Miguel de Unamuno used Huarte in order to define Don Quixote's temperament as choleric, and Rafael Salillas remarked on the relation between the two texts.[34] Later, in 1938, Mauricio de Iriarte, in his important book on Huarte, once again stressed the close connection between the *Examen* and the *Quixote*.[35] Then, in 1957, an essay by Otis H. Green, based on Iriarte's book, concluded that Don Quixote, although he eventually dies of melancholy, is a choleric personality type.[36] Harald Weinrich, on the other hand, had found that the Knight of the Sad Countenance was a melancholic.[37] The ample study by Iriarte had already indicated that, seen from Huarte's point of view, Don Quixote – of a hot and dry temperament – would be both choleric and melancholy;[38] Green – who did not make direct use of Huarte's text – emphasized the fact that the pages of the *Quixote* were pervaded by humoral theory, but used as the basis of his analysis the English treatises on melancholy, and this was a severe limitation on his study.[39] Javier García Gibert's interpretation takes up Green's ideas without modification, despite the fact that they were of no use to him and tend, rather, to impair his otherwise stimulating study of melancholy in Cervantes.[40]

A study by Yvonne David-Peyre proposes that Cervantes used the model of melancholy defined by Huarte and Alonso Ponce de Santa Cruz, but inclines toward a diagnosis taken from twentieth-century psychiatry as a way to understanding Don Quixote's madness.[41] Another study, that of Chester Harka, upholds that Huarte virtually created a new temperament, the melancholic-choleric, and that this was to be the model used by Cervantes in his characterization of Don Quixote.[42] Actually, Harka confuses the choleric character with the adust melancholy produced by burnt choler (yellow bile). According to the Galenic tradition, melancholy could be either natural or adust, the former resulting from the natural black humour, and the latter being occasioned by the combustion of any of the natural humours, with the exception of the phlegm; the 'adust' humours were thus burned blood, choler or bile. Another study, by William Melczer, arrives at the conclusion that, although melancholy was the cause of his death, Don Quixote was created as an essentially anti-melancholy character, manic, exuberant, vital and imaginative.[43] Deborah Kong realized that Don Quixote's melancholy is caused by his yellow bile, that has first been burnt and has later cooled.[44] Teresa Soufas, on the other hand, diagnoses in Don Quixote the knight an active melancholy, adust and manic, but recognizes in Alonso Quijano the man, who is aware of his identity as an hidalgo, a natural, inactive and contemplative melancholy.[45]

The first thing that needs to be established, it seems to me, is that *Don Quixote* is immersed in a new intellectual texture that vindicates the positive although risk-laden nature of the black humour. An example of this new attitude is found in a 'Sonnet to Melancholy', recorded in one of the minutes of the poets who met in the Academia de los Nocturnos at Valencia; this poem, after describing the ills, the complaints, the loneliness and other tribulations suffered by those afflicted with this humour, finishes by pointing out its positive aspects:

> Who shall not say they in part do love the pain,
> since they displeasure take from what is glory,
> fleeing from pleasure that is glorious good.
>
> I hold him to be of a happy fortune,
> the melancholic in his temperament,
> having the power to reason without torment.[46]

In this connection Huarte's idea that St Paul himself could have been a melancholic – endowed by God with the great understanding and acute imagination necessary to reveal to the world the arrival of Christ – is revealing.[47] Huarte describes the painful oscillations of the melancholic: when the melancholy humour becomes heated people are lustful, proud, astute and vengeful, although fond of conversation and affable; but when the humour cools the opposite virtues appear: 'chastity, humility, awe and reverence for God, charity, pity and great contrition in recognition of their sins with sighs and tears.'[48] For this reason, says Huarte, when God decided to create in the womb of a woman the man capable of proving that Christ was the promised Messiah, he made him 'choleric adust'. It should be clarified here that Huarte was referring to the melancholic by adustion, as he himself explains.[49] In another part of the book Huarte describes the two types of melancholy:

> One natural, which is the excrement of the blood, which temperament is cold and dry, of a very coarse substance and of no use for wit; rather it makes men stubborn, clumsy and prone to laughter because they lack imagination. And there is that which they call black bile (*atrabilis*) or choler adust, of which Aristotle said that it makes men passing wise, and whose temperament is as variable as vinegar: at times it produces effects of heat, fomenting the earth[50] and at others it cools.[51]

The Apostle Paul, Huarte explains, felt a tremendous struggle between his mind, subject to the divine law, and his bodily parts, slaves to the law of sin (he refers to Romans 7:23). Huarte concludes that melancholics, like St Paul, may be good at preaching, although they suffer from a lack of heat and only moderate dryness, factors that make it difficult for them to become great orators, since they do not have a natural 'gift of the gab'. The capacity for oratory is not common among melancholics, whether natural or by adustion.[52] Also, and this is important, melancholy may be acquired through contemplation, prayer and meditation, since these activities cool and dry the body; he sustains this by reference to *Problem XXX, 1*, in order to demonstrate that all men who are outstanding for their genius are melancholics,[53] and agrees with the moral philosophers who recommend meditation and the contemplation of divine things in order to acquire 'the temperament of which the rational soul stands in need'.[54] It is worth noting that Don Quixote compares himself to St Paul, although he acknowledges himself a sinner and not a saint.[55]

Don Quixote dried out his brains, not through prayer and contemplation, but by reading so many chivalric romances and spending sleepless nights meditating on his obsessive attempts to 'understand and unbowel their sense'.[56] The result is that he loses his wits and decides to become, neither a preacher nor a saint, but a knight errant. The difficulty of identifying the peculiarities of Don Quixote's melancholy is due not only to complexity of Cervantes's novel, but also to the contradictory nature of the temperaments associated with the black humour, and which are, as Huarte points out, extremely various. It is evident that Cervantes frequently plays with metaphors and images that make allusion to melancholy, but it is not always possible to make the melancholic model fit the Knight of the Sorrowful Countenance. It should also be noted that, if it was the reading of chivalric romances that drove Don Quixote mad, Cervantes points out from the beginning that his story intends 'that the melancholy man, by the reading thereof, may be urged to laughter'.[57] In one of the first mentions of the subject, Don Quixote himself cannot refrain from laughing when he sees that his tremendous fear at the horrible noises heard during the night was occasioned by the innocent rhythmic blows of a fuller's mill

> Don Quixote looked also on his squire, and saw his cheeks swollen with laughter, giving withal evident signs that he was in danger to burst if he vented not that passion; whereat all Don Quixote's melancholy little prevailing, he could not, beholding Sancho, but laugh also himself.[58]

On another occasion, Sancho's ludicrous kisses bestowed on the Gentleman of the Green Kaftan also sets off Don Quixote's laughter despite his 'profound melancholy'.[59] In a conversation with the Canon, Don Quixote himself recommends the cleric to read books of chivalry, for 'you shall find that they will exile all the melancholy that shall trouble you, and rectify your disposition, if by fortune it be depraved'.[60] What is important in this Quixotic recommendation is that it is preceded by a strange image that provides us with clues for understanding the metaphor of melancholy in the novel. In order to help the canon appreciate the importance of the books of chivalrous adventure, Don Quixote invites him to imagine, 'A great lake of pitch boiling hot, and many serpents, snakes, lizards, and other kinds of cruel and dreadful beasts swimming athwart it, and in every part of it . . .'

From within it a 'most lamentable voice' is heard, inviting the knight to submerge himself in what we might call the lake of melancholy:

> if thou desirest to obtain the good concealed under these horrid and black waters, show the valour of thy strong breast, and throw thyself into the midst of this sable and inflamed liquor; for if thou dost not so, thou shalt not be worthy to discover the great wonders hidden in the seven castles of the seven fates, which are seated under these gloomy waves.

The knight, Don Quixote goes on, hurls himself into the boiling lake and soon finds himself in a flowery meadow more beautiful than the Elysian Fields. He crosses the verdant expanse, walking beside a rivulet 'whose fresh waters [resemble] liquid crystal' and a fountain of jasper and marble, and arrives at a castle with walls of solid gold and crenellations of diamonds: there he is led by a group of maidens to a genuine erotic paradise. The principal maiden takes the bold knight by the hand and leads him 'into the rich castle or palace without speaking a word' and then she has him strip 'naked as he was when his mother bore him, and bathe[s] him in very temperate waters, and afterwards anoint[s] him all over with precious ointments'. After dining on the most delicious foods and listening to the most delightful music, another damsel arrives 'on a sudden', more beautiful than all the rest, and sits beside the knight.[61] The narrator leaves what remains of the story floating in the imagination and its message is also insinuated: in order to reach the marvellous experience of an erotic happiness without limits it is necessary first to throw oneself into the black and awful lake of melancholy.

This lake is a simulacrum of the damaging infernal waters that appear in medieval literature as a derivation of the river Styx of Greek mythology, and of course reminds us of the swampy lagoon of the acedious sinners of Dante. But Don Quixote's lake of melancholy is the gate of entry to a marvellous paradisaical space; in another adventure, while passing through a wood, the knight of La Mancha encounters some beautiful girls disguised as shepherdesses; they explain that the hidalgos and the other leading residents of a nearby village have formed a 'new and pastoral Arcadia' to which they invite him to enter as their guest, and tell him: 'for the moment into this place neither grief nor melancholy shall enter.'[62]

The idea that melancholy surrounds the man who is unable to attain the erotic satisfaction he desires seems to be insinuated in an explanation that Don Quixote gives of his sadness to the Duchess, amazed at the 'madness and wit' of the knight: 'The Duchess became aware of his melancholy and asked him what it was that made him sad, whether it was on account of the absence of Sancho.' The knight answers that 'this is not the principal cause that makes me appear sad', a typical allusion to the play of appearances that characterizes the novel. Melancholy is an appearance whose cause is guarded in silence; but when the Duchess offers him four damsels, beautiful as flowers, to serve him, the knight expresses his wish to isolate himself in his chambers: 'for I put a wall between my desires and my honesty', and he prefers to sleep in all his clothes than allow the maidens to undress him.[63] The desire the damsels awaken in him, or the erotic memory they arouse in him of his unreachable Dulcinea, oblige him to carry out a simulacrum of melancholy, a genuine solitary exercise of artificial sorrow.[64] This is precisely the recommendation of Huarte: besides praying, contemplating and meditating, in order to attain the cold and dry melancholy it is necessary to 'go aside from women'.[65]

This mimetic and ingenious melancholy is, it seems to me, the key to the diagnosis of Don Quixote, who has made imitation his principal coinage. We could say that Don Quixote performs an Imitation – rather than a Praise – of Folly. René Girard is of the opinion that the essence of Don Quixote's vision of chivalry is in the imitation of Amadis of Gaul, in the same way that the essence of Christianity is in the imitation of Jesus Christ.[66] Indeed, Don Quixote, in the Sierra Morena, imagines for himself two alternatives: 'whether were it better to imitate Orlando in his unmeasurable furies, than Amadis in his melancholy moods.'[67] And he puts these two types of madness into practice: he first strips himself naked and becomes an artificial savage (or wild man) in the style of Ariosto's *Orlando the Furious*,[68] and afterwards opts for the life of sorrow: 'Let the remembrance of Amadis live', he exclaimed, 'and be imitated in everything as much as may be, by Don Quixote of the Mancha.'[69] And the imitation now takes the form of a religious melancholy, like that of Amadis when he withdrew to the Peña Pobre in the company of a hermit, and where, paradoxically, he achieved the fame of a man in love by virtue of praying, weeping and commending himself to God. In his fit of artificial sorrow, Don Quixote fashions a rosary out of a strip torn from his shirt, full of knots, and writes – between sobs and sighs and appeals to the nymphs, fauns and sylvans of the forest – the most amusing verses:

> Love doth him cruelly wrest
> With a passion of evil descent
> Which robb'd Don Quixote of rest,
> Till a cask with tears was full prest,
> Dulcinea's want to lament
>   Of Toboso.[70]

What differentiates the imitation of the melancholy of Amadis from the imitation of Christ is that Cervantes introduces playfulness and humour, and along with these qualities – and more important – artificiality: Don Quixote imitates the melancholy of Amadis, but this is no more than an artifice since he does so without cause or reason, in the same way as he knots a rosary out of his shirt-tail with which he vainly prays 'a million Ave Marias'. Cervantes was aware of the scarcely respectful (indeed indecent) nature of this method of putting together a rosary and censored himself for the second edition:[71] he changed the rags to acorns of the cork-oak and eliminated the million Ave Marias. This only serves to emphasize the fact that we are dealing with a play of imitations in which religious sorrow is feigned without there being any active reason for playing the part of a hermit. This melancholy is as fictitious as the fervour with which the knight fashions a rosary with his shirt-tail. Marcel Bataillon is right to compare this way of praying to Pedro de Urdemalas's affirmation that he prays 'out of courtesy'.[72]

Thus, the difficulty of explaining Don Quixote's melancholy arises from the fact of its being inserted within a simulacrum, and also from the fact that its very diverse symptoms obey not only the variety of forms acquired by the adustion of the humours, but also the diversity of literary artifices that the action of the novel requires. It is therefore not easy to know for certain whether the Quixotic simulacrum of melancholy expresses a genuine sorrow or is merely an ingenious invention. I cannot agree with Melczer's interpretation, according to which in the mind of Cervantes Don Quixote does not appear as a melancholic, but, rather, that melancholy is what dominates the anti-Quixotic world that the knight is trying to reform and cure.[73] It is true that on a number of occasions the text refers to the melancholy that exists in the world. For example: the Princess Micomicona is fatigued by '*malenconía*';[74] a bad omen causes 'melancholy to pour into the heart' of a superstitious person;[75] a poor galley-slave burdened with chains has scarcely the strength to reply to Don Quixote, 'he went so sad and melancholy';[76] there are some governments that are '*malencónicos*';[77] the river Guadiana 'everywhere it went, betrayed its sadness and melancholy';[78] the sound of music, on one occasion, was 'very sad and melancholy';[79] and even Rocinante appears 'melancholy and sad'.[80] But it is precisely the simulacrum of artificial melancholy – together with other ingenious follies – that may delight the world and offer the hope of salvation, in a peculiar application *avant la lettre* of modern homeopathic medicine: *simila similibus curantur*.

His melancholy enables Don Quixote to understand that there is a malignant enchanter that turns the world upside down. It is possible that the image of this wise enchanter may have inspired the famous malign spirit ('*genius malignum*') of Descartes,[81] but the French thinker was horrified at the idea that melancholic delirium might have a positive function in the comprehension of the world. The Cartesian demon causes havoc in the senses of the thinker and sows doubt in him; but the wise enchanter of Don Quixote not only deceives the knight, but is also capable of turning the external world upside down. Descartes would seem expressly to reject Don Quixote's melancholic mimesis when he says in his *Meditations*:

> Perhaps I could compare myself to madmen whose brains are so damaged by the persistent vapours of melancholy, that they firmly believe that they are kings when they are paupers, or that they go dressed in purple when they are naked, or that their heads are made of porcelain or that they are pumpkins or that they are made of glass. But these people are demented and I would be taken for one equally insane if I took something from them as a model for myself.[82]

Faced with the terrible malignant genie of doubt Descartes opposes his immutable conviction; even though he might be deceived, at least he is sure of one thing: that he exists. In contrast, Don Quixote, from the cage in which he is being driven upon a cart, says, 'I know, and do verily persuade myself, that I am enchanted, and that is sufficient for the discharge of my conscience'. Sancho, who has tried to make him doubt by pointing out to him his hardly enchanting bodily needs to evacuate 'lesser and greater waters', ends up acknowledging that Rocinante 'also seems enchanted, so sad and melancholy he goes'.[83]

Finally, Don Quixote is defeated by the 'bachelor' Sansón Carrasco, who – in an attempt to cure him – obliges him to retire from the life of the knight errant. The very playful Catalan gentleman, who has amused himself immensely with Don Quixote, protests to Sansón:

> 'Oh, sir', said Don Antonio, 'God forgive you the injury you have done the whole world in wishing to make sane the most amusing madman there is in it! Do you not see, sir, that the benefit caused by the sanity of Don Quixote can never equal the pleasure he gives with his follies? [. . .] and if it were not against charity I would say "may Don Quixote never be cured!" because with his health we not only lose his own graces but those of this squire, for either of them might delight melancholy itself.'[84]

There is a significant aspect that is worth emphasizing here: the mocking and playful attitude with which the sad knight and his squire are received throughout the novel is not a caprice of Cervantes, but rather corresponds to one of the most significant forms of courtly behaviour of the period, as can be gathered from Baldassare Castiglione's influential *Book of the Courtier*.[85] The rules of courtly life defined the accepted forms of exercising the art of mockery without falling into what Hoby, in his first English translation of the book, renders as 'immoderate jesting' and the poet Boscán, the translator of the first Spanish version, as *truhanería* (which could be translated as knavishness or roguery, but also buffoonery), so that the courtier might learn how to be a 'a man of wit' (*hombre gracioso*, according to Boscán) and thus escape from tedium and melancholy.[86] This courtly mockery is 'a deceit that may come to pass between friends regarding things that in nothing offend, or at the least in little'.[87] The victims of courtly jests were often common people, like the case related by Castiglione of a villager from near Bergamo, who could almost be Sancho Panza, whom they disguised in order to introduce him to some unsuspecting ladies, who were thus made the butt of the jest, as the 'best courtier in all Spaine'.[88]

In the context of these courtly jests, we may better understand the way in which, in *Don Quixote*, artificial melancholy may serve to cure the real thing. But when artificial melancholy is overcome, true melancholy causes havoc. Don Quixote's two types of melancholy bear the same name, but we may assume that the one that kills him is a manifestation of the ancient and perilous acedia, which has prostrated him in indifference.

After his defeat, Don Quixote represents the 'saddest and most melancholy figure that sadness could form'.[89] When he finally returns home and is cured of his madness, he falls seriously ill: 'whether it was on account of the melancholy produced in him on seeing himself vanquished, or by disposition of Heaven which ordered it so, a fever took hold of him, which had him laid in bed for six days.' When the doctor examines him he immediately recognizes the danger, and his diagnosis is 'that melancholies and loss of pleasure in life were putting an end to him'.[90] The paradox is that in his melancholy Don Quixote asks Sancho to forgive him for having led him into error and caused him to appear mad like himself, to which his squire replies with some words that are the key to the whole book:

> Don't die Sir, my lord, but take my advice and live many years because the greatest folly that a man can commit in this life is to let himself die just like that, without being killed by anyone, nor by any hands but those of melancholy.[91]

And in order to make clear the difference between this negative form of melancholy and his state of luminous chivalrous madness, Sancho immediately follows up with a reference to the less spiritual version of acedia: he begs his master not to be lazy, to get out of bed and set off in search of the no-longer enchanted Dulcinea.

It seems to me important to emphasize the fact that *Don Quixote* was both an expression of, and a vehicle for, the popularization of the new forms of the canon of melancholy. Cervantes brought together in his novel the rich baggage of the Italian and Spanish Renaissance on melancholy, the same that was concentrated in the work of Huarte, but which came to his hands through the medical and popular tradition that surely must have been passed on to him by his father, a modest itinerant surgeon and apothecary. As for the subsequent influence of Quixotic melancholy, we also find complex and contradictory tendencies. During the seventeenth century *Don Quixote* was seen by many intellectuals as a fierce criticism of the immoralities disseminated by the novels of chivalry. Even as late as 1737, for example, Gregorio Mayans understood *Don Quixote* as a powerful brake on the pernicious influence of novels of chivalry, that both 'effeminize' and 'stir up' the spirits by inciting to dishonest passionate amours and the most monstrous feats of bravery or folly.[92] Mayans believed that the malign influence of these novels was a continuation of the pernicious Milesian fables and of other reprehensible texts, among which he mentions Italian sybaritic fables, the Talmudic or Cabbalistic stories, the Mohammedan Koran, the inventions of the Anabaptists and picaresque novels:[93] in other words, all the expressions of otherness that alarmed the conservative Spain of the eighteenth century. I mention the example of Mayans as symptomatic; although he refers only to the genre of the picaresque, he offers the type of critique that could in fact also be applied to *Don Quixote* itself: 'on the pretext of warning against the picaresque life, it teaches it.'[94] Irrespective of the intentions of Cervantes – upon which I do not wish to speculate – the fact is that *Don Quixote* presents a highly attractive and amusing model to its readers. The enormous fascination it has exercised is due above all to its extraordinary psychological subtlety and the alluring complexity of its ironies, parodies and paradoxes.

As for the subject of melancholy, the Quixotic model remains captivating because of its comic manner of stringing together a multitude of planes. Presented as a book for amusing melancholics, it does so by means of an artificially sad character who imagines all sorts of illusions in order to console us, to the point of making the world around him organize and represent for him the comic–melancholic simulacra that give life to the novel – until the down-to-earth bachelor Sansón Carrasco arrives and, by means of another simulacrum, cures the hidalgo's artificial sorrow and causes him to fall into the gloomy abyss of a terminal melancholy. In this way *Don Quixote* taught the readers of its period how to enjoy melancholy in a new way. Here, melancholy is not a sin, nor is it the work of the Devil: it is a fashion, a way of being modern while imitating – and even criticizing – the ancients. Nevertheless, Cervantes – as Erich Auerbach has observed – does not hold this model up for our admiration, nor does he use it to describe existential tensions in the face of destiny or to criticize the social milieu; he simply plays with it and invites us to be amused.[95]

Thus, in *Don Quixote* we not only see the dichotomy melancholy–sorrow operating in a secular space. There is another ingredient, the mimetic reflection, which gives melancholy a new dimension and contributes to the expansion of the melancholic canon throughout Europe and its readoption in other periods as a symbol of the Enlightenment, Romanticism and Modernism. This new ingredient, the *mimesis*, does not have its origin in the medical tradition, which is governed by the Hippocratic axiom: *contraria contrariis curantur*. The imitation of madness could not be a remedy recommended by doctors to cure the sicknesses of the secular world.

We may, on the other hand, find the roots of imitation and simulation in theology, in the theatre and in the world of the court. The sorrow inspired by God might help cure secular and worldly sorrow, in the same way that a certain type of melancholy – or something very similar – might be encountered on the path taken by mystics in the attempt to come closer to God. We cannot in any case avoid noting the influence of the theatrical metaphors, so common at the time, that envisaged the world as a great theatre; Don Quixote himself refers to this in his reflections after a chance meeting with a group of actors who were on their way to perform the '*auto sacramental*', *Las Cortes de la Muerte*: their simulation is a mirror held up to human life.[96] Better than any comparison, the players represent 'in a more living form what we are and what we should be'.[97] The courtly world, in contrast, was governed by customs and rules aimed at adorning personal life with forms suitable for attaining the favour of princes, serving them with grace and earning the praise of everyone else, as was recognized by Baldassare Castiglione in *The Book of the Courtier*.[98] Although the increasing complexity of courtly ceremony tended to conceal beneath its multiple appearances the harshness of life, courtiers, like theatrical players, had to be past masters of pretence. We can thus trace a connecting line between the cultivation of bodily dryness in order to help attain mystical ecstasy, the acting of a member of a company of mummers disguised as Death, and the play of prudent or courtly appearances of the 'man free of illusions'[99] referred to by Baltasar Gracián.[100] What they all have in common is artifice and imitation, so characteristic of Baroque culture.

It is worth pausing at this point, nevertheless, to compare Don Quixote's sophisticated simulacrum of melancholy with the crude dissimulation portrayed in a comedy attributed to Lope de Vega, the *Comedia del príncipe melancólico*, written between 1588 and 1595.[101] Although Lope de Vega's authorship of this play is doubtful, it is worth examining it as an interesting reflection of the

Baroque culture of dissimulation. The contrast with *Don Quixote* will help us to highlight the peculiarities which Cervantes impresses on melancholy, even while recognizing an affinity in the predilection of Baroque literature for the play of simulations.[102] The comedy ascribed to Lope de Vega portrays the rivalry between two brothers, sons of the King of Hungary, who are in competition for the love of their cousin, the Duchess Rosilena. She prefers the younger prince Leonido, which gives rise to the anger of the heir to the throne (referred to throughout as the Príncipe), who wishes to kill his brother. But later on the disdained Príncipe changes his strategy and, with the complicity of his valet Fabio, decides to pretend to have fallen prey to a terrible melancholy. And so, the Príncipe begins to scream and shout, falls into a pit of infinite despair, affirms he is being consumed by fire, that he wants to die, and blames his father the King for his strange bicephalous condition: 'Why, my lord, have you commanded / two heads to grow upon me?' (344: 2). When it is demonstrated to him that he has only one head, he accuses them of having stolen the other one and hidden it away. Unlike the feigned melancholy of Don Quixote, that of the Príncipe is an opportunistic madness whose purpose is to cause consternation in all and thus obtain the hand of the Duchess Rosilena. As a final touch in the pattern of his symptoms, the Príncipe declares that he has become invisible, that he is a giant or a woman, refuses to eat and is obviously raving:

> I am thoughts and smoke
> And woman, which is much less,
> And my breasts are full
> Of the evil that consumes me.
> I am insufferable thought,
> I am pain that never ends
> And a ferocious beast
> Hard and incomprehensible. [347: 1]

The diagnosis given by another character in the play, Count Marcelo, is clear: ''Tis great melancholy, / That cools the heart / And doth fill the breast.'[103] The Príncipe's simulated melancholy sets in motion a grotesque succession of dissimulations: two servants disguise themselves as corpses in winding-sheets in order to convince the melancholic that he must eat, since even the dead like themselves experience hunger (they are driven out to the accompaniment of blows); Count Marcelo pretends he is Rosilena's husband in order to prevent the King marrying her; but Rosilena in turn pretends to be pregnant by the Count, in order to test the love of Leonido (who suffers terrible fits of jealousy); afterwards she pretends to love the Príncipe, but lays a trap for him and makes him confess his imposture:

> ROSILENA: Is't possible? A mockery has been
> This melancholy?
> PRÍNCIPE: Yes, by your life and mine,
> A counterfeit 't has been. [362: 2]

Of course, everything works out badly for the dissimulating prince. As the play draws to its conclusion he himself tires of the 'job of pretending' [356: 2], and the spectators will also, perhaps, have become bored with the long and involved plot of pretence and deceit. Quixotic melancholy is based on simulacrum and imitation and lacks any utilitarian purpose. Melancholy in the *comedia* attributed to Lope de Vega, on the other hand, shows the corruption of the court in the deceitful simulation of the impostor who takes advantage of his friends and his family. In *El príncipe melancólico* there is a critique and an indictment of simulated melancholy; in *Don Quixote* we find a sublimation of the Baroque play of simulations that transcends the mere stereotype of pretence.

Thus Don Quixote's artificial sorrow is a Baroque melancholy that synthesizes in a parodic canon certain very diverse cultural traditions of the Spanish Renaissance: the new medicine, mysticism, dramaturgy and courtly behaviour. The best of the Golden Age is brought together in Baroque melancholy, which we may proceed to anatomize by studying its essential components, using *Don Quixote* as a point of vantage, then examining Huarte, St John of the Cross, Tirso de Molina and Baltasar Gracián, writers who reflected, in their different ways, on the 'humour of wits' ('el humor de los ingenios'), the dark nights of the soul, the noble melancholic, and the artificial prudence of the men of their times. This is a melancholy deeply immersed in Christian culture, and its great novelty resides in its flexible and many-faceted nature.

To gain a more complete appreciation of the singularity of Spanish Baroque melancholy we can hardly do better than to contrast it with its English manifestations, strongly tinged with Puritanism. Thus, as Cervantes surely read Dr Huarte's *Examen de ingenios*, it seems that Shakespeare knew the *Treatise of Melancholie* written by Dr Timothy Bright, and possibly used it as a model for the character of Hamlet. The melancholy that gnaws the Prince of Denmark from within, tormenting his soul, besieged by the mysteries of the world and bitter doubts, is very different from that suffered by Don Quixote, in the same way that the melancholy described by Bright is different in many ways from that which interested Huarte.

Timothy Bright was born around 1550; he was first a physician and then a man of the cloth. His treatise on melancholy was published in 1586 by a Huguenot refugee who had established himself in London as a publisher and was concerned to disseminate the expressions of Puritanism. Bright's treatise gives direct expression to the typical anxieties of Protestants, haunted by the phantom of original sin and denied the alleviating effect of confession and expiation as enjoyed by Catholics. While the latter could attain absolution of their sins, Protestants must endure the weight of guilt and aspire only to consolation. Bright explains in his treatise that it is possible to cure melancholics, but that those attacked by the weight of a religious sorrow, originating in the consciousness of guilt, can be consoled but never cured. For Bright, melancholy is a pernicious ill and, unlike Huarte, he does not accord it any relation with genius or wit; he is primarily concerned to establish a clear distinction between the sickness produced by the black humour and the desolation of the conscience afflicted by sin; the latter, according to Bright, is not, properly speaking, melancholy. Following the tradition, he distinguishes the natural melancholy from the adust; the combusted form is presented as three different kinds of inflammation: that of the black humour, which generates sadness; that of the blood, which produces an absurd joy; and that of choler or yellow bile, which induces rages, furies and desires for vengeance. Later he describes, doubtless without being aware of the analogy, the havoc wrought by the inflammation of the divine choler. In the same way as the burnt yellow bile in human beings, the inflamed choler of God unleashes desires for vengeance against the guilty soul of the sinner.[104] But there is a fundamental difference between the inflammation of the humour in human beings and the adustion of the divine choler: in the first case the soul is not essentially affected,[105] while the vengeance of God destroys the entire nature of man, both body and soul.[106] Melancholy may 'importune the soul',[107] but the inflamed choler of God produces total confusion, extreme terror and anguish without limits; there is no remedy for this suffering that derives from original sin and from the fear of divine chastisement. To the degree that all men are sinners, explains Bright, nobody is spared this threat. But those who suffer from melancholy are more exposed than others to the dangers of absolute desperation, and are drawn to study, erudition and natural philosophy; the anxiety of the melancholic leads him to enter into mysteries that surpass human capacities of understanding: he must then suffer the due punishment for the rash investigation of sacred arcana that the Lord has reserved for His own contemplation alone, and to his bodily illness are added the intolerable effects of the choler of God.[108]

Of course, Hamlet's melancholy is of an extraordinary richness and complexity when compared with what was in the mind of Dr Bright. In Hamlet, melancholy is not only the source of his disillusion, his discontent, his bitterness and his misogyny; it is also, as Bridget Gellert Lyons observes, the origin of the superior forms of imagination, knowledge and meditation that characterize the protagonist.[109] Nonetheless, a moral vision of melancholy is what predominates: one which grows as an answer to the corruption of the world that surrounds the Prince. We cannot at this point fail to recognize that Shakespeare praises in Hamlet – as Harold Jenkins has so well pointed out – the man who, after questioning the sense of creation, finally accepts that it comprises a design beyond our understanding, and after abhorring life is happy to accept it as it is, to accept in the end that 'readiness is all'.[110]

I think that we can link this peculiar 'readiness'[111] attained by Hamlet at the end of the play with the vocation or calling (*Beruf*) which for Max Weber is the foundation-stone of the construction of the modern capitalist soul. To attain this readiness it was necessary to pass first through the anxieties and sufferings of that profound sorrow described by Bright. Robert Burton, who was less rigorous than Bright, did not hesitate to accept that this religious affliction was a form of melancholy, and even defined it as a variant of love melancholy, due to the loss or privation of the object of one's desires. Burton was an Anglican and thus looked with distaste on the severity of the Puritans, which could well lead to very dangerous melancholic conditions; he recommended moderation in the face of religious excess.[112]

The melancholic of the southern tradition, unlike the Protestant of the north, lived immersed in the treacherous whirlpool of decisions that his awareness of free will imposed upon him.¹¹³ In Don Quixote, melancholy itself is a choice, an act of will and an affirmation of liberty. Another extraordinary example is the melancholic peregrination along the roads of the world undertaken by Andrenio and Critilo, in Gracián's *El criticón*. These travellers of life go from one crossroads to another, always running the risk of losing their way. If they should err, choosing for example the paths of Falismundo, Volusia, Falsirena, Céprope or Hipocrinda, the responsibility falls on the shoulders of the travellers and not on the heritage of original sin: for the same reason, the pilgrims of the world may return to the path that leads them towards the island of immortality. But on the threshold of the final station, melancholy takes hold of Andrenio and Critilo; they arrive at old age at the feet of the white-topped Alps in the cold kingdom of ill humours:

> 'What an ill-tempered region is this!' bemoaned Andrenio.
>
> 'And how unhealthy!' retorted Critilo. 'The fervours of the blood here give way to the horrors of melancholy, laughter for cries of lamentation: everything is coldness and sorrow.'¹¹⁴

These men have interiorized in a tragic way their condition of free choosers of life and bear in their souls the crossroads; all men in old age are Janus: 'at this terminus of life all of us tread two different worlds simultaneously and walk with two faces.'¹¹⁵

In contrast with Protestant man, Gracián's critical heroes move through life in a permanent act of migration, from one difficult choice to another in search of salvation, like Don Quixote behind his chimeras. Not even melancholy is capable of calling a halt to life, a wantonness that would have horrified the Puritan man who lived like a tree, clinging with his roots to the original sin in which they were plunged, and resisting, immutable, the tempests of life. In England a tolerant and humanist spirit like John Milton was necessary in order to recognize in Melancholy a way for inspiration, as he did in his poem *Il Penseroso*; the fact is that Milton – author of the greatest epic poem on original sin – in spite of his Calvinism, recognized the importance of free will and reason. Before him, John Dowland, the great English lutenist and composer – who had strong leanings towards Catholicism – had published in 1604 the disquieting collection of seven pavanes that, under the title of *Lacrimae*, explore the labyrinths of melancholy in obsessive circles and take us from the ancient (*Lachrimae antiquae*) and moaning (*gementes*) tears to the amorous (*amantes*) and genuine ones (*verae*), by way of the sad tears (*tristes*) and, ironically, the false tears of the crocodile (*coactae*).[116]

With justice, the melancholy of the sixteenth and seventeenth centuries has been seen as an exacerbation of self-consciousness, and Milton has been regarded as a prime example of this.[117] The authors of *Saturn and Melancholy* observe that since the second half of the sixteenth century, under the terrible pressure of religious conflict, melancholy had a determining effect on even the physical appearance of the people of the time, and opened the way to new tensions.

> This unleashing of dynamic forces occurred for the first time in the Baroque period and – something of great significance – bore its richest harvest of fruit in the countries where the tension, which was to feed artistic expression, was most alive: in the Spain of Cervantes, where the Baroque expanded under the rod of iron of a particularly severe form of Catholicism, and even more so in the England of Shakespeare and Donne, where it reaffirmed itself in the face of a proudly self-assured Protestantism. These two countries came to occupy – and there they remained – the privileged sphere of this properly modern, and consciously cultivated, melancholy.[118]

Unfortunately, this is the last mention of Cervantes in the vast work on *Saturn and Melancholy*, but it is highly revealing of the problem that I am dealing with here.[119] Nevertheless, to understand the connections that link Renaissance melancholy to the modern variety exemplified in John Milton, Thomas Gray and John Keats – and whose culmination is in Romanticism – it is absolutely indispensable to study the fundamental role of *Don Quixote* and other expressions of the Saturnine humour during the Spanish Golden Age. Cervantes's work contributes that peculiar combination of comic irony and stubborn free will so characteristic of the Baroque culture of the Spanish Counter-reformation, and without which it was difficult for modern melancholy to develop as a new form of acute consciousness of individuality: it is that speculative and meditative Quixoticism, that maintains a marked distance from religion of which Miguel de Unamuno spoke, and which connects with introspective individualism.[120] Without these peculiarities it is impossible to conceive of those romantic and modern ways of deliberately cultivating the adust humour and of positively evaluating the pain produced by the closeness of death and unattainability of love.

One of the best-known interpretations of the melancholy of *Don Quixote* maintains that its root is to be found in the great sense of disillusion experienced by the Spanish of the Golden Age on seeing how their venerable and cherished ideals fell to pieces on coming into collision with modernity. Ramiro de Maeztu had already perceived in Don Quixote 'the melancholy that a man and a people feel on losing faith in their ideal'.[121] Lukács had arrived at a similar conclusion through his Marxist analysis: Don Quixote embodied 'the deep melancholy of the very course of history', a course in which the 'eternal contents' lose their meaning before the inexorable passing of time.[122] The new era converts man into a solitary being, torn apart by the great transition towards modernity. A study by Javier García Gibert on melancholy in Cervantes follows this same line of interpretation, and proposes that Don Quixote's madness is the beautiful but ridiculous chimera of a Spain ensconced in outdated ideals, while his final opting for good judgement is the necessary but lethal alternative making it possible to cross the threshold into modernity. According to this interpretation, Quixotic melancholy is thus the great epistemological divide separating the ancient from the modern.[123]

Certainly, this explanation allows us to understand different facets of Cervantes's black humour and may also apply to the whole broad renaissance of melancholy that extends from Ficino in the fifteenth century to Burton in the seventeenth. But it is a general interpretation that may not help us very much to understand the concrete forms in which melancholy makes its appearance at the dawn of modernity. As regards *Don Quixote*, for example, it is necessary not only to observe that Cervantes's novel reflects the great tragedy of the transition to modernity, but to appreciate also, and above all, its original contributions – genuine mutations – that ensure the continuity of the great myth of melancholy. The black humours that darken the mind of Don Quixote are not only the expression of a rupture: they are also the luminous link in a long chain which continues to connect us to Antiquity, the Middle Ages and the Renaissance.

Melancholy evolved, at the dawn of modernity, to take on the form of a great myth. This myth – given impulse paradoxically by the medical sciences – on being adopted by Christian culture became, in turn, a great amplifier and accelerator of individualizing tendencies. Melancholy contributed decisively to give impulse to this peculiar enthronement of the ego and personal identity, which is found at the heart of modern subjectivity. I do not believe that the Christian tradition alone could have opened the way to this modern individualism: it was first necessary for Christianity to be impregnated by certain structures of pre-Christian mythical thought. On being fertilized by melancholy, Christianity turned its gaze back to the Bible and the exegetes found prefigurations of the myth, principally in Paul's Second Epistle to the Corinthians, where, as I have already mentioned, the apostle establishes the existence of two types of sorrow. But this does not mean that the myth of melancholy has its origin in St Paul. Western modernity is not to be found – in complete though embryonic form – in the biblical texts.

As I have argued, this process did not take place simply as the continuation of an ancient tradition, whose ancient genealogy and evolution can be traced across the millennia. Certain mutations to the ancient canon were also necessary, which permitted the survival of the myth of melancholy and its 'refunctionalizing'. Don Quixote's melancholy is one of those mutations. Cervantes's novel harvests the exotic fruit of melancholy, but submits it to a mutation so extraordinary that he succeeds in implanting it in lasting form at the heart of European culture.

Thus, to return to the image with which I began this chapter: if we wish to go exploring the family tree of Christianity, we should, like Eve in the Garden of Eden, not forget to sample its forbidden fruit. And let us remember that such fruit were not created to survive for a long time, but only succeed in propagating themselves when someone picks them.

NOTES

[1] Published in English as *The Survival of the Pagan Gods* (New York, 1953).
[2] Published in London by Nelson, 1964. Panofsky and Saxl had already published, in German, their research into Dürer, Saturn and melancholy in 1923. My references here are to the more recent French edition of 1989: *Saturne et la Mélancolie*.
[3] See Frances A. Yates, *The Occult Philosophy in the Elizabethan Age* (London: Routledge & Kegan Paul, 1979), ch. 2.
[4] See the essay by José Ramón Enríquez, 'Gerión el mestizo y el teatro del Siglo de Oro', in *Pánico escénico* (Mexico City: Dirección de Literatura, UNAM, 1997), which puts forward the idea that Fernando

de Rojas makes a brilliant use of the *taqiyya* to conceal what at base is an invitation to mad love.
5   See Klibansky, Panofsky and Saxl, *Saturne et la Mélancolie*.
6   Teresa Scott Soufas, *Melancholy and the Secular Mind in Spanish Golden Age Literature* (Columbia: University of Missouri Press, 1990). Christine Orobitg has also make an important contribution to the study of Spanish melancholy in her extremely useful monograph, *L'humeur noire, Mélancolie, écriture et pensée en Espagne au XVIe et au XVIIe siècle* (Bethesda, MD: International Scholars Publications, n.d., *c.*1997). Orobitg's book contains a considerable amount of valuable references, but does not address the subject of *Don Quixote*.
7   Wind, *Pagan Mysteries in the Renaissance* (Harmondsworth: Peregrine, 1967), p. 69
8   Ibid., p. 83.
9   *Melancholy and the Secular Mind in Spanish Golden Age Literature*, p. 36.
10 Ibid., pp. 5 and 71.
11 *Stanze, La parola e il fantasma nella cultura occidentale* (Turin: Einaudi, 1977), ch. 2.
12 Siegfried Wenzel, *The Sin of Sloth: Acedia in Medieval Thought and Literature* (Chapel Hill: University of North Carolina Press, 1967).
13 In the English text of this psalm, which is number 91 in the Authorized Version, there is no mention of this 'demon', which has been rendered in less concrete form as 'the destruction that wasteth at noonday'.
14 *De institutis coenobiorum et de octo principalium vitiorum remediis libri XII*, X, p. 1. Cited by Reinhard Kuhn, *The Demon of Noontide. Ennui in Western Literature* (Princeton: Princeton University Press, 1976), p. 50. The eight vices, according to Cassianus, are: gluttony (*gastrimargía, gula*), lust (*pornéia, fornicatio*), avarice (*philargyría, avaritia*), sorrow (*lupé, tristitia*), anger or wrath (*orgé, ira*), acedia or sloth (*akedia, acedia*), vainglory (*kenodoxía, inanis gloria*) and pride (*hyperēphanía, superbia*). Before Cassianus, Evagrio del Ponto had spoken of the demon of acedia, that attacked monks around midday, when the shadows of things are short but time is longer: 'it engenders hatred for the place, even for the way of life', says Evagrio, leading to a longing for other spaces, inciting them to think that the Lord may be worshipped anywhere and that pleasing Him is not dependent on a particular place. This demon emphasizes the pains of the ascetic life and makes life itself seem of very long duration. Cited by Rémi Brague, 'L'acédie selon Évagre de Pontique: image, histoire et lieu', *Esthétique el mélancolie*, ed. Christophe Carraud (Orléans: Institut d'Arts Visuels, 1992); see also by the same author the extended version of his essay: 'L'image et l'acédie. Remarques sur le premier «Apophtegme»', *Revue Thomiste*, 85, 2 (1985). A fascinating historical follow-up of the noontide demons is also to be found in Roger Caillois, 'Les démons du midi', *Revue de l'histoire des religions*, 115; 116; 117 (1937), 142–73, 54–83, 143–86.
15 The seven sins, according to Gregory, are: vainglory (*inanis gloria*), envy (*invidia*), wrath (*ira*), sorrow (*tristitia*), avarice (*avaritia*), gluttony (*ventris ingluvia*) and lust (*luxuria*). As can be seen, Gregory merged pride with vainglory and acedia with melancholy, but added a new vice:

envy. For mnemonic ends it was customary to refer to the set of seven deadly sins by the term SALIGIA, constructed on the basis of the initial letters in Latin: *superbia, avaritia, luxuria, invidia, gula, ira* and *acedia* (this term was often used to point to the Gregorian fusion of sorrow with acedia).

[16] (Quae enim secundum Deum tristitia est paenitentiam in salutem stabilem operatur saeculi autem tristitia mortem operatur) II Corinthians, 7:10.

[17] Siegfried Wenzel, *The Sin of Sloth: Acedia in Medieval Thought and Literature*, pp. 186–7.

[18] Rainer Jehl, *Melancholie und Acedia. Ein Beitrag zu Anthropologie und Ethik Bonaventuras* (Paderborn: Ferdinand Schöningh, 1984), p. 305. I owe to this work the description of the problems presented by St Bonaventure's theology.

[19] Noel L. Brann, 'Is acedia melancholy? A re-examination of this question in the light of Fra Battista da Crema's *Della cognitione et vittoria de se stesso* (1531)', *Journal of the History of Medicine*, 34 (1979), p. 183. One variant of these two tendencies can be seen in the opposition between melancholy and despair, observed in the allegorical figures typical of the French literature of the fifteenth century. Dominique Gangler-Mundwiller ('Mélancolie et désespérance: medicine et morale au quinzième siècle') has demonstrated that the two notions are very different and are in fact mutually exclusive in the literature of religious dissemination. In writings of Christian morality the idea of despair predominates, as the final stage in the suffering of the faithful, whose excessive repentance may drive them to suicide (as is also the case of the acedious). On the other hand, lyrical poetry adopts the theme of melancholy, and although its medical origin can be perceived, its moral meaning predominates, linked to the pain of love or to generalized sadness. But we are already dealing with a worldly and aristocratic melancholy that escapes from theology, although it adopts forms of religious vocabulary.

[20] Petrarch, *Secretum meum, II*, cited by Brann, 'Is acedia melancholy?', p. 182.

[21] 'Un saturnino overo è un angelo, overo è un demonio', ibid., p. 193.

[22] Melchor Cano, *Tratado de la victoria de sí mismo* (Madrid: Biblioteca de Autores Españoles, 1873), vol. 65, p. 310. The image of acedia as a 'noontide demon' was common in Spain; see Joseph E. Gillet, 'El mediodía y el demonio meridiano en España', *Nueva Revista de Filología Hispánica*, 7 (1953).

[23] There is a fascinating example of translation of the medieval concept of acedia into a completely different cultural universe: for this purpose Fray Andrés de Olmos used precisely the close relation between acedia and sorrow in his *Tratado sobre los siete pecados capitales (1551–1552)* (Mexico City: Universidad Nacional Autónoma de México, 1996), written in Nahuatl with the aim of converting the indígenous people of Mexico. In this work there is a chapter entitled 'De peccato accidie', in which Olmos translates *acedia* as *tlatziuhuizotl*; the verb *tlatzihui*, according to Angel María Garibay, was used to describe what would happen

to the sun if, for lack of nourishment, it were to cease to work on the world, and also had an implicit reference to tiredness and sloth. Olmos cites St Thomas in Latin but explains the idea in Nahuatl: 'Acedia est quaedam tristitia agravans. Quitoznequi ca yehuatl yn tlatçiuiçotl yuhqui huei tetl huei quahuitl [...] yectli yehua yn tlatçiuçotl huel tlaocoyatiztli, ynic ce tlacatl tlaocoya yn iquac ilhuilo aço notçallo ynic tlein qualli quichihuaz, anoço ic nahuatilo çan ic tlatemati, cuitlaçotlahua huel ayyel yuhqui yn coyametl'. (Acedia est quaedam tristitia agravans. Which means: that acedia is like a great stone, a large stick [...] and that acedia is really a sorrow, and, thus a man is sad when it is said, he is called to do something good, or even for this reason is referred to as negligent, without value, lazy, dejected, like a pig). Sorrow is here tlaocoya, the same quality that permeated Nahua culture and which finds expression in the well-known poem of Nezahualcóyotl that begins: 'Nitlayocoya, nictotlamatiya' (I have sorrow, I suffer bitterness). As one can see, Olmos connected acedia with concepts that had profound cosmic and existential resonances in the Nahua ambiance. See the edition of Olmos's text prepared and translated by Georges Baudot (I quote from his translation, although I substitute acedia for *pereza*; the emphases are added); on the verb *tlatzihui*, used to refer to melancholy among the Nahuas, and Nezahualcóyotl, see Angel María Garibay, *Historia de la literatura náhuatl* (Mexico City: Porrúa, 1953), glossary and pp. 188 ff. and 201 of
vol. I.
[24] Sigfried Wenzel, 'Petrarch's *Accidia*', *Studies in the Renaissance*, 7 (1961), p. 46.
[25] 'Tristi fummo / ne l'aere dolce che dal sol s'allegra, / portando dentro accidioso fummo: / or ci attristiam nella belletta negra', *Inferno*, VII, pp. 121–4 (English version adapted from the Temple Classics translation; here the word 'acedious' is substituted for the original translator's 'lazy'). In Rima 25 Dante is visited by Melancholy, who arrives accompanied by Anger and Pain.
[26] *Stanze. La parole e il fantasma nella cultura occidentale*, ch. 2, n. 7. Actually, St Jerome does not mention acedia; in Epistle 125, he says: 'There are those who fall into melancholy due to the dampness of their cells, immoderate fasting, the tedium of solitude and the excess of reading, which causes their ears to hum day and night, and they would stand in need of the remedies of Hippocrates more than our counsels' (*Epistolarium*, II, pp. 601–2).
[27] *Saturne et la Mélancolie*, p. 465.
[28] *The Protestant Ethic and the Spirit of Capitalism*, trans. Talcott Parsons (New York: Charles Scribner's Sons, 1958), p. 105.
[29] As Julius H. Rubin (*Religious Melancholy and Protestant Experience in America* (Oxford: Oxford University Press, 1994), p. 18) has pointed out. For a long time, especially since the mid seventeenth century, the Puritans' critics in England used the melancholic madness that motivated their fits of religious passion as an argument against them; see the description of these criticisms prepared by John F. Sena, 'Melancholic madness and the Puritans', *Harvard Theological Review*, 66 (1973).

30. *The Book of Life* (Liber de vita) tr. Charles Boer (Woodstock, CT: Spring Publications, 1994), especially the first book. In his study of Ficino, Kristeller has shown the importance of melancholy in the definition of interior experience; in this experience Ficino combines two theories that share the same sensibility but totally lack any logical connection. These are the medieval Christian theory of inner restlessness (*inquies*), typically found in St Augustine but the roots of which go back to Plotinus, and the ancient explanation of melancholy; Ficino thus gives birth to a modern idea that lacks the metaphysical background of the Augustinian notion of restlessness. Melancholy derives from empirical causes (the body, the stars); men lament it and at the same time suffer it with a certain pride, as a necessary correlate of their spiritual vocation. The illogical and incoherent combination of these two theories is a peculiar characteristic of Ficino and gives him his historical specificity. See Paul Oskar Kristeller, *Il pensiero filosófico di Marsilio Ficino* (Florencia: Sansoni, 1953), pp. 218–27.

31. In *Il messaggiero*, a dialogue written in hospital, he refers to his '*soverchia maninconia*', and explains the different types of melancholy, following the tradition of Ficino. It is worth mentioning that complex feelings of guilt led Tasso to confess his alleged heresy in 1577; the inquisitor of Ferrara hold him prisoner for a few days, but pronounced him guiltless on the grounds of his melancholy; this upset Tasso, who wished to be absolved of the sin of heresy. In a protest to the Cardinals of the Inquisition, he denounced the fact of having been 'assoluto più tosto come peccante di umor melancolico che come sospetto d'eresia'. Quoted by Juliana Schiesari, *The Gendering of Melancholia. Feminism, Psychoanalysis, and the Symbolics of Loss in Renaissance Literature* (Ithaca: Cornell University Press, 1992), p. 194.

32. Translated by Richard Carew from the Italian version, this highly successful book went through four English editions between 1594 and 1616 under the title *Examen de Ingenios: The Examination of Mens Wits*. In 1698, Edward Bellamy published a new translation, direct from the Spanish, entitled *Examen de Ingenios, or the Tryal of Wits*.

33. Jackie Pigeaud, a great scholar of Greek antiquity, in the text that prefaces her translation of *Problem XXX, I* (Marsella: Rivages, 1988), stresses the importance of Huarte's work (*L'homme de génie et la mélancolie. Problème XXX, I*, pp. 63 and 77, n. 56). The extraordinary success of the *Examen* throughout Europe in the seventeenth and eighteenth centuries popularized the Aristotelian problem regarding melancholy. Huarte's book was translated into French in 1580 and went through thirty-five editions in that language up to 1675; there were seven Italian, six English and three Latin editions, and also one in Dutch.

34. Miguel de Unamuno, *Vida de don Quijote y Sancho*, in *Ensayos*, vol. II (Madrid: Aguilar, 1951), p. 85; Rafael Salillas, *Un inspirador de Cervantes: el doctor Huarte de San Juan*.

35. *El doctor Huarte de San Juan y su 'Examen de ingenios'. Contribución a la historia de la psicología experimental* (Madrid: Consejo Superior de Investigaciones Científicas, 1948).

36. 'El Ingenioso Hidalgo.'

37 *Das Ingenium Don Quijotes, ein Beitrag zur Literarischen Characterkunde* (Munster: Aschendorffsche Verlagbuchhandlung, 1956).
38 *El doctor Huarte de San Juan y su 'Examen de ingenios'*, pp. 320–1.
39 Chester Harka, in '*Don Quijote* in the light of Huarte's *Examen de ingenios*: a reexamination', *Anales cervantinos*, 19 (1981), has demonstrated that Green did not know Huarte's text except through Iriarte's study, and that his sources for the subject of melancholy came from the book by Lawrence Babb, *The Elizabethan Malady. A Study in English Literature from 1580 to 1642* (East Lansing: Michigan State College Press, 1951).
40 Javier García Gibert, *Cervantes y la melancolía* (Valencia: Edicions Alfons el Magnànim, 1997), pp. 97–9. He also finds support for his conclusions in an article by Dolores Romero López ('Fisonomía y temperamento de don Quijote de la Mancha', in *Estado actual de los estudios sobre el Siglo de Oro*, ed. M. García Martín (Salamanca: Universidad de Salamanca, 1993)); she maintains that the knight was portrayed by Cervantes as a choleric who had acquired, through his voracious reading of books, an adust melancholy. The essay by Augustín Redondo, 'La melancolía y el Quijote de 1605', *Varia lingüística y literaria*, II: 215–41, ed. Martha Elena Venier (Mexico City: El Colegio de México, 1997) is also interesting.
41 Yvonne David-Peyre, 'L'observation psycho-pathologique et la fiction dans la folie de Don Quichotte', in *Hommage a Amédée Mas*, ed. R. A. Lawton (Paris: Presses Universitaire de France, 1972); the clinical interpretation is based on a study by Dr B. J. Logre, 'La folie de Don Quichotte', *Ouest Médical*, 23 (1956).
42 '*Don Quijote* in the light of Huarte's *Examen de ingenios*: a reexamination', p. 10.
43 'Did Don Quijote die of melancholy?', in *Folie et déraison à la Renaissance*, Colloque International, Novembre 1973 (Bruselas: Éditions de l'Université de Bruxelles, 1976).
44 'Don Quijote, melancholy knight', in *A Study of the Medical Theory of the Humours and its Application to Selected Spanish Literature of the Golden Age*, pp. 201–34 (unpub. Ph.D. thesis, University of Edinburgh, 1980).
45 *Melancholy and the Secular Mind*, pp. 35–6.
46 [¿Quién no dirá que en parte aman la pena, / pues toman de lo qu'es gloria disgusto, / huyendo del plazer qu'es bien glorioso? // Téngole por dichoso / al melancólico en temperamento / pues raciocina sin ningún tormento.] Minutes of the Academia de los Nocturnos, II, session 24, 11 March, 1592. This sonnet has been commented on by Pedro Ruiz Pérez in 'El discurso elegiaco y la lírica barroca: pérdida y melancolía'.
47 *Examen de ingenios para las ciencias*, critical edn by Guillermo Serés (Madrid: Cátedra, 1989), ch. 10, p. 463.
48 ['castidad, humildad, temor y reverencia de Dios, caridad, misericordia y gran reconocimiento de sus pecados con suspiros y lágrimas'] Ibid., ch. 10, p. 462. This passage was expurgated by the Inquisition and no longer appears in the edition of 1594.
49 Ibid., ch. 10, p. 463.

50 '*tierra*', perhaps in the sense of 'mortal clay' or in that of the solid element.
51 ['Una natural, que es la hez de la sangre, cuyo temperamento es frialdad y sequedad con muy gruesa sustancia, y ésta no vale para el ingenio, antes hace los hombres necios, torpes y risueños porque carecen de imaginativa. Y la que se llama *atra bilis* o *cólera adusta*, de la cual dijo Aristóteles que hace a los hombres sapientísimos, cuyo temperamento es vario como el del vinagre: unas veces hace efectos de calor, fomentando la tierra, y otras enfría'] Ibid., ch. 5, p. 372. The word *choler*, of Greek origin, is used here as a synonym for *bilis* or humour; *atrabilis* or the black bile is the black humour; choler adust is black because it is burnt. [*Translator's note:* In this chapter the word 'wit' is used throughout to translate the Spanish word 'ingenio', as was normal in the early seventeenth century, there being no word in modern English that comes close enough to it in meaning.]
52 Ibid., ch. 5, p. 372.
53 Ibid., ch. 3, p. 265. 'Homines qui ingenio claruerunt', according to the Latin translation of the Greek term *perittoí* (exceptional, surpassing what is normal). This is the interpretation of Cicero who, in the *Tusculan Disputations* (I, Ch. 33, p. 80), says: 'Aristoteles quidem ait omnes ingeniosos melancholicos esse' (indeed Aristotle says that all creative people (*ingeniosos*) are melancholics).
54 *Examen de ingenios para las ciencias*, ch. 3, p. 274.
55 *Don Quixote*, II, ch. 58, pp. 1096–7. (The references are to the normal division of the '*Quijote*' into two volumes, treating the four books of the original editions of the *El ingenioso hidalgo don Quixote de la Mancha* (1605), as 'Part I', and the second part, of 1615 (*Segunda parte del ingenioso cavallero don Quixote de la Mancha*), as 'Part II'; the page references are to the Spanish edition edited by Francisco Rico.)
56 '... entenderlas y desentrañarles el sentido.' Ibid., I, ch. 1, p. 38. (All quotations from the First Part of Cervantes's novel are taken from Thomas Shelton's first English translation published in 1612. The translations from the Second Part are original.)
57 (que ... el melancólico se mueva a risa ...). Ibid., Author's Preface to the Reader, p. 18.
58 Ibid., I, ch. 20, p. 219. Later on, when Don Quixote and Sancho are resting, breakfasting and drinking water from the brook beside the fuller's mill, they feel that all the 'choleric and melancholic humours' that the fear had produced in them have been 'cut away' (I, ch. 21, p. 228). This passage has been adduced as an indication that Don Quixote was of a choleric disposition, as well as melancholic; but what the passage really refers to is the annoyance or 'choleric mood' that overcame them at seeing themselves made fools of by the sounds of the mill (Jesús García Gibert, *Cervantes y la melancolía*, p. 99).
59 [...habiendo sacado a plaza la risa de la profunda malencolía de su amo ...] *Don Quixote*, II, ch. 16, p. 755.
60 [... y verá cómo le destierran la melancolía que tuviere y le mejoran la condición, si acaso la tiene mala ...] Ibid., I, ch. 50, p. 571.
61 Ibid., I, ch. 50, pp. 569–71.

62 [... una nueva y pastoril Arcadia ... por agora en este sitio no ha de entrar la pesadumbre ni la melancolía.] Ibid., II, ch. 58, p. 1102.
63 Ibid., II, ch. 44, pp. 982–3.
64 In another passage Don Quixote's melancholy is mentioned as being 'buried in the thoughts of his amours'. In contrast, that of Sancho is due to his having had to pay fifty *reales* (II, ch. 30, p. 874).
65 *Examen de ingenios para las ciencias*, ch. 5, p. 263.
66 *Mensonge romantique et vérité romanesque* (Paris: Grasset, 1961), p. 16.
67 [... imitar a Roldán en las locuras desaforadas que hizo, o Amadís en las malencónicas] *Don Quixote*, I, ch. 26, p. 290.
68 On this kind of madness, see my book *Wild Men in the Looking Glass: The Mythic Origins of European Otherness* (Anne Arbor: Michigan University Press, 1994), ch. 7.
69 *Don Quixote*, I, ch. 26, p. 291.
70 [Tráele amor al estricote, / que es de muy mala ralea; / y, así, hasta henchir un pipote, / aquí lloró don Quijote / ausencias de Dulcinea / del Toboso.] Ibid., I, ch. 26, p. 293 (version adapted from Thomas Shelton's translation).
71 Thomas Shelton's translation was based on one of the later editions; the reference to the shirt tails is thus missing in the first English edition, the rosary being made of 'beads of great galls'.
72 Marcel Bataillon, *Erasmo y España. Estudios sobre la historia espiritual del siglo XVI* (Mexico City: Fondo de Cultura Económica, 1966), p. 788. Another passage that was once expurgated by the Inquisition touches on the same problem: 'works of charity that are done in a lukewarm and indolent manner are without merit and are worth nothing' (*Don Quixote*, II, ch. 36, p. 930). Bataillon finds in this expression an Erasmist influence (*Erasmo y España*, p. 784, n. 39).
73 'Did Don Quixote die of melancholy?', pp. 164–5.
74 *Don Quixote*, I, ch. 29, p. 339.
75 Ibid., II, ch. 58, p. 1098.
76 Ibid., I, ch. 22, p. 237.
77 Ibid., II, ch. 13, p. 727.
78 Ibid., II, ch. 23, p. 822.
79 Ibid., II, ch. 36, p. 933.
80 Ibid., I, ch. 43, p. 511. ('In the meanwhile it happened that one of the horses whereon they rode drew near to smell Rozinante, that, melancholy and sadly, with his ears cast down, did sustain without moving his outstretched lord' (Shelton).)
81 As suggested by Steven Nadler, 'Descartes's demon and the madness of Don Quixote', *Journal of the History of Ideas*, 58, (1997).
82 *Meditationes de prima philosophia. Oeuvres de Descartes*, vol. 6, eds Charles Adam and Paul Tannery (Paris: J. Vrin, 1897–1910), p. 19.
83 *Don Quixote*, I, ch. 49, p. 560. ('the good Rozinante, who also seems enchanted, so sad and melancholy he goes' (Shelton).)
84 Ibid., II, ch. 65, p. 1162.
85 *Il libro del cortegiano*; the book was widely translated during the sixteenth century, an important example being the translation by the Spanish poet Juan Boscán published in 1534 (*Los cuatro libros del*

cortesano compuestos por el conde Baltasar Castellón y agora nuevamente traducidos por Boscán); reference is also made here to the first English translation, by Thomas Hoby, first published in 1561. A considerable portion of Book II is dedicated to forms of mockery or 'Meerie Pranckes'. The influence of Castiglione on Cervantes was pointed out by Américo Castro, *El pensamiento de Cervantes*. The subject has since been treated by Joseph G. Fucilla, 'The role of the *Cortegiano* in the second part of *Don Quijote*', *Hispania*, 33 (1950).

86 Translating from Boscán's version: 'But it seems that the mockery of the Courtier still ought to distance itself somewhat more from knavishness, and in no way ought to degenerate into ribald deceits or to take advantage (of others)' (Second Book, VII, p. 271); Hoby's translation has '... the Meerie Pranckes that the Courtier ought to use, must ... be somewhat wyde from immoderate jesting. He ought also to take heed that his Meerie Pranckes tourne not to pilferinge ...' (p. 197). The reference to the 'man of wit' (*hombre gracioso*) appears on p. 274 in the Spanish version; the corresponding passage in Hoby reads: 'forsomuch as my part hath bin to entreat onlie of Jestes' (p. 199). These were ways of combating that melancholy boredom so criticized by Antonio de Guevara in his *Menosprecio de corte y alabanza de aldea* (1539), but which finally became a fashion among the nobility throughout Europe, reflected in the spleen of the English or the *tristesse* of the French: honourable and aristocratic ways of bearing with the advent of modernity, absolutism and the bourgeoisie.

87 *Los cuatros libros del cortesano compuestos*, VII, p. 261 ('a friendlye deceit in matters that offende not at all or verie little', Hoby, p. 190).

88 Ibid., VII, p. 262 (Hoby, p. 191).

89 *Don Quixote*, II, ch. 60, p. 1119. In another passage: 'The sorely wounded Don Quixote was downcast and melancholy, his face bandaged and marked, not by the hand of God, but by the claws of a cat, misfortunes strange to errant knighthood' [estaba mohíno y malencólico el mal ferido don Quijote, vendado el rostro y señalado, no por la mano de Dios, sino por la uñas de un gato, desdichas anejas a la andante caballería] (II, ch. 48, p. 1014).

90 Ibid., II, ch. 74, pp. 1215–16. Another reference to death from melancholy appears in the inserted novel, the *History of the Curious – Impertinent*: it is that of Camilla on learning of the death of her lover Lothario, 'the which being known to Camilla, she made a profession, and shortly after deceased between the rigorous hands of sorrow and melancholy' [acabó en breves días la vida a las rigurosas manos de tristezas y melancolías] (I, ch. 35, p. 423).

91 [No se muera vuestra merced, señor mío, sino tome mi consejo y viva muchos años, porque la mayor locura que puede hacer un hombre en esta vida es dejarse morir sin más ni más, sin que nadie le mate ni otras manos le acaben que las de la melancolía.] Ibid., II, ch. 74, p. 1219.

92 Gregorio Mayans, *Vida de Miguel de Cervantes Saavedra*, 5th edn (Madrid: Pedro Joseph Alonso i Padilla, 1750), pp. 19–20.

93 Ibid., pp. 17–20.

94 Ibid., p. 20. Once again we find ourselves face to face with the cautious

use of dissimulation, the Arabic *taqiyya*, which, according to José Ramón Enríquez ('Gerión el mestizo y el teatro del Siglo de Oro') is characteristic of the literature of the Golden Age.

95 Erich Auerbach, *Mimesis: The Representation of Reality in Western Literature*, tr. Willard Trask (Princeton, NJ: Princeton University Press, 1953), ch. 14. Anthony Close, in *The Romantic Approach to Don Quixote* (Cambridge: Cambridge University Press, 1978), has analysed the romantic distortions in the interpretation of *Don Quixote*. Close thinks that comedy is the essential nature of the novel. My stress on the melancholy figure is not an alternative proposal of the essential nature of Cervantes's work – if such 'essential' substance exists, which I doubt – but a study of the culture and attitudes that surrounded Don Quixote's illness.

96 *Auto sacramental*: a type of religious play performed at Corpus Christi.

97 [más al vivo [. . .] lo que somos y lo que habemos de ser] *Don Quixote*, II, ch. 12, p. 719. This has been emphasized by Mark Van Doren, *Don Quijote's Profession* (New York: Columbia University Press, 1958).

98 See the beginning of the First Book: 'You then require me to wryte, which is (to my thynkynge) the trade and maner of Courtyers, whyche is most fyttynge for a Gentilman that lyveth in the Court of Princes, by the whiche he maye have the knowledge how to serve them perfectlye in everye reasonable matter, and obtaine thereby favour of them and prayse of other men. Fynallye, of what sort he ought to be that deserveth to be called so perfet a Courtyer . . .' (Hoby, p. 21).

99 The word used by Gracián is '*desengañado*'.

100 Baltasar Gracián, *Oráculo manual y arte de prudencia*, in *Obras completas*, II, Biblioteca Castro (Madrid: Turner, 1993), maxim 100, II, p. 228.

101 *Obras de Lope de Vega*, vol. I of the *Obras dramáticas*, published by the Real Academia Española in 1916. On the question of attribution and dating see Griswold S. Morley and Courtney Bruerton, *Cronología de las comedia de Lope de Vega* (Madrid: Gredos, 1968), pp. 59 and 590.

102 It is curious that this play attributed to Lope de Vega has been commented on by almost none of the authors who have been interested in melancholy in Spain. I am aware only of the suggestive comments made by Jorge Urrutia in his 'Glosa a la inacción', in *Humoures negros: del tedio, la melancolía, el esplín y otros aburrimientos*, eds Rosa de Diego and Lydia Vázquez (Madrid: Biblioteca Nueva, 1998). See also the essay by J. Homero Arjona, who throws doubt on the ascription of this *comedia* to Lope de Vega ('Did Lope de Vega write the extant *El príncipe melancólico?*', *Hispanic Review*, 24 (1956)).

103 He explains that 'love later cools' (*el amor luego resfría*) (347, p. 2), and further on repeats the opinion: 'It is great melancholy, / that presses on his entrails / and makes subject his heart' [Ella es gran melancolía, / que las entrañas le aprieta / y el corazón le sujeta] (348, p. 2).

104 Timothy Bright, *A Treatise of Melancholie* (London: Thomas Vautrollier, 1586), ch. 32.

105 Ibid., ch. 10.

106 Ibid., ch. 33.

107 Ibid., ch. 10.

108 Ibid., ch. 35.
109 Bridget Gellert Lyons, *Voices of Melancholy. Studies in Literary Treatments of Melancholy in Renaissance England* (London: Routledge & Kegan Paul, 1971), ch. 4.
110 Harold Jenkins, 'Introduction', Arden edn of *Hamlet* (London: Routledge, 1989), p. 159. See also Gustav Arthur Bieber, *Der Melancholikertypus Shakespeares un sein Ursprung* (Heidelberg: Carl Winter's Universitätsbuchhandlung, 1913).
111 *Hamlet*, V, ii, 218.
112 Robert Burton, *The Anatomy of Melancholy*, ed. Floyd Dell and Paul Jordan Smith (New York: Tudor, 1955), partition 3, section 4, member 2, subsect. 6, p. 970. Luther himself, many of whose followers had suffered melancholy in the face of an obscure predestination, advised them to leave aside their thoughts concerning free will: 'Only anxiety will come about from tormenting oneself with the question of choice/ free will' (letter quoted by H. C. Erik Midelfort, *A History of Madness in Sixteenth-Century Germany* (Stanford: Stanford University Press, 1999), p. 106).
113 In a highly stimulating essay ('Fatalisme des temperaments et liberté spirituelle dans l'*Examen des esperits* de Huarte de San Juan'), Jackie Pigeaud remarks on the enormous importance of the problem of free will in the work of Huarte, who tries to reconcile biological fatalism with the freedom of men (and God!). Thus, melancholy is a key element, since the black humour is on the side of liberty and improvisation, without contravening the natural laws implied by humoral determinism. Huarte – as Pigeaud points out – does not find in Galen the idea of the victory of the soul over the body, a Christian notion that makes it possible to highlight the merit of those who, like St Paul, succeed in mastering (and drawing benefit from) the restrictions of the bodily temperaments and humours without tearing down the edifice of Nature created by God. Pigeaud concludes that in Huarte we see the triumph of dynamism over the combinatory.
114 Baltasar Gracián, *El criticón*, III, i, p. 446.
115 [En este remate de la vida todos discurrimos a dos luces y andamos a dos haces.] Ibid., III, i, p. 448.
116 John Dowland, *Lacrimae, or Seaven Teares figured in Seaven Passionate Pavans* (London: Windet, 1604). This work uses as a kind of leitmotiv a descending series of four notes (which could be described as the lower tetrachord of the Phrygian scale). Dowland adopted this phrase as a kind of personal 'signature' and it became identified as an archetypal representation of melancholy in music. Another English composer, Anthony Holborne, composed many pieces in a melancholy tone, including an explicit reference in 'The Image of Melancholy', in his collection of *Pavans, Galliards, Almains, and other short Aeirs both grave, and light* (London: W. Barley, 1599). To counteract melancholy, a large collection of popular songs was accumulated in England under the title of *Pills to Purge Melancholy*, the first volume of which was published by John Playford in 1698, later editions in several volumes being

published by Thomas D'Urfey. These are jocose and amusing songs, some of an obscene or picaresque tone.

[117] Klibansky, Panofsky and Saxl, *Saturne et la Mélancolie*, dedicate a special section to the subject (pp. 371–87).

[118] [Cette libération des forces dynamiques s'opéra pour la première fois à l'époque baroque; et, chose significative, elle porta le plus pleinement ses fruits dans les pays où la tension, qui allait alimenter la production artistique, était la plus vive: dans l'Espagne de Cervantes, où le baroque s'épanouit sous la férule d'un catholicisme particulièrement sévère, et plus encore dans l'Angleterre de Shakespeare et de Donne, ou il s'affirma face à un protestantisme orgueilleusement sûr de lui-même. Ces deux pays devinrent, et restèrent, la sphère privilégiée de cette mélancolie proprement moderne, que l'on cultivait en toute conscience.] Ibid., pp. 377 ff.

[119] In the preface to the 1989 edition, Raymond Klibansky mentions the Spain of Cervantes as an important link in the modern history of melancholy, a history that is still waiting to be written and which will be like 'writing the history of the sensibility of contemporary man' (p. 19).

[120] Miguel de Unamuno, *Del sentimiento trágico de la vida*, in *Ensayos*, vol. II (Madrid: Aguilar, 1951), pp. 1007 and 1009. In *Saturne et la Mélancolie* the importance of the combination of humourism with melancholy is recognized (p. 380).

[121] Ramiro de Maeztu, *Don Quijote, don Juan y la Celestina* ([1926]; Madrid: Espasa-Calpe (Austral), 1981), p. 22.

[122] Georg Lukács, *Teoría de la novela* ([1920]; Barcelona: Edhasa, 1971), p. 111.

[123] Javier García Gibert, *Cervantes y la melancolía*, p. 117. This excellent essay also deals with other aspects of the complex phenomenon, and gives us a panorama of Cervantine melancholy throughout his works. Pierre Vilar had already pointed out that Don Quixote seems to embody the idea of Martín Gonzalez de Cellorigo, according to which there was a divorce between certain Spaniards who lived outside the natural order of things – in an illusory, mythical and mystical world – and another Spain, sunk in pillage, corruption and misery (Pierre Vilar, 'Le temps du Quichotte').

Bibliography

Actas de la Academia de los Nocturnos, ed. J. L. Sirera and E. Rodríguez (Valencia: Edicions Alfons el Magnànim, 1990).
Acuña, Hernando de, *Poesías*, ed. Lorenzo Rubio González (Valladolid: Diputación Provincial, 1981).
Agamben, Giorgio, *Stanze, La parola e il fantasma nella cultura occidentale* (Turin: Einaudi, 1977).
Aguilar, Gaspar de, 'La gitana melancólica', in *Dramáticos contemporáneos a Lope de Vega*, ed. Ramón de Mesonero Romanos, vol. I (Madrid: Biblioteca de Autores Españoles, 1857).
Alcázar, Jorge, 'La figura emblemática de la melancolía en *El sueño* de Sor Juana', *Poligrafías*, 1 (1996), 123–50.
Álvarez, Javier, *Mística y depresión: san Juan de la Cruz* (Madrid: Trotta, 1997).
Álvarez de Toledo, Luisa Isabel, *Alonso Pérez de Guzmán: General de la Invencible* (Cádiz: Servicio de Publicaciones de la Universidad, Consejería de Educación y Ciencia de la Junta de Andalucía, 1994).
Amato Lusitano (João Rodrigues de Castelo Branco), *Centúrias de curas medicinais*, 4 vols, tr. Firmino Crespo (Lisboa: Universidade Nova de Lisboa, n.d. c.1980).
Andrés, Melquiades, *Historia de la mística de la Edad de Oro en España y América* (Madrid: Biblioteca de Autores Cristianos, 1994).
Anglo, Sydney, 'Melancholia and witchcraft: the debate between Wier, Bodin, and Scot', in *Folie et déraison à la Renaissance*, Colloque International, November 1973 (Bruselas: Éditions de l'Université de Bruxelles, 1976).
Arbesmann, Rudolph, 'The "daemonium meridianum" and Greek and Latin patristic exegesis', *Traditio*, 14 (1958), 17–31.
Aristóteles (pseudo-), *L'homme de génie et la mélancolie, Problème XXX, 1*, ed. Jackie Pigeaud (Marsella: Rivages, 1988).
Arjona, J. Homero, 'Did Lope de Vega write the extant *El príncipe melancólico?*', *Hispanic Review*, 24 (1956), 42–9.
Armas, F. A. de, '*La Celestina*: an example of love melancholy', *Romanic Review*, 66, 4 (1975), 288–95.
Arnau de Vilanova, *Regiment de sanitat*, in *Obres catalanes*, ed. Miquel Batllori, vol. II, (Barcelona: Barcino, 1947).
Arnold, Matthew, *Culture and Anarchy. An Essay in Political and Social Criticism* ([1869]; New York: Macmillan, 1916).

Auerbach, Erich, *Mimesis: The Representation of Reality in Western Literature*, tr. Willard Trask (Princeton, NJ: Princeton University Press, 1953).

Augustine (Saint), *The City of God against the Pagans*, ed. and tr. R. W. Dyson (Cambridge: Cambridge University Press, 1998).

Azouvi, François, 'The Plague, Melancholy and the Devil', *Diogenes*, 108 (1979), 112–30.

Babb, Lawrence, *The Elizabethan Malady. A Study in English Literature from 1580 to 1642* (East Lansing: Michigan State College Press, 1951).

Barlow, T. D., *The Medieval World Picture and Albert Dürer's Melancholia* (Cambridge: The Roxburghe Club, 1950).

Barondes, Samuel H., *Mood Genes: Hunting for Origins of Mania and Depression* (New York: W. H. Freeman, 1998).

Bartra, Roger, 'Ludonomicon: el poder burlado', *Casa del Tiempo*, 54 (1985), 69–71.

—— *La jaula de la melancolía* (Mexico City: Grijalbo, 1987).

—— *The Cage of Melancholy. Identity and Metamorphosis in the Mexican Character* (New Brunswick: Rutgers University Press, 1992).

—— *Wild Men in the Looking Glass: The Mythic Origins of European Otherness* (Anne Arbor: Michigan University Press, 1994).

—— *The Artificial Savage: Modern Myths of the Wild Man* (Anne Arbor: Michigan University Press, 1997).

—— *El Siglo de Oro de la melancolía. Textos españoles y novohispanos sobre las enfermedades del alma* (Mexico City: Universidad Iberoamericana, Departamento de Historia, 1998).

Barrenechea, Francisco, 'Modelos para romper: Velásquez y la crítica de la autoridad en la medicina del Siglo de Oro', in Roger Bartra, *El Siglo de Oro de la melancolía. Textos españoles y novohispanos sobre las enfermedades del alma* (Mexico City: Universidad Iberoamericana, Departamento de Historia, 1998).

Barrios, Juan de, *Verdadera medicina, cirugía, y astrología* (Mexico City: Fernando Balli, 1607). Chapters 9 and 10, 'De melancolía' and 'Del amor', publ. in Roger Bartra, *El Siglo de Oro de la melancolía. Textos españoles y novohispanos sobre las enfermedades del alma* (Mexico City: Universidad Iberoamericana, Departamento de Historia, 1998).

Bataillon, Marcel, '¿Melancolía renacentista o melancolía judía?', in *Estudios hispánicos. Homenaje a Archer M. Huntington* (Wellesley, MA: Spanish department, Wellesley College, 1952).

—— 'Andrés Laguna, Autor del *Viaje a Turquía* a la luz de las recientes investigaciones', *Estudios segovianos*, 15 (1963), 5–69.

—— *Erasmo y España. Estudios sobre la historia espiritual del siglo XVI* (Mexico City: Fondo de Cultura Económica, 1966).

Baxter, Christopher, 'Johann Weyer's *De praestigiis daemonum*: unsystematic psychopathology', in Sydney Anglo (ed.), *The Damned Art. Essays in the Literature of Witchcraft* (London: Routledge & Kegan Paul, 1977).

—— 'Jean Bodin's *De la démonomanie des sorciers*: the logic of persecution', in Sydney Anglo (ed.), *The Damned Art. Essays in the Literature of Witchcraft* (London: Routledge & Kegan Paul, 1977).

Beecher, Donald A., 'Lovesickness, diagnosis, and destiny in the renaissance theaters of England and Spain: the parallel development of a

medico-literary motif', in Louise and Peter Fothergill-Payne (eds), *Parallel Lives. Spanish and English National Drama* (Lewisburg: Bucknell University Press, 1991).
Beinart, Haim, *Andalucía y sus judíos* (Córdoba: Monte de Piedad-Caja de Ahorros, 1986).
—— 'The Conversos and their fate', in Elie Kedourie (ed.), *Spain and the Jews, The Sephardi Experience. 1442 and After* (London: Thames and Hudson, 1992).
Bel Bravo, María Antonia, *El auto de fe de 1593. Los conversos granadinos de origen judío* (Granada: Universidad de Granada, 1988).
Benjamin, Walter, *The Origin of German Tragic Drama* (London: Verso, 1977).
Bertalanffy, Ludwig von, *General System Theory* (New York: Braziller, 1968).
Bettelheim, Bruno, *The Empty Fortress: Infantile Autism and the Birth of the Self* (New York: Free Press, 1967).
Bieber, Gustav Arthur, *Der Melancholikertypus Shakespeares un sein Ursprung* (Heidelberg: Carl Winter's Universitätsbuchhandlung, 1913).
Bieñko, Doris, *Azucena mística. Isabel de la Encarnación, una monja poblana del siglo XVII* (Mexico: Escuela Nacional de Antropología e Historia, 2001).
Binswanger, Ludwig, *Mélancolie et manie. Etudes phénoménologiques* (Paris: Presses Universitaires de France, 1987),
Blackmore, Susan, *The Meme Machine* (Oxford: Oxford University Press, 1999).
Blázquez Miguel, Juan, *Sueños y procesos de Lucrecia de León* (Madrid: Tecnos, 1987).
Bleznick, Donald W., 'La teoría clásica de los humores en los tratados políticos del Siglo de Oro', *Hispanofila*, 2, 2 (1959), 1–9.
Blumenberg, Hans, *Work on Myth* (Cambridge, MA: MIT Press, 1985).
Böhme, Jacob, *Aurora (Morgenröthe im Aufgang)*, in *Sämtliche Schriften*, vol. I, ed. W. E. Peuckert (Stuttgart: F. Fromann, 1955–61).
Böhme, Jacob (Jacob Behmen), *A Consolatory Treatise of the Four Complexions, that is, an Instruction in the Time of Temptation for a Sad and Assaulted Heart*... (London: H. Blunden, 1654).
Bolaños, María, *Pasajes de la melancolía. Arte y bilis negra a comienzos del siglo XX* (Madrid: Junta de Castilla y León, 1996).
Bonuzzi, Luciano, 'Il contributo dei ricercatori padovani allo studio della «melancholia» nel '500', *Acta Medicae Historiae Patavina*, 15 (1968–9), 35–46.
Brague, Rémi, 'L'image et l'acédie. Remarques sur le premier «Apophtegme»', *Revue Thomiste*, 85, 2 (1985), 199–228.
—— 'L'acédie selon Évagre de Pontique: image, histoire et lieu', *Esthétique el mélancolie*, ed. Christophe Carraud (Orléans: Institut d'Arts Visuels, 1992).
Brailowsky, Simón, *Las sustancias de los sueños. Neuropsicofarmacología* (Mexico City: Fondo de Cultura Económica, 1995).
Brann, Noel L., 'Is acedia melancholy? A re-examination of this question in the light of Fra Battista da Crema's *Della cognitione et vittoria di se stesso* (1531)', *Journal of the History of Medicine*, 34 (1979), 180–99.

Braudel, Fernand, *El Mediterráneo y el mundo mediterráneo en la época de Felipe II*, 2 vols (Mexico City: Fondo de Cultura Económica, 1976). Originally published in French in 3 vols as *La Méditerranée et le monde Méditerranéen à l'epoque de Philippe II* (1949).

Bright, Timothy, *A Treatise of Melancholie* (London: Thomas Vautrollier, 1586).

—— *Traité de la Mélancolie*, tr. and ed. Eliane Cuvelier (Grenoble: Jérôme Millon, 1996).

Brown, G. S. and Harris, T. *The Social Origins of Depression: A Study of Psychiatric Disorder in Women* (New York: Free Press, 1978).

Burke, James F., 'The *Estrella de Sevilla* and the tradition of saturnine melancholy', *Bulletin of Hispanic Studies*, 51, 2 (1974), 137–56.

Burke, Peter, *The Fortunes of the Courtier* (University Park, PA: Pennsylvania State University Press, 1995).

Burkert, Walter, *Creation of the Sacred: Tracks of Biology in Early Religions* (Cambridge, MA: Harvard University Press, 1996).

Burton, Robert, *The Anatomy of Melancholy*, eds Floyd Dell and Paul Jordan Smith (New York: Tudor, 1955).

Butcher, Samuel Henry, 'The Melancholy of the Greeks', in *Some Aspects of the Greek Genius* (London: Macmillan, 1891).

Bynum, Caroline Walker, 'The body of Christ in the later Middle Ages: a reply to Leo Steinberg', *Fragmentation and Redemption, Essays on Gender and the Human Body in Medieval Religion* (New York: Zone Books, 1992).

Cælius Aurelianus, *On Acute Diseases and On Chronic Diseases*, edition of the Latin text and English tr. by I. E. Drabkin (Chicago: University of Chicago Press, 1950).

Caillois, Roger, 'Les démons du midi', *Revue de l'histoire des religions*, 115; 116; 117 (1937), 142–73, 54–83, 143–86.

Calvesi, Maurizio, *La Melanconia di Albrecht Dürer* (Turin: Einaudi, 1993).

Cano, Melchor, *Tratado de la victoria de sí mismo* (Madrid: Biblioteca de Autores Españoles, 1873) vol. 65, pp. 303–24.

Cardaillac, Louis, *Moriscos y cristianos. Un enfrentamiento polémico (1542–1640)* (Mexico City: Fondo de Cultura Económica, 1979).

Cárdenas, Juan de, *Problemas y secretos maravillosos de las Indias* (Mexico City: Pedro Ocharte, 1591).

Cardoner i Planas, Antoni, *Història de la medicina a la corona d'Aragó (1162–1479)* (Barcelona: Scientia, 1973).

Castiglione, Baltasar de, *El cortesano*, 1534 Spanish tr. by Juan Boscán (Mexico City: Universidad Nacional Autónoma de Mexico, 1997).

—— *The Book of the Courtier*, tr. by Thomas Hoby ([1561]; London: J. M. Dent, 1994).

Castro, Américo, *El pensamiento de Cervantes* (Madrid: Anejos de la Revista de Filología Española, 1925), vol. VI.

—— 'La mística y humana feminidad de Teresa la Santa', in *Santa Teresa y otros ensayos* (Santander: Historia Nueva, 1929).

—— *España en su historia. Cristianos, moros y judíos* (Buenos Aires: Losada, 1948).

—— *Aspectos del vivir hispánico. Espiritualismo, mesianismo, actitud personal en los siglos XIV al XVI* (Santiago de Chile: Cruz del Sur, 1949).
Céard, Jean, 'The Devil and lovesickness: views of 16th century physicians and demonologists', in Donald A. Beecher and Massimo Civolella (eds), *Eros and Anteros: The Medical Traditions of Love in the Renaissance* (Toronto: University of Toronto Italian Studies 9, Dovehouse Editions, 1992).
Certeau, Michel de, *La possession de Loudun* (Paris: Julliard, 1970).
Cervantes, Miguel de, *Don Quijote de la Mancha*, ed. Francisco Rico (Barcelona: Instituto Cervantes/Crítica, 1998).
—— *Don Quixote de la Mancha*, Thomas Shelton's translation of the First Part of *Don Quixote* can be accessed via the Internet, at *www.bartleby.com*.
Ciruelo, Pedro, *Tratado en el qual se repruevan todas las supersticiones y hechizerías: muy útil y necessario a todos los buenos Christianos zelosos de su salvación*, compuesto por el Doctor y Maestro Pedro Ciruelo, Canónigo de la Santa Iglesia Cathedral de Salamanca (Barcelona: Sebastián de Cormellas, 1628).
Clapier-Valladon, Simone, 'L'homme et le rire', in *Histoire des moeurs*, ed. Jean Poirier (Paris: Gallimard, 1991), vol. II, pp. 247–97.
Clark, Stuart, 'The scientific status of demonology', in Charlotte F. Otten, *A Lycanthropy Reader. Werewolves in Western Culture* (Syracuse, NY: Syracuse University Press, 1986).
Close, Anthony, *The Romantic Approach to Don Quixote* (Cambridge: Cambridge University Press, 1978).
Cohen-Solal, Annie, *Sartre, 1905–1980* (Barcelona: Edhasa, 1990).
Constantino el Africano, *Della melancolia*, Latin edn and Italian tr. by M. T. Malato and U. de Martini (Roma: Istituto di Storia della Medicina dell'Università di Roma, 1959).
Coronas Tejada, Luis, *Conversos and Inquisition in Jaén* (Jerusalem: Magnes Press/Hebrew University, 1988).
Couliano, Ioan P., *Eros and Magic in the Renaissance*, trans. Margaret Cook (Chicago: University of Chicago Press, 1987).
Covarrubias, Sebastián de, *Tesoro de la lengua castellana o española* [1611], ed. F. C. R. Maldonado (Madrid: Castalia, 1995).
Cuevas, José and Jesús de las, *Arcos de la Frontera* (Cádiz: Departamento de Publicaciones de la Diputación Provincial, 1967).
Dante, *Dante's Inferno*, Italian text and English tr. (London: J. M. Dent and Sons, 1900).
David-Peyre, Yvonne, *Le Personage du médecin et la relation médecin-malade dans la littérature ibérique XVIe et XVIIe siècle* (thesis for *doctorat ès lettres*) (Paris: Ediciones Hispano-Americanas, 1971).
—— 'L'observation psycho-pathologique et la fiction dans la folie de Don Quichotte', in *Hommage a Amédée Mas*, ed. R. A. Lawton (Paris: Presses Universitaire de France, 1972).
—— 'D. Duarte Roi du Portugal: une névrose exemplaire', *Littérature, medecine, societé*, 1 (1979), 73–114.
—— 'Deux examples du mal d'amour dit «héroïque» chez Cervantès. Du langage médical a la transcription rhétorique', *Bulletin de l'Association Guillaume Budé*, 4 (1982), 383–404.

Dawkins, Richard, *The Selfish Gene* (Oxford: Oxford University Press, 1976 (rev. edn, 1989)).
Delgado y Orellana, José Antonio, 'Tres insólitos arcenses', *Hidalguía*, 31, 178–9 (1983), 401–20.
del Río, Martín, *La magia demoníaca (Libro II de las Disquisiciones mágicas)*, tr. and annotated by Jesús Moya (Madrid: Hiperión, 1991).
Dennett, Daniel C., *Darwin's Dangerous Idea. Evolution and the Meanings of Life* (New York: Simon & Schuster, 1995).
—— 'Appraising grace. What evolutionary good is God?', *The Sciences* (January–February 1997), 39–44.
Descartes, René, *Meditationes de prima philosophia. Oeuvres de Descartes*, vol. 6, ed. Charles Adam and Paul Tannery (Paris: J. Vrin, 1897–1910).
Deyermond, Alan, 'The text-book mishandled: Andreas Capellanus and the opening scene of *La Celestina*', *Neophilologus*, 45 (1961), 218–21.
Díaz-Plaja, Guillermo, *Tratado de las melancolías españolas* (Madrid: Sala, 1975).
Domínguez Ortiz, Antonio, *Los judeoconversos en España y América* (Madrid: Istmo, 1971).
—— *La clase social de los conversos en Castilla en la Edad Moderna* (Granada: Universidad de Granada, 1991).
Down, J. Langdon, *Mental Affections of Childhood* ([1887]; Oxford: MacKeith Press, Blackwell Scientific Publications, 1990).
Dronke, Peter, *Women Writers of the Middle Ages. A Critical Study of Texts from Perpetua (†203) to Marguerite Porete (†1310)* (Cambridge: Cambridge University Press, 1984).
Duminil, Marie-Paule, 'La mélancolie amoureuse dans l'Antiquité', in Jean Céard (ed.), *La folie et le corps* (Paris: Presses de l'École Normale Supérieure, 1985).
Duncan, Marc, *Discours de la possession des religieuses ursulines de Lodun*, 1634 (printed pamphlet of 64 pp., no publisher's or printer's imprint, in the Bibliotèque nationale de France, 16-LB36-3961).
—— *Apologie pour Monsieur Duncan docteur en médecine. Contre le Traitté de la Mélancholie. Tiré des Réflexions du Sieur de la Mre.* (printed document of 295 pp., no date or imprints, in the Bibliotèque nationale de France, 4-TD86-14).
Elliott, J. H., 'The Court of the Spanish Habsburgs: a peculiar institution?', in *Spain and Its World, 1500–1700* (New Haven: Yale University Press, 1989).
—— 'Self-perception and decline in early seventeenth-century Spain', in *Spain and Its World, 1500–1700* (New Haven: Yale University Press, 1989).
Enríquez, José Ramón, 'Gerión el mestizo y el teatro del Siglo de Oro', in *Pánico escénico* (Mexico City: Dirección de Literatura, UNAM, 1997).
Escudero Ortuño, Alberto, *Concepto de la melancolía en el siglo XVII (un comentario a las obras de Robert Burton y Alfonso de Santa Cruz)* (Huesca: Imprenta provincial, 1950).
Estes, Leland L., 'The medical origins of the European witch craze: a hypothesis', in Charlotte F. Otten, *A Lycanthropy Reader. Werewolves in Western Culture* (Syracuse, NY: Syracuse University Press, 1986).

Evans, Bergen, *The Psychiatry of Robert Burton* (New York: Columbia University Press, 1944).
Farfán, Agustín, *Tratado breve de medicina y de todas las enfermedades* (Mexico City: Pedro Ocharte, 1592), Chapter 6, 'De la melancolía', pub. in Roger Bartra, *El Siglo de Oro de la melancolía. Textos españoles y novohispanos sobre las enfermedades del alma* (Mexico City: Universidad Iberoamericana, Departamento de Historia, 1998).
Farinelli, Arturo, *Dos excéntricos: Cristobal de Villalón – El Dr. Juan Huarte* (Madrid: Revista de Filología Española, Anejo 24, 1936).
Fédida, Pierre, 'Le cannibale mélancolique', *Nouvelle Revue de Psychanalyse*, 6 (1972), 123–7.
Ferrand, Jacques, *Traité de l'essence et guérison de l'Amour ou mélancolie érotique* (Toulouse: Veuve de J. Colomiez, 1610).
—— *De la maladie d'Amour, ou mélancolie érotique, discours curieux qui enseigne à cognoistre l'essence, les causes, les signes, et les remèdes de ce mal fantastique* (Paris: Denis Moreau, 1623). [A Spanish translation also exists: *Melancolía erótica o enfermedad de amor*, tr. Julián Mateo Ballorca (Madrid: Asociación Española de Neuropsiquiatría, 1996).]
—— *A Treatise on Lovesickness*, tr., ed. and critical introduction by Donald A. Beecher and Massimo Ciavollela (Syracuse, NY: Syracuse University Press, 1990).
Ficino, Marsilio, *The Book of Life (Liber de vita)*, tr. Charles Boer (Woodstock, CT: Spring Publications, 1994).
—— *Sobre el amor. Comentarios al* Banquete *de Platón*, tr. M. Lamberti and J. L. Bernal (Mexico City: Universidad Nacional Autónoma de México, 1994).
Folch Jou, Guillermo, Pedro García Domínguez and Sagrario Muñoz Calvo, 'La Celestina: ¿hechicera o boticaria?', in *La Celestina y su contorno social*, ed. Manuel Criado del Val, Actas del I Congreso Internacional sobre La Celestina (Barcelona: Borrás, 1977).
Földényi, László F., *Melancolía*, tr. into Spanish from Hungarian by Adan Kovacsics (Barcelona: Círculo de Lectores, 1996).
Fontenelle, Bernard, *De l'origine des fables [1724]*, ed. J.-R. Carré (Paris: Félix Alcan, 1932).
Foucault, Michel, *Histoire de la folie à l'âge classique* (Paris: Gallimard, 1972).
Franco Toriz, Germán, 'Una singular aportación indiana al tema de la melancolía: la cura de la «merarquía» por cauterios', in Roger Bartra, *El Siglo de Oro de la melancolía. Textos españoles y novohispanos sobre las enfermedades del alma* (Mexico City: Universidad Iberoamericana, Departamento de Historia, 1998).
Freud, Sigmund, 'Mourning and Melancholy', in *Standard Edition of the Complete Psychological Works*, XIV (Toronto: Hogarth Press, 1957), pp. 237–58.
—— 'A seventeenth-century demonological neurosis', in *Standard Edition of the Complete Psychological Works*, XIX (Toronto: Hogarth Press, 1961), pp. 67–105.
—— 'Draft G. Melancholia' (1895), in *Standard Edition of the Complete Psychological Works*, I: Pre-Psychoanalytic Publications and Unpublished Drafts (1886–1899) (Toronto: Hogarth Press, 1966),

pp. 200–6, orig. pub. as *Aus den Anfängen der Psychoanalyse. Briefe an Wilhelm Fliess. Abhandlungen und Notizen aus den Jahren 1887–1902* (London: Imago, 1950).

Freylas, Alonso de, *Si los melancólicos pueden saber lo que está por venir, o adivinar el suceso bueno o malo de lo futuro, con la fuerza de su ingenio, o soñando*, in *Conocimiento, curación, y preservación de la peste* (Jaén: Fernando Díaz de Montoya, 1606 [according to the colophon the date is 1605]).

Friedenwald, Harry, 'Andres a Laguna, a pioneer in his views on witchcraft', in *The Jews and Medicine. Essays*, 2 vols (Baltimore: Johns Hopkins Press, 1944).

—— 'Montalto, A Jewish physician at the court of Marie de Médicis and Louis XIII', in *The Jews and Medicine. Essays*, 2 vols (Baltimore: Johns Hopkins Press, 1944).

—— 'Concerning the diseases of the Jews', in *The Jews and Medicine. Essays*, 2 vols (Baltimore: Johns Hopkins Press, 1944).

—— 'Two Jewish physicians of the sixteenth century', in *The Jews and Medicine. Essays*, 2 vols (Baltimore: Johns Hopkins Press, 1944).

Fucilla, Joseph G., 'The role of the *Cortegiano* in the second part of *Don Quijote*', *Hispania*, 33 (1950), 291–6.

Gállego, Julián, *Visión y símbolos en la pintura española del Siglo de Oro* (Madrid: Cátedra, 1987).

Galzigna, Mario, 'L'enigma della malinconia. Materiali per una storia', *Aut aut*, 195–6 (1983), 75–97.

Gambin, Felice, *Azabache. Il dibattito sulla malinconia nella Spagna dei Secoli d'Oro* (Pisa: Edizioni ETS, 2005).

Gangler-Mundwiller, Dominique, 'Mélancolie et désespérance: medicine et morale au quinzième siècle', *Littérature, medecine, societé*, 1 (1979), 46–72.

García Ballester, Luis, *Los moriscos y la medicina. Un capítulo de la medicina y la ciencia marginadas en la España del siglo XVI* (Barcelona: Labor, 1984).

García Gibert, Javier, *Cervantes y la melancolía* (Valencia: Edicions Alfons el Magnànim, 1997).

Garibay, Angel María, *Historia de la literatura náhuatl* (Mexico City: Porrúa, 1953).

Gellner, Ernest, 'Origins of society', in *Anthropology and Politics. Revolutions in the Sacred Grove* (Oxford: Blackwell, 1995).

Gillet, Joseph E., 'El mediodía y el demonio meridiano en España', *Nueva Revista de Filología Hispánica*, 7 (1953), 307–15.

Ginzburg, Carlo, *El queso y los gusanos* (Mexico City: Oceano/Muchnik, 1997).

Girard, René, *Mensonge romantique et vérité romanesque* (Paris: Grasset, 1961).

Godínez [Wadding], Miguel, *Practica de la Theologia Mystica* (Sevilla: Juan Vejarano a costa de Lucas Martín de Hermosilla, 1682).

Gorceix, Bernard, 'La mélancolie aux XVIe et XVIIe siècles. Paracelse et Jacob Böhme', *Recherches germaniques*, 9 (1979), 18–29.

Gould, Stephen Jay, 'Caring groups and selfish genes', in *The Panda's Thumb* (New York: Norton, 1980).

—— 'Darwinian Fundamentalism', part 1, *New York Review of Books*, 44, 10 (12 June 1997), 34–7.
—— 'Evolution: the pleasures of pluralism', part 2, *New York Review of Books*, 44, 11 (26 June 1997), 47–52.
Gracián, Baltasar, *Oráculo manual y arte de prudencia*, in *Obras completas*, II, Biblioteca Castro (Madrid: Turner, 1993).
Granjel, Luis S., 'Los «Diálogos» de Pedro Mercado', in *Médicos españoles* (Salamanca: Universidad de Salamanca, 1967).
Green, Otis H., 'El *Ingenioso* Hidalgo', *Hispanic Review*, 25 (1957), 175–93.
—— *Spain and the Western Tradition, The Castilian Mind in Literature from El Cid to Calderón*, 4 vols (Madison: University of Wisconsin Press, 1963–8).
—— '*El Licenciado Vidriera*: its relation to the *Viaje del Parnaso* and the *Examen de Ingenios* of Huarte', in *The Literary Mind of Medieval & Renaissance Spain* (Lexington: University Press of Kentucky, 1970).
Gruner, Oskar Cameron, *A Treatise on the Canon of Medicine of Avicenna, Incorporating a Translation of the First Book* (London: Luzac, 1930).
Guevara, Antonio de, *Menosprecio de corte y alabanza de aldea*, edición de Asunción Rallo (Madrid: Cátedra, 1984).
Gurméndez, Carlos, *La melancolía* (Madrid: Espasa-Calpe, col. Austral, 1990).
Hagnel, Olle, Jan Lanke, Birgitta Rorsman and Leif Öjesjö, 'Are we entering an age of melancholy?', *Psychological Medicine*, 12 (1982), 279–98.
Harka, Chester, '*Don Quijote* in the light of Huarte's *Examen de ingenios*: a reexamination', *Anales cervantinos*, 19 (1981), 3–13.
Harvey, E. Ruth, *The Inward Wits. Psychological Theory in the Middle Ages and the Renaissance* (London: Warburg Institute, 1975).
Heinze, Gerardo and Martha Ontiveros, 'La fitofarmacología como tratamiento alterno en psiquiatría', *Salud mental*, 21, 6 (1998), 33–42.
Herffernan, Carol Falvo, *The Melancholy Muse. Chaucer, Shakespeare and Early Medicine* (Pittsburgh: Duquesne University Press, 1995).
Hildegard de Bingen, *El arte de sanar de santa Hildegarda* [*Causae et curae*], ed. Manfred Pawlik (Gerona: Tikal, n.d. c.1997).
Hofstadter, Douglas R., *Gödel, Escher, Bach. An Eternal Golden Braid* (New York: Basic Books, 1979).
Hölldobler, Bert and Edmund O. Wilson, *The Ants* (Cambridge, MA: Harvard University Press, 1990).
Huarte de San Juan, Juan, *Examen de ingenios para las ciencias*, critical edn by Guillermo Serés (Madrid: Cátedra, 1989).
Huxley, Aldous, 'Accidie', in *On the Margin* (London: Chatto & Windus, 1923).
Idel, Moshe, 'Religion, thought and attitudes: the impact of the expulsion on the Jews', in Elie Kedourie (ed.), *Spain and the Jews. The Sepharadi Experience. 1442 and After* (London: Thames and Hudson, 1992).
Iriarte, Mauricio de, *El doctor Huarte de San Juan y su 'Examen de ingenios'. Contribución a la historia de la psicología experimental* (Madrid: Consejo Superior de Investigaciones Científicas, 1948). [Orig. pub. 1938 in *Spanische Forschungen der Goerresgesellschaft*.]

Jackson, Stanley W., *Melancholia and Depression. From Hippocratic Times to Modern Times* (New Haven: Yale University Press, 1986).
Jacquart, Danielle, 'La maladie et le remède d'amour dans quelques écrits medicaux du Moyen Age', in Danielle Buschinger and André Crepin (eds), *Amour, mariage et transgression au Moyen Age* (Göppingen: Centre d'Études Médiévales de l'Université de Picardie-Kümmerle Verlag, 1984).
Jacquart, Danielle, and Claude Thomasset, 'L'amour «héroïque» à travers le traité d'Arnaud de Villeneuve', in Jean Céard (ed.), *La folie et le corps* (Paris: Presses de l'École Normale Supérieure, 1985).
—— *Sexualité et savoir médical au Moyen Age* (Paris: Presses Universitaires de France, 1985).
Jahoda, Gustav, *Psychology and Anthropology. A Psychological Perspective* (London: Academic Press, 1982).
Jehl, Rainer, *Melancholie und Acedia. Ein Beitrag zu Anthropologie und Ethik Bonaventuras* (Paderborn: Ferdinand Schöningh, 1984).
Jenkins, Harold, 'Introduction', Arden edn of *Hamlet* (London: Routledge, 1989).
Jerónimo (san), *Epistolario*, ed. Juan Bautista Valero (Madrid: Biblioteca de Autores Cristianos, 1995).
Juan de la Cruz (san), *Obras completas* (Madrid: Biblioteca de Autores Cristianos, 1982).
Juana Inés de la Cruz, sor, *El sueño*, in *Obras completas, I. Lírica personal*, ed. Alfonso Méndez Plancarte (Mexico City: Fondo de Cultura Económica, 1951), pp. 335–59.
Kagan, Jerome, *Galen's Prophecy. Temperament in Human Nature* (New York: Basic Books, 1994).
Kagan, Richard L., *Students and Society in Early Modern Spain* (Baltimore: Johns Hopkins University Press, 1974).
—— *Lucrecia's Dreams. Politics and Prophecy in Sixteenth-Century Spain* (Berkeley: University of California Press, 1990).
Kahn, Jack, *Job's Illness: Loss, Grief and Integration. A Psychological Interpretation* (Oxford: Pergamon Press, 1975).
Kaplan, Bert, 'Acedia: the decline of desire as the ultimate life crisis', in D. Capps, W. H. Capps and M. G. Bradford (eds), *Encounter with Erikson. Historical Interpretation and religious biography* (Missoula, Montana: Scholars Press/The American Academy of Religion, 1977).
Kleinman, Arthur and Bryan Good (compilers), *Culture and Depression. Studies in the Anthropology and Cross-Cultural Pasychiatry of Affect and Disorder* (Berkeley: University of California Press, 1985).
Klerman, G. L., 'Is this the Age of Melancholy?', *Psychology Today*, 12 (1979), 36–42, 88–9.
Klibansky, Raymond, Erwin Panofsky and Fritz Saxl, *Saturne et la Mélancolie* (Paris: Gallimard, 1989).
Kong, Deborah, 'Don Quijote, Melancholy Knight', in *A Study of the Medical Theory of the Humours and its Application to Selected Spanish Literature of the Golden Age*, pp. 201–34 (unpub. Ph.D. thesis, University of Edinburgh, 1980).
Koyré, Alexandre, *La Philosophie de Jacob Boehme* (Paris: J. Vrin, 1979).

Kramer, Heinrich and Johann Sprenger, *El martillo de las brujas* [*Malleus maleficarum*] (Madrid: Felmar, 1976).
Kraus, Arnoldo, 'Suffering. A vital experience', *Journal of Clinical Rheumatology*, 4, 1 (1998).
Kristeller, Paul Oskar, *Il pensiero filosófico di Marsilio Ficino* (Florencia: Sansoni, 1953).
Kristeva, Julia, *Soleil noir, Dépression et mélancolie* (Paris: Gallimard, 1987).
Kuhn, Reinhard, *The Demon of Noontide. Ennui in Western Literature* (Princeton: Princeton University Press, 1976).
Kuhn, T. S., *La estructura de las revoluciones científicas* (Mexico City: Fondo de Cultura Económica, 1971).
Labriole, Pierre de, 'Le "démon de midi"', *Bulletin du Cange*, 9 (1934), 46–54.
Laguna, Andrés, *Pedacio Dioscórides Anazarbeo acerca de la materia medicinal y los venenos mortíferos, traducido de la lengua Griega en la vulgar castellana, & ilustrado con claras y sustantiales Annotaciones y con las figuras de innúmeras plantas, exquisitas y raras* (Amberes: Iuan Latio, 1555).
Laignel-Lavastine, M., 'Concomitance des états pathologiques et les «trois signes»', in *Illuminations et sécheresses*, ed. Bruno de Jésus-Marie (Paris: Desclée de Brouwer, 1937).
Laín Entralgo, Pedro, *La historia clínica, Historia y teoría del relato patográfico* (Barcelona: Salvat, 1961).
León, Luis de (fray), *Exposición del Libro de Job*, in *Obras completas castellanas* (Madrid: Biblioteca de Autores cristianos, 1944).
Lepenies, Wolf, *Melancholy and Society* (Cambridge: Harvard University Press, 1992).
Lieber, Elinor, 'Galen in Hebrew: the transmission of Galen's works in the medieval Islamic world', in Vivian Nutton (ed.), *Galen: Problems and Prospects* (London: Wellcome Institute for the History of Medicine, 1981).
Lloyd, G. E. R., *Demystifying Mentalities* (Cambridge: Cambridge University Press, 1990).
Logre, B. J., 'La folie de Don Quichotte', *Ouest Médical*, 23 (1956).
López de Hinojosos, Alonso, *Suma y recopilación de cirugía, con un arte para sangrar muy útil y provechosa* (Mexico City: Pedro Balli, 1595). Chapter 53, 'De merarquía y tristezas', pub. in Roger Bartra, *El Siglo de Oro de la melancolía. Textos españoles y novohispanos sobre las enfermedades del alma* (Mexico City: Universidad Iberoamericana, Departamento de Historia, 1998).
López de Villalobos, Francisco, *Algunas obras del Doctor Francisco López de Villalobos* (Madrid: Sociedad de Bibliófilos Españoles, 1886).
López Estrada, Francisco, 'Estudio y texto de la narración pastoril «Ausencia y soledad de amor», del «Inventario» de Villegas', *Boletín de la Real Academia Española* 29, 126 (1949), 99–133.
López Ibor, Juan José, 'Ideas de Santa Teresa sobre la melancolía', *Revista de espiritualidad*, 22 (1963), 432–43.
López Piñero, José María and Calero, Francisco, *Los temas polémicos de la medicina renacentista: las* Controversias *(1556), de Francisco Vallés* (Madrid: Consejo Superior de Investigaciones Científicas, 1988).

Loureiro, Ángel G., 'España maníaca', *Quimera*, 167 (1998), 15–20.
Lowes, John Livingston, 'The Loveres Maladye of Hereos', *Modern Philology*, 11 (1914), 491–546.
Luhmann, Niklas, *Love as Passion* (Cambridge, MA: Harvard University Press, 1986).
Lukács, Georg, *Teoría de la novela* ([1920]; Barcelona: Edhasa, 1971).
Lyons, Bridget Gellert, *Voices of Melancholy. Studies in Literary Treatments of Melancholy in Renaissance England* (London: Routledge & Kegan Paul, 1971).
Maeztu, Ramiro de, *Don Quijote, don Juan y la Celestina* ([1926]; Madrid: Espasa-Calpe (Austral), 1981).
Maimónides, Moses, *On the Causes of Symptoms (Maqālah fī bayān ba'ḍ al-'arāḍ wa-al-jawāb 'anhā – Ma'amar ha-hakra'ah – De causis accidentium)*, Hebrew text with English trans. ed. J. O. Leibowitz and S. Marcus (Berkeley: University of California Press, 1974).
Mancheño y Olivares, Miguel, *Apuntes para una historia de Arcos de la Frontera* (Arcos: Tipografía El Arcobricense, 1893).
Maravall, José Antonio, *Estado moderno y mentalidad social*, 2 vols (Madrid: Alianza Editorial, 1986).
Marco Merenciano, Francisco, 'Psicoanálisis y melancolía en Santa Teresa', in *Ensayos médicos y literarios* (Madrid: Ensayos Cultura Hispánica, 1958).
Marsella, Anthony J., Norman Sartorius, Assen Jablensky and Fred R. Fenton, 'Cross-cultural studies of depressive disorders: an overview', in *Culture and Depression. Studies in the Anthropology and Cross-Cultural Psychiatry of Affect and Disorder*, comp. Arthur Kleinman and Byron Good (Berkeley: University of California Press, 1985).
Martínez de Toledo, Alfonso, *Arcipreste de Talavera o Corbacho*, ed. Michael Gerli (Madrid: Cátedra, 1992).
Martínez Ruiz, Juan and Joaquina Albarracín Navarro, 'Farmacopea en *La Celestina* y en un manuscrito árabe de Ocaña', in *La Celestina y su contorno social*, ed. Manuel Criado del Val, Actas del I Congreso Internacional sobre La Celestina (Barcelona: Borrás, 1977).
Mayans, Gregorio, *Vida de Miguel de Cervantes Saavedra*, 5th edn (Madrid: Pedro Joseph Alonso i Padilla, 1750).
Meadow, Mary, 'The dark side of mysticism: depression and the "dark night"', *Psychology and Christianity*, 5 (1991), 233–53.
Melczer, William, 'Did Don Quixote die of melancholy?', in *Folie et déraison à la Renaissance*, Colloque International, November 1973 (Bruselas: Éditions de l'Université de Bruxelles, 1976).
Ménardière, Hippolite Pilet de la, *Traité de la mélancholie. Savoir si elle est la cause des Effets que l'on remarque dans les Possédées de Loudun* (La Flèche, no pub., 1635).
Mercado, Pedro de, *Diálogos de filosophia natural y moral* (Granada: Hugo de Mena and René Rabilio, 1558). The sixth dialogue, 'De la melancolía', is pub. in Roger Bartra, *El Siglo de Oro de la melancolía. Textos españoles y novohispanos sobre las enfermedades del alma* (Mexico City: Universidad Iberoamericana, Departamento de Historia, 1998).

Merola, Hieronymo, *República original sacada del cuerpo humano* (Barcelona: Pedro Malo, 1587).
Michëlis de Vasconcellos, Carolina, *A Saudade Portuguesa, Divagações Filológicas e Literar-Históricas em Volta de Inês de Castro e do cantar Velho 'Saudade Minha – ¿Quando te veria?'* (second edn, rev. and expanded) (Porto: Renasença Portuguesa, 1922).
Midelfort, H. C. Erik, *A History of Madness in Sixteenth-Century Germany* (Stanford: Stanford University Press, 1999).
Montalto, Filoteo Elião de, *Archipathologia, in qua internarum capitis affectionum essentia, causae, signa, praesagia et curatio accuratissima indagine edisserunter* (Paris: F. Jacquin, 1614).
Morley, Griswold S. and Courtney Bruerton, *Cronología de las comedia de Lope de Vega* (Madrid: Gredos, 1968).
Müller, Friedrich Max, *Comparative Mythology [1856]*, ed. A. S. Palmer (New York: Dutton, 1909).
Murillo y Velarde, Thomás, *Aprobación de ingenios y curación de hipocondríacos, con observaciones y remedios muy particulares* (Zaragoza: Diego de Ormer, 1672).
Nadler, Steven, 'Descartes's Demon and the madness of Don Quixote', *Journal of the History of Ideas*, 58, 2 (1997), 41–55.
Nordström, Folke, *Goya, Saturn, and Melancholy* (Estocolmo: Alquist & Wiksell, 1962).
Obeyeserkere, Gananath, 'Depression, Buddhism, and the work of culture in Sri Lanka', in *Culture and Depression. Studies in the Anthropology and Cross-Cultural Pasychiatry of Affect and Disorder*, comp. Arthur Kleinman and Byron Good (Berkeley: University of California Press, 1985).
Olmedilla y Puig, Joaquín, *Estudio histórico de la vida y escritos del sabio español Andrés Laguna, médico de Carlos I y Felipe II y célebre escritor y botánico del siglo XVI* (Madrid: El Correo, 1887).
Olmos, Andrés de (fray), *Tratado sobre los siete pecados capitales (1551–1552)*, palæography of Nahuatl text, Spanish version, intro. and notes by Georges Baudot (Mexico City: Universidad Nacional Autónoma de México, 1996).
Orfalí, Moisés, 'El judeoconverso hispano: historia de una mentalidad', in Carlos Barros (ed.), *Xudeus e conversos na historia*, Actas do Congreso Internacional, Ribadavia, 14–17 October 1991 (Santiago de Copostela: Editorial de la Historia, 1994).
Orobitg, Christine, 'Between evil and malady: cures of melancholy in Spanish Golden Age', Conference on *Healing, Magic and Belief in Europe, 15th–20th Centuries*, vol. II, 178–208 (Zeist, Holanda: Conference Centre Woudschoten, 1994).
—— 'La typologie des nations et l'espagnol mélancoligue: notes pour l'interpretation d'un cliché', *Revue de synthese*, 4, 1 (1995), 99–128.
—— *L'humeur noire. Mélancolie, écriture et pensée en Espagne au XVIe et au XVIIe siècle* (Bethesda, MD: International Scholars Publications, n.d., c.1997).
—— *Garcilaso et la mélancolie* (Toulouse: Presses Universitaires du Mirail, 1997).

Ortega, Eusebio and Benjamín Marcos, *Francisco Vallés (El Divino)* (Madrid: Biblioteca Filosófica, 1914).
Paz, Octavio, *Sor Juana Inés de la Cruz o las trampas de la fe* (Mexico City: Fondo de Cultura Económica, 1982).
Pedro Hispano, *Obras médicas*, ed. Maria Helena da Rocha Pereira (Coimbra: Universidad de Coimbra, 1973).
Pérez Bautista, Florencio L., 'La medicina y los médicos en el teatro de Calderón de la Barca', *Cuadernos de Historia de la Medicina Española*, 7 (1968), 149–245.
Pérez Regordán, Manuel, 'El doctor don Andrés Velázquez y su libro de la melancolía', unpub. typescript (Arcos de la Frontera, 1972).
—— *La Real Justicia y el Santo Oficio de la Inquisición en Arcos de la Frontera* (Arcos de la Frontera: author's own publication, 1992).
—— *Historias y leyendas de Arcos*, 3 vols (Arcos de la Frontera: published by the Arcos town council, 1988 and 1994).
Pérez-Rincón, Héctor, 'Reflexiones melancólicas (un paseo bibliográfico)', *Ciencia y desarrollo*, 28, 105 (1992), 33–41.
—— 'Del leteo al beleño. Un hipnótico mitológico y uno natural en dos fragmentos poéticos del Siglo de Oro', *La Gaceta del Fondo de Cultura Económica*, 300 (1995), 55–6.
Pérouse, Gabriel A., *L'Examen de Esprits du Docteur Juan Huarte de San Juan. Sa diffusion et son influence en France aux XVIe et XVIIe siècles* (Paris: Les Belles Lettres, 1970).
Peset Llorca, Vicente, 'Las maravillosas facultades de los melancólicos (Un tema de psiquiatría renacentista)', *Archivos de neurobiología*, 18, 4 (1955), 980–1002.
—— 'La psiquiatría de un médico humanista (Francisco Vallés, 1524–1592)', *Archivos de neurobiología*, 23, 1 and 2; 24, 1 (1961), 55–70, 155–83, 60–78.
Piga Sánchez-Morate, B., 'Sobre algunas ideas interesantes acerca de la melancolía morbus en la medicina española del siglo XVI', *Medicina*, 11, 5 (1943), 437–9.
Pigeaud, Jackie, 'Fatalisme des temperaments et liberté spirituelle dans l'*Examen des esperits* de Huarte de San Juan', *Littérature, medecine, societé*, 1 (1979), 115–59.
—— *La maladie de l'âme. Etude sur la relation de l'âme et du corps dans la tradition médico-philosophique antique* (Paris: Les Belles Lettres, 1981).
—— 'De la mélancolie et de quelques autres maladies dans les *Etymologies* IV d'Isidore de Seville', in *Textes médicaux latins antiques*, ed. G. Sabbah (Saint-Étienne: Publications de l'Université de Saint-Étienne, 1984).
—— *L'homme de génie et la mélancolie, Problème XXX, 1* (Paris: Rivages, 1988).
—— 'Reflections on Love-Melancholy in Robert Burton', in *Eros and Anteros: The Medical Traditions of Love in the Renaissance*, Donald A. Beecher and Massimo Ciavolella (eds) (Toronto: University of Toronto Italian Studies Dovehouse Editions, 1992).
Quevedo, Francisco de, *Historia de la vida del Buscón llamado Don Pablos*, in *Obras completas*, vol. I (Madrid: Aguilar, 1958).
Redondo, Augustin, 'La métaphore du corps de la république à travers le traité du médecin Jerónimo Merola (1587)', *Le corps comme métaphore*

dans l'Espagne des XVIe et XVIIe siècles, ed. A. Redondo (Paris: Publications de la Sorbonne Nouvelle, 1992).

—— 'La melancolía y el *Quijote* de 1605', in *Varia lingüística y literaria*, II: 215–41, ed. Martha Elena Venier (Mexico City: El Colegio de México, 1997).

Reguera, Isidoro, *Objetos de melancolía (Jacob Böhme)* (Madrid: Ediciones Libertarias, 1985).

Rhazes (Abú Bakr Muhammad ibn Zakariyá al-Razi), *Liber ad Almansorem decem tractatus continens (Kitab al-Mansuri)*, in *Opera*, trans. Gerardo de Cremona (Ludguni: no pub., 1510).

Ribeiro, João, *Curiosidades verbais* (São Paulo, no pub., n.d. [1927?]).

Roberts, Kimberley S. and Sacks, Norman P., 'Dom Duarte and Robert Burton: two men of Melancholy', *Journal of the History of Medicine*, 9 (1954), 21–37.

Rodríguez Marín, Francisco, *Estudios cervantinos* (Madrid: Patronato del IV centenario de Cervantes, Ediciones Atlas, 1947).

Rojas, Fernando de, *La Celestina*, ed. Bruno Mario Daminani (Madrid: Cátedra, 1985).

Romero López, Dolores, 'Fisonomía y temperamento de don Quijote de la Mancha', in *Estado actual de los estudios sobre el Siglo de Oro*, ed. M. García Martín (Salamanca: Universidad de Salamanca, 1993).

Roth, Cecil, *A History of Marranos* (New York: Sepher-Herman Press, 1974).

Roth, Norman, *Jews, Visigoths, and Muslims in Medieval Spain. Cooperation and Conflict* (Leiden: E. J. Brill, 1994).

Rubin, Julius H., *Religious Melancholy and Protestant Experience in America* (Oxford: Oxford University Press, 1994).

Rubio, Luciano, 'El temperamento «melancólico» de fray Luis de León y sus actuaciones prácticas', in S. Álvarez Turienzo (ed.), *Fray Luis de León. El frayle, el humanista, el teólogo* (Real Monasterio de El Escorial: Ediciones Escurialenses, 1992).

Ruiz Pérez, Pedro, 'El discurso elegiaco y la lírica barroca: pérdida y melancolía', in *La elegía*, III international conference on the poetry of del Siglo de Oro, ed. Begoña López Bueno (Sevilla: Universidad de Sevilla, 1996).

Ruy Sánchez, Alberto, *Con la literatura en el cuerpo. Historias de literatura y melancolía* (Mexico City: Taurus, 1995).

Sabuco de Nantes, Miguel, *Nueva filosofía de la naturaleza del hombre [y otros escritos]* (Madrid: Editora Nacional, 1981).

Sacks, Oliver, 'An anthropologist on Mars' and 'Prodigies', in *An Anthropologist on Mars* (New York: Knopf, 1995).

—— 'The Autist Artist', 'The Twins' and 'A Walking Grove', in *The Man Who Mistook His Wife for a Hat* (New York: HarperCollins, 1985).

Sacristán, María Cristina, *Locura e Inquisición en Nueva España, 1571–1760* (Mexico City: Fondo de Cultura Económica, 1992).

Said, Edward W., *Culture and Imperialism* (New York: Knopf, 1993).

Salillas, Rafael, *Un inspirador de Cervantes: el doctor Huarte de San Juan* (Madrid: Eduardo Arias, 1905).

Sánchez-Albornoz, Claudio, *España, un enigma histórico*, 8th edn, 2 vols (Barcelona: EDHASA, 1981).

Sancho de San Román, Rafael, *La medicina y los médicos en la obra de Tirso de Molina* (Salamanca: Universidad de Salamanca, 1960).
Santa Cruz, Alfonso de, *Dignotio et cura afectuum melancholicorum* (Madrid: Tomás de Junta, 1622); Spanish trans. Raúl Lavalle, in *Sobre la melancolía. Diagnóstico y curación de los afectos melancólicos*, ed. Juan Antonio Paniagua (Pamplona: Ediciones Universidad de Navarra, 2005).
Schiesari, Juliana, *The Gendering of Melancholia. Feminism, Psychoanalysis, and the Symbolics of Loss in Renaissance literature* (Ithaca: Cornell University Press, 1992).
Schleiner, Winfried, *Melancholy, Genius, and Utopia in the Renaissance* (Wiesbaden: Otto Harrassowitz, 1991).
Scot, Reginald, 'A discourse upon divels and spirits', appendix to *The Discoverie of Witchcraft* ([London: William Brome, 1584] facs. edn Da Capo Press, Amsterdam, 1971).
Screech, M. A., *Montaigne and Melancholy* (London: Penguin, 1991).
Searle, John R., 'Minds, brains and programs', *Behavioral and Brain Sciences*, 3 (1980), 417–57.
Sena, John F., 'Melancholic madness and the Puritans', *Harvard Theological Review*, 66 (1973), 293–309.
Seznec, Jean, *La survivance des dieux antiques* (London: Studies of the Warburg Institute, vol. XI, 1940).
—— *The Survival of the Pagan Gods* (New York, 1953).
Simon, J. R., *Robert Burton (1577–1640) et l'Anatomie de la Mélancholie* (Paris: Didier, 1964).
Singer, Irving, *The Nature of Love. 2: Courtly and Romantic* (Chicago: University of Chicago Press, 1984).
Siraisi, Nancy G., *Avicenna in Renaissance Italy. The* Canon *and Medical Teaching in Italian Universities after 1500* (Princeton: Princeton University Press, 1987).
Sober, Elliot and David Sloan Wilson, *Unto Others: The Evolution and Psychology of Unselfish Behavior* (Cambridge, Massachusetts: Harvard University Press, 1998).
Sokal, Alan and Jean Bricmont, *Impostures intellectuelles* (Paris: Odile Jacob, 1997).
Soufas, Teresa Scott, 'Calderón's melancholy wife-murderers', *Hispanic Review*, 52, 2 (1984), 181–203.
—— *Melancholy and the Secular Mind in Spanish Golden Age Literature* (Columbia: University of Missouri Press, 1990).
Speak, Gill, 'An odd kind of melancholy: reflections on the glass delusion in Europe (1440–1680)', *History of Psychiatry*, 1 (1990), 191–206.
—— '*El licenciado Vidriera* and the glass men of early modern Europe', *Modern Language Review*, 85, 4 (1990), 850–65.
Starobinski, Jean, *Histoire du traitement de la mélancolie des origines à 1900* (Basilea: J. R. Geigy, 1960).
Steinberg, Leo, *The Sexuality of Christ in Renaissance Art and in Modern Oblivion*, 2nd edn rev. and amended (Chicago: University of Chicago Press, 1996).

Strohmaier, Gotthard, 'Galen in Arabic: problems and prospects', in Vivian Nutton (ed.), *Galen: Problems and Prospects* (London: Wellcome Institute for the History of Medicine, 1981).

Surin, Jean-Joseph, *Lettres spirituelles* (Toulouse: Cavallera, 1928).

Tamani, Giuliano, *Il 'Canon medicinae' di Avicenna nella tradizione ebraica. Le miniature del manoscritto 2197 della Biblioteca Universitaria di Bologna* (Padua: Editoriale Programma, 1988).

Tellenbach, Hubertus, *La mélancolie* (Paris: Presses Universitaires de France, 1979) [Orig. pub. as *Melancholie: Problemgeschichte, Endogenität, Typologie, Pathogenese, Klinik* (Berlín: Springer-Verlag, 1961)].

Temkin, Owsei, 'On Galen's pneumatology', in *The Double Face of Janus and Other Essays in the History of Medicine* (Baltimore: Johns Hopkins University Press, 1977).

Teresa de Ávila (Saint), *Obras completas* (Madrid: Biblioteca de Autores Cristianos, 1986).

Thomas, Hugh, *La trata de esclavos. Historia del tráfico de seres humanos de 1440 a 1870*, (Barcelona: Planeta, 1998). Pub. as *The Slave Trade: The History of the Atlantic Slave Trade, 1440–1870* (London: Phoenix, 2006).

Tirso de Molina, *El melancólico* [1611], in *Obras dramáticas completas*, vol. I (Madrid: Aguilar, 1946).

Torre, Esteban, *Averroes y la ciencia médica. La doctrina anatomofuncional del «Colliget»* (Madrid: Ediciones del Centro, 1974).

Torroja Menéndez, Carmen and María Rivas Palá, 'Teatro en Toledo en el siglo XV. Auto de la pasión de Alonso del Campo', *Boletín de la Real Academia Española*, Anejo 35 (1977), 24–34.

Trabulse, Elías, *Ciencia y religión en el siglo XVII* (Mexico City: El Colegio de México, 1974).

—— 'El hermetismo y Sor Juana Inés de la Cruz', in *El círculo roto* (Mexico City: Lecturas Mexicanas, 1984).

Treffert, Darold A., *Extraordinary People. Understanding 'Idiot Savants'* (New York: Harper and Row, 1989).

Turner, Denis, 'St John of the Cross and depression', *Downside Review*, 106 (1988), 157–70.

Ullersperger, J. B., *La historia de la psicologia y de la psiquiatría en España desde los más remotos tiempos hasta la actualidad* (Madrid: Editorial Alhambra, 1954); trans. of *Die Geschichte der Psychologie un der Psychiatrik in Spanien von dem ältesten Zeiten bis aur Gegenwart* (Würzburg: A. Stuber's Buchhandlung, 1871).

Ullman, M., *Islamic Medicine* (Edinburgh: Edinburgh University Press, 1978).

Unamuno, Miguel de, *Vida de don Quijote y Sancho*, in *Ensayos*, vol. II (Madrid: Aguilar, 1951).

—— *Del sentimiento trágico de la vida*, in *Ensayos*, vol. II (Madrid: Aguilar, 1951).

Urrutia, Jorge, 'Glosa a la inacción', in *Humores negros: del tedio, la melancolía, el esplín y otros aburrimientos*, ed. Rosa de Diego and Lydia Vázquez (Madrid: Biblioteca Nueva, 1998).

Váez, Pedro, *Petri Vaezi, excellentissimi principis ducis Machedae et pro regis Cathaloniae medici* (Barcelona: Sebastián Cormellas, 1593).
Van Doren, Mark, *Don Quijote's Profession* (New York: Columbia University Press, 1958).
Vega, Lope de, *Comedia del príncipe melancólico*, in *Obras de Lope de Vega*, Obras dramáticas, vol. I (Madrid: Real Academia Española, 1916).
Velásquez, Andrés, *Libro de la melancholia, en el qual se trata de la naturaleza desta enfermedad, assi llamada Melancholia, y de sus causas y simptomas. Y si el rustico puede hablar Latin, ò philosophar, estando phrenetico ò maniaco, sin primero lo aver aprendido* (Sevilla: Hernando Díaz, printer, and Alonso de Mata, bookseller, 1585). Pub. in Roger Bartra, *El Siglo de Oro de la melancolía. Textos españoles y novohispanos sobre las enfermedades del alma* (Mexico City: Universidad Iberoamericana, Departamento de Historia, 1998).
Vilar, Pierre, 'Le temps du Quichotte', *Europe*, 121–2 (1956), 3–15.
Villalón, Cristóbal de, *El Crótalon de Cristóforo Gnofoso*, ed. Asunción Rallo (Madrid: Cátedra, 1990).
Vincent, Jean-Didier, *Biología de las pasiones* (Barcelona: Anagrama, 1987).
Vives, Juan Luis, *Tratado del alma*, in *Obras completas*, Spanish trans. Lorenzo Riber, vol. II (Madrid: Aguilar, 1948).
Vossler, Karl, *La poesía de la soledad en España* (Buenos Aires, 1946).
Wack, Mary F., 'The *Liber de heros morbo* of Johannes Afflacius and its implications for medieval love conventions', *Speculum*, 62 (1987), 324–44.
—— *Lovesickness in the Middle Ages. The* Viaticum *and Its Commentaries* (Philadelphia: University of Pennsylvania Press, 1990).
Weber, Max, *The Protestant Ethic and the Spirit of Capitalism*, trans. Talcott Parsons (New York: Charles Scribner's Sons, 1958).
Weinrich, Harald, *Das Ingenium Don Quijotes, ein Beitrag zur Literarischen Characterkunde* (Munster: Aschendorffsche Verlagbuchhandlung, 1956).
Wenzel, Siegfried, 'Petrarch's *Accidia*', *Studies in the Renaissance*, 7 (1961), 36–48.
—— *The Sin of Sloth: Acedia in Medieval Thought and Literature* (Chapel Hill: University of North Carolina Press, 1967).
Wier, Jean, *Histoires, disputes et discours des illusions et impostures des diables, des magiciens infâmes, sorcières et empoisonneurs: des ensorcelez et demoniaques et de la guérison d'iceux: item de la punition que méritent les magiciens, les empoisonneurs et les sorcières*, 2 vols (Paris: A. Delahaye et Lecrosnier, 1885).
Williams, Raymond, *Culture and Society, 1780–1950* (Harmondsworth: Penguin, 1961).
Wind, Edgar, *Mystères païens de la Renaissance* (Paris: Gallimard, 1992).
—— *Pagan Mysteries in the Renaissance* (Harmondsworth: Peregrine, 1967).
Worrell, William H., 'The demon of noonday and some related ideas', *Journal of the American Oriental Society*, 88 (1918), 160–6.
Yates, Frances A., *The Occult Philosophy in the Elizabethan Age* (London: Routledge & Kegan Paul, 1979).

Yerushalmi, Yosef Hayim, *From Spanish Court to Italian Ghetto. Isaac Cardoso: A Study in Seventeenth-Century Marranism and Jewish Apologetics* (New York: Columbia University Press, 1971).

Zilboorg, Gregory, *A History of Medical Psychology* (New York: Norton, 1941).

Index

acedia 23, 36ff, 70, 84ff, 95, 100, 169–174, 179, 197
Acuña, Hernando de 106ff, 156
adustion (or combustion) of humours 25, 27ff, 31ff, 47, 50, 53, 61, 64, 72, 75, 81, 103, 112, 141, 144, 159, 173, 177ff, 281, 189ff
Aëtius 61, 91, 148
Agamben, Giorgio 85, 126, 145, 170, 174
Aguilar, Gaspar 151
Albarracín Navarro, Joaquina. 155
Albucasis (Abū al-Qasim al-Zaharaui Khalaf ibn Abbas), 159
Alcalá university 68
Alcázar, Jorge 52, 129
Alexander of Tralles 61
Alfonso el Sabio 65

Álvarez de Toledo, Luisa Isabel 163
Álvarez, Javier 147
Álvarez, Javier 88

Amato Lusitano (João Rodrigues de Castelo Branco), 40, 109ff, 158
Andreas Capellanus 102
Andrés, Melquiades 146

anger 44ff, 93, 102, 107, 163, 187, 195
Anglo, Sydeney 73ff, 138ff, 140, 145
anguish 16, 51, 190ff
Antonio, Nicolás 136
ants 24ff
anxiety 1, 3, 5, 14, 20, 26ff 31, 49, 92, 139, 190, 204
Aquinas, Thomas 162
Arbesmann, Rudolph 37
Aretæus of Cappadocia 15, 61, 116
Ariosto, Ludovico 180
Aristotle 15, 22, 45, 61, 105, 114, 200
Arjona, J. Homero 203
Armas, F. A. de 154
Arnold, Matthew 3, 7
Auerbach, Erich 185, 203
Augustine, St 22, 42, 99, 152
autism 121, 162
Averroes 57, 94, 110, 149
Avicenna 5, 11, 28, 31ff, 57, 60ff, 94, 100, 103, 162, 173
Azouvi, François 141

Babb, Lawrence 156, 199
Barlow, T. D., 137
Barondes, Samuel H., 35
Barrenechea, Francisco 129
Barrios, Juan de 104ff, 156

228 Index

Bataillon, Marcel 55, 107ff, 131, 142, 150, 157, 181, 201
Baudelaire, Charles 36
Baudot, Georges 197
Baxter, Christopher 73ff, 138ff
Beecher, Donald A., 38, 141, 151, 155
Beinart, Haim 157ff
Bel Bravo, María Antonia 158
Benjamin, Walter 134
Bernini, Giovanni Lorenzo 85
Bertalanffy, Ludwig von 12, 34
Bettelheim, Bruno 162
Bieber, Gustav Arthur 204
Bieńko, Doris 150
Binswanger, Ludwig 4, 8
black bile 14, 27–33, 39, 49ff, 53, 64, 74, 97, 110, 114, 173–175, 177, 200
Blackmore, Susan 36
Blázquez Miguel, Juan 147ff
bleeding 72, 89, 111, 158ff
Bleznick, Donald W, 131
blood, red bile (see also sanguine humour), 14, 28ff, 31, 45, 95ff, 103, 105, 111, 113, 145ff, 152, 160, 173, 176ff, 189, 191
Blumenberg, Hans 20, 24, 36
Bodin, Jean 73, 77, 83, 133, 138
Böhme, Jakob 92ff, 149, 166
Bolaños, María 134
Bonaventure (Saint), 171ff, 196
Bonuzzi, Luciano 40
Boscán, Juan 183, 202
Bossuet, Jacques-Bénigne 171
Brague, Rémi 195
Brailowsky, Simón 35
Brann, Noel L., 150
Braudel, Fernand 59, 132
Bricmont, Jean 7
Bright, Timothy 2, 7, 188ff, 204
Brown, G. S., 4, 7
Bruerton, Courtney 203

Buddhism 4
Burke, James F., 155
Burke, Peter 136
Burkert, Walter 18, 35
Burton, Robert 2, 5, 36, 105, 154, 166, 174, 190, 193, 204
Butcher, Samuel Henry 151
Bynum, Carline W., 152

Cælius Aurelianus 49ff, 129
Caillois, Roger 195
Calderón de la Barca, Pedro 54, 134, 166, 170
Calero, Francisco 150
Calvesi, Maurizio 137
Campanella, Tomasso 144, 160
Cano, Melchor 95, 150, 158, 173, 196
Cardaillac, Louis 133, 155
Cardano, Girolamo 73
Cardoner i Planas, Antoni 39
Cardoso, Isaac 108, 158
Cassianus (Cassian), John 23, 84, 166, 170, 202
Castells, Ricardo 154
Castiglione, Baldassare 183, 186, 202
Castro, Américo 91, 108, 157, 202
cauterization 40, 89, 147, 157
Céard, Jean 40, 140ff
Ceballos, Jerónimo de 122
cerebral ventricles 29, 42ff, 46, 48, 50, 57, 141
Certeau, Michel de 140
Cervantes, Miguel de 2, 40, 106, 124, 132, 142, 161, 163, 166, 169, 175–185, 188, 192ff, 202ff
Charles V, 68, 130
Chaucer, Geoffrey 36
choler, choleric 28ff, 81, 93, 95, 102, 112, 149, 173, 175ff, 177, 189ff, 199ff
Ciavollela, Massimo 38, 141, 151

Cicero 118, 172, 200
Ciruelo, Pedro 82, 145
Clapier-Valladon, Simone 127
Clark, Stuart 143, 145
Close, Anthony 203
Cohen-Solal, Annie 8
cold humour or temperament 13, 33, 46ff, 61, 73, 79ff, 94, 118, 128, 177, 180, 191
communication 21, 23
Concini, Concino (Marquis d'Ancre), 113
Constantinus Africanus 26ff, 38
continuity of myths 165
conversos 54ff
Coronas Tejada, Luis 157
Couliano, Ioan P., 127
Crema, Battista da 150, 173
Cuevas, José and Jesús de las 135

D'Urfey, Thomas 205
Dante Alighieri 174, 197
Darwinian interpretation 18ff, 20
David-Peyre, Yvonne 134, 155, 176
David-Peyre, Yvonne 40, 199
Dawkins, Richard 17ff, 35
Delgado y Orellana, José Antonio 132, 135ff, 163ff
dementia 16, 37, 128
Dennett, Daniel C., 18ff, 35
depression 3ff, 16ff, 27
Descartes, René 45, 182
devil 37, 71ff
Deyermond, Alan 153
Díaz-Plaja, Guillermo 7,134
Dioscorides 35, 77
diuretics 111
Domínguez Ortiz, Antonio 158
Donne, John 205
Dowland, John 191, 204
Down, J. Langdon 120, 162
Drake, Francis 121, 162
Dronke, Peter 146

dryness, dry temperament 13, 47ff, 50, 61, 73, 88ff, 94, 112, 119, 128, 176ff, 180, 186,
Duarte, Dom (King of Portugal), 63ff
Duminil, Marie-Paule 151
Duncan, Marc 139, 160
Dürer, Albrecht 5, 51ff, 54, 135, 194

ecstasy 85, 92, 94ff, 186
Elias, Norbert 69
Elliott, J. H., 122, 136, 162
emetics 89, 111
Empedocles 80
Enríquez, José Ramón 103, 155, 194, 203
entropy 11
epilepsy 46, 86
Erasistratus 96, 154
erotic melancholy 30, 86, 96ff, 103, 106, 134, 151, 155, 168
Escolano, Gaspar 8
Escudero Ortuño, Alberto 162
Estes, Leland L., 144
Evagrius Ponti (Evagrio del Ponto), 23, 195
Evans, Bergen 156
evolution, evolutionism 2, 17ff, 19ff, 36, 132,166ff, 194

Farfán, Agustín 153
Farinelli, Arturo 130
fear, terror 14, 22, 27, 29ff, 32, 38, 44, 46ff, 53, 61, 64, 75ff, 85, 91, 93ff, 107, 109ff, 117, 123, 144, 149, 173, 178, 189ff, 200
Fédida, Pierre 35
Fénelon, François 171
Ferdinand (King), 58, 130
Fernel, Jean 30ff, 40

Ferrand, Jacques 2, 38ff, 105ff, 151
Ficino, Marsilio 20, 23, 47, 54, 115ff, 151, 153, 162, 166, 173ff, 193, 198
Fleury, Claude 171
Folch Jou, Guillermo 155
Földényi, László F., 8
Fontenelle, Bernard 25, 38
Foucault, Michel 13ff, 34, 139
Franco Toriz, Germán 40
frenzy, frenetic 33, 38, 71ff, 78, 115ff, 119ff, 130, 142, 160
Freud, Sigmund 15, 34, 37
Freylas, Alonso de 80ff, 9, 1574, 144, 150
Friedenwald, Harry 143, 159

Galen 9ff, 11, 15ff, 20, 26, 42ff, 45–48, 52, 57, 61, 91, 93, 96ff, 111ff, 122, 148, 162, 204
Galigai, Leonora 113ff
Gállego, Julián 152
Galzigna, Mario 139
Gamaza, Baltasar de 101
Gambin, Felice 7
Gangler-Mundwiller, Dominique 196
García Ballester, Luis 133
García Combado, Juan 99
García Domínguez, Pedro 155
García Gibert, Javier 175, 193, 199ff, 205
Garcilaso de la Vega 156
Garibay, Angel María 196ff
Gellner, Ernest 24, 37
Gillet, Joseph E., 196
Ginzburg, Carlo 134
Girard, René 180
Godínez, Miguel (Michael Wadding), 94ff, 150
Góngora, Luis de 40, 156ff, 158ff

González de Cellorigo, Martín 122, 205
Good, Bryan 7
Gorceix, Bernard 149
Gould, Stephen Jay 19, 36
Gracián, Baltasar 186, 188, 191, 203ff
Gracián, Jerónimo (Fray), 87
Gray, Thomas 192
Green, Matthew 36
Green, Otis 124, 130, 132ff, 163, 175
Gregory (Pope), 170
Gruner, Oskar Cameron 39
Guainerio, Antonio 115ff, 117, 161
Guevara, Antonio de 64ff, 69ff, 134ff, 137, 202
Gurméndez, Carlos 8

Hagnel, Olle 6
Haly Abbas 27ff, 38ff
Harka, Chester 176, 199
Harris, T., 4, 7
Hartzenbusch, Juan Eugenio 134
Harvey, E. Ruth 39
Heinze, Gerardo 35
Hercules 80
Herffernan, Carol Falvo 156
Hildegard von Bingen 20, 146, 166
Hippocrates 26, 61, 96, 162, 174, 197
Hippocratic theory 9, 13, 16, 28, 33, 41, 57
Hofstadter, Douglas R., 128
Holborne, Anthony 204
Hölldobler, Bert 24, 37
Huarte de San Juan, Juan 9, 13, 16, 20, 26, 41–45, 47–49, 71ff, 75, 97ff, 112, 114–118, 121, 126ff, 130, 137ff, 158ff, 161ff,

175–178, 180, 184, 188ff,
    198ff, 204
humoral theory 11, 13ff, 16, 22,
    26–34, 41, 47ff, 50ff, 55,
    61, 79, 102, 123, 168,
    172ff, 176, 190
Huxley, Aldous 36
hypocondria 28–31, 38, 40, 97,
    110, 120, 138, 158

Idel, Moshe 157
idiot savants 120
individualism 174
individuality 12
individualization 169, 193ff
Iriarte, Mauricio de 136, 138, 175
Isaac Judaeus (Ishāq ibn Sulaymān
    al-Isra'īli), 130
Ishāq ibn Imrān 27ff
Isidoro de Sevilla 46

Jackson, Stanley W., 1, 35, 38, 127
Jacquart, Danielle 39, 152ff
Jahoda, Gustav 48, 129
Jeanne of the Angels (sister), 139
Jehl, Rainer 171, 196
Jenkins, Harold 190, 204
Jerome, St 22, 174, 197
Jerónimo de Ceballos 162
Jews 54ff, 90, 107–126
Jiménez de Cisneros, Francisco
    (Cardinal), 58
Johannitius (Hunayn ibn Ishaq),
    76, 151
John of the Cross (St), 9, 87ff, 91,
    93, 139, 147, 188
Juana Inés de la Cruz (sor), 51ff,
    129, 146

Kagan, Jerome 35
Kagan, Richard L., 135, 147
Kahn, Jack 148
Kaplan, Bert 145
Keats, John 192

Kierkegaard, Søren 166
Kircher, Athanasius 52
Kleinman, Arthur 7
Klerman, G. L., 6
Klibansky, Raymond 1, 3, 6, 36,
    39, 137, 153, 159ff, 166,
    174, 195, 205
Kong, Deborah 176
Koyré, Alexandre 93, 149
Kraus, Arnoldo 35
Kristeller, Paul Oskar 198
Kristeva, Julia 1, 7, 14, 34
Kuhn, Reinhard 145, 195
Kuhn, T. S., 9, 34

Labriole, Pierre de 35
Laguna, Andrés 77ff, 77, 80, 142ff
Laignel-Lavastine, M., 147
Laín Entralgo, Pedro 40
Lamarckian process 19, 98
laugher 28, 42–45, 56, 128, 177ff
laxatives 89, 111
Ledesma, Alonso de 146
León, Lucrecia de 90, 147
León, Luis de (fray), 90ff, 92,
    147ff
Leone Hebreo 108
Lepenies, Wolf 1, 3, 7, 69, 136
Lieber, Elinor 131
Lloyd, G. E. R., 129
Logre, B. J., 199
López de Hinojosos, Alonso 40
López de Villalobos, Francisco 130
López Estrada, Francisco 156
López Ibor, Juan José 146
López Piñero, José María 150
Loureiro, Ángel G, 8
love-sickness 27, 96ff, 106, 154
Lowes, John Livingston 151
Luhmann, Niklas 12, 34
Lukács, Georg 193
Luther, Martin 93, 204
lycanthropy 5ff, 27ff, 144
Lyons, Bridget Gellert 190, 204

Machado, Antonio 166
Maeztu, Ramiro de 193, 205
Maimonides, Moses 64, 110, 130, 134
Mancheño y Olivares, Miguel 132, 135, 145, 153, 162ff
mania, maniac 16ff, 29, 32, 34ff, 46, 64, 72ff, 80, 115ff, 119ff, 126, 128ff, 140, 144, 161
Maravall, José Antonio 128, 132
Marco Merenciano, Francisco 145
Marcos, Benjamín 133
Marie de Medici 113,
Marsella, Anthony J., 6
Martínez de Toledo, Alfonso (Archpriest of Talavera), 102, 153
Martínez Ruiz, Juan 155
Martyr, Peter 83
Mayans, Gregorio 184ff, 202
Meadow, Mary 147
melancholy: black colour 47, 61, 93, 110, 142, 149, 174; courtly disease 63ff; frontiers 58; imagination 13, 42–46, 56, 61, 74, 76, 80ff, 85, s 88, 91, 98ff, 163, 177, 180, 190; Latin-speaking frenetics 116, 119; moral problem 75ff; mystics 85ff, 92–95; myth 17ff, 21; preternatural symtoms 46; prophetic power 71ff; story of the hangman's wife; symptoms 16, 27ff, 29ff, 32ff, 46ff, 49, 53, 64, 72ff, 82, 85ff, 89, 109ff, 114, 128, 175, 181, 187; therapeutic coitus 28, 100ff, 153; violence 102; wit 47; women 49, 73ff, 86, 102, 112, 138ff, 146

Melczer, William 176, 181
memes (new replicators), 17ff
Ménardière, Hippolite Pilet de la 139
Menasseh ben Israel 109
Mendoza, Alonso de 90
Menéndez Pidal, Ramón 154
merarchia 40
Mercado, Pedro de 75ff, 77, 82, 117, 141, 161
Merola, Hieronymo 131
methaphors 11ff, 15, 50
Methodist medicine 49ff
Michëlis de Vasconcellos, Carolina 39
Midelfort, H. C. Erik 133, 138, 140ff, 204
Milton, John 191ff
Montaigne, Michel de 2, 169
Montalto, Filoteo Elião de 113, 159
Montanus (Giovanni da Monte), 31ff, 40
Montemayor, Jorge 108
Morisco uprising 59
Morley, Griswold S., 203
Müller, Friedrich Max 25, 38
Muñoz Calvo, Sagrario 155
Murillo, Thomás 80, 143, 162
mutations 19, 22ff, 63, 168–171, 193ff
myth 17ff, 25ff

Nadler, Steve 201
Najab ud-din Unhammad 38
nakedness 152, 179ff, 183
Nemesius (bishop of Emesa), 42, 126
Nerval, Gérard de 20
nervous liquors 43
neurotransmitters 3, 14ff
Newton, Isaac 127
Nezahualcóyotl 197

Index

Noonday demon (daemonium meridianum), 22
Nordström, Folke 134

Obeyeserkere, Gananath 4, 7
Olmedilla y Puig, Joaquín 142
Olmos, Andrés de (fray), 196
Ontiveros, Martha 35
Orfalí, Moisés 157
Origen 23, 37
Orobitg, Christine 7ff, 143, 145, 156, 195
Ortega, Eusebio 133
Osuna university 68
otherness 21ff, 168, 185

Pacheco, Francisco 152
Palá, María Rivas 153
Panofsky, Erwin 1, 3, 6, 36, 39, 137, 153, 159ff, 166, 174, 194ff, 205
Paracelsus 10ff
Paul (Saint), 170, 177ff, 194, 204
Paul de Ægina 61
Paz, Octavio 51, 129, 145ff
penis erection 45, 152
Peramato, Pedro de 136
Pérez Bautista, Florencio L., 155
Pérez de Guzmán, Alonso (Duke of Medina Sidonia), 123, 125, 163
Pérez Regordán, Manuel 130, 132ff, 135ff, 152ff, 158, 164
Pérez-Rincón, Héctor 35, 129
Peset Llorca, Vicente 127, 138
Petrarch, Francesco 23, 172ff, 196
Petrus Hispanus 100ff, 104, 153
Phillip II, 56, 63, 68, 123, 130
phlegm, phlegmatic 25, 28ff, 32, 61, 64, 102, 110, 149, 172ff, 176
Pico de la Mirandola, Giovanni 167

Piga Sánchez-Morate, B., 132
Pigeaud, Jackie 46, 128, 151, 156, 198, 204
Plato 80, 105
Playford, John 205
Ponce de León, Cristóbal (Duke), 58ff, 65, 67
Ponce de León, Rodrigo (Duke), 122, 125
Ponce de Santa Cruz, Alonso 176
Porta, Giovanni Battista della 73, 81
Pratz (Pratensis), Jason 47, 75, 140
Prozac 15
purity of blood 55, 84

Quevedo, Francisco de 68ff, 136

Redondo, Augustin 131, 137, 199
Reguera, Isidoro 149
Renaissance 57ff, 99
Reuchlin, Johannes 108
Rhazes (Abú Bakr Muhammad ibn Zakariyá al-Razi), 28, 38ff, 56, 61, 131
Ribeiro, João 39
Río, Martín del 140
Riquer, Martín de 154
Roberts, Kimberley S., 134
Rodríguez Marín, Francisco 135ff
Rojas, Fernando de 103, 108, 154ff, 168, 194ff
romanticism 5, 13, 20, 186, 192, 203
Rossi, Azariah dei 109ff
Roth, Cecil 158
Roth, Norman 133
Rubin, Julius H., 197
Rubio, Luciano 148
Rufus of Ephesus 100
Ruiz Pérez, Pedro 199
Ruy Sánchez, Alberto 8

Sabuco de Nantes, Miguel 122ff, 162ff

Index

Sacks, Norman P., 134
Sacks, Oliver 121, 161
Sacristán, María Cristina 156
sadness 2, 4, 14, 23, 29ff, 32ff, 37ff, 45ff, 61, 63ff, 69, 75, 85ff, 91–95, 103, 107ff, 110, 112, 116, 118,s 123, 135, 149ff, 158, 162ff, 165ff, 170ff, 175, 180, 182, 184, 189
Said, Edward W., 3, 7
Salillas, Rafael 175, 198
San José, María de 146
San Pedro, Diego de 108
Sánchez-Albornoz, Claudio 157
Sancho de San Román, Rafael 151
sanguine humour (see also blood), 44, 46, 102, 129, 149
Santa Cruz, Alfonso de 48, 128
Sartre, Jean-Paul 5
saudade 38ff, 64
Saxl, Fritz 1, 3, 6, 36, 39, 137, 153, 159ff, 166, 174, 194ff, 205
Schiesari, Juliana 198
Schleiner, Winfried 152
Scot, Reginald 74, 83, 145
Screech, M. A., 1, 7
Searle, John 21, 36
Segorbe, Jerónimo de 146
semantics 12, 21, 24ff
Sena, John F., 197
Seneca 172
Serés, Guillermo 130
Seznec, Jean 165
Shakespeare, William 2, 137ff, 169, 188, 205
Shelton, Thomas 201
Singer, Irving 153
sins, see vices
Siraisi, Nancy G., 39, 131
slavery 59ff
Sober, Elliot 36
Socrates 80

Sokal, Alan 7
solitude and loneliness 12, 24, 26, 33, 69ff, 88, 90ff, 104, 123, 170, 174, 198
Soranus of Ephesus 49
Soufas, Teresa Scott 7, 133, 155, 169ff, 176, 195
Speak, Gill 132
spleen 5, 31, 36, 44, 110, 202
Starobinski, Jean 1, 6ff, 33, 40
Steinberg, Leo 152
Strohmaier, Gotthard 131
suicide 49, 91, 196
Surin, Jean-Joseph 139ff
survivals 165ff
syntax 18, 21, 23ff
syphilis 53

Tamani, Giuliano 131
Tarántula, Mathiolo de la 162
Tasso, Torquato 175, 198
Tellenbach, Hubertus 1, 7, 147
Temkin, Awsei 151
Teresa de Ávila (Saint), 85ff, 91, 93, 145
Thomas (St), 197
Thomas, Hugh 132
Thomasset, Claude 40, 153
Tirso de Molina 63, 96ff, 134, 188
Tobar, Rodrigo de 101
Torre, Esteban 131
Torroja Menéndez, Carmen 153
Trabulse, Elías 52, 129, 156
translation 10ff, 21, 47, 51, 196
Treffert, Darold A., 162
Turner, Denis 147

Ullersperger, J, B, 39ff, 133
Ullman, M., 38
Unamuno, Miguel de 175, 192, 198, 205
Urrutia, Jorge 203

Váez, Pedro 40

Index

Valleriola, François 47
Vallés, Francisco 61, 75, 127ff, 133, 149
Vega, Lope de 63, 170, 186ff, 203
Velásquez, Andrés 2, 14, 16, 26, 29ff, 41–49, 52–63, 71ff, 79, 83ff, 93ff, 97ff, 101, 108, 114–121, 123–126, 126–133, 135–138, 149, 151ff, 160ff
Velázquez, Diego 152
Vesalius, Andreas 33
vices (capital), 84, 102, 170, 195
Vilanova, Arnau de 29ff, 39, 150, 166
Vilar, Pierre 205
Villalón, Cristóbal de 70, 137
Villegas, Antonio de 104, 107
Vincent, Jean-Didier 14, 34
Vives, Juan Luis 118ff, 161ff
Vossler, Karl 39

Wack, Mary F., 38ff, 101, 134, 152ff
Weber, Max 174, 190
Weinrich, Harald 175
Wenzel, Siegfried 145, 171, 173ff, 195ff,
Wier, Jean 73ff, 77, 139
Williams, Raymond 3, 7
Willis, Thomas 13, 43
Wilson, David Sloan 36
Wilson, Edmund O., 24, 37
Wind, Edgar 169ff, 195
witch-hunting, witches 72ff, 74, 77, 79ff, 82, 113, 140
Wolf, Elcan Isaac 158
Worrell, William H., 36

Yates. Frances 52, 129, 158, 194
yellow bile 27ff, 31, 176, 189
Yerushalmi, Yosef Hayim 131, 158

Zilboorg, Gregory 38